Management for Professionals

The Springer series Management for Professionals comprises high-level business and management books for executives, MBA students, and practice-oriented business researchers. The topics span all themes of relevance for businesses and the business ecosystem. The authors are experienced business professionals and renowned professors who combine scientific backgrounds, best practices, and entrepreneurial vision to provide powerful insights into how to achieve business excellence.

Tracy Dathe • Volker Müller • Marc Helmold

Business Opportunities and Risks in China

Strategies and Recommendations from a European Perspective

Springer

Tracy Dathe
Macromedia University
Berlin, Germany

Marc Helmold
IU International University of
Applied Sciences
Berlin, Germany

Volker Müller
European Chamber of Commerce
Beijing, China

ISSN 2192-8096 ISSN 2192-810X (electronic)
Management for Professionals
ISBN 978-3-031-31932-7 ISBN 978-3-031-31933-4 (eBook)
https://doi.org/10.1007/978-3-031-31933-4

This Springer imprint is published by the registered company Springer Nature Switzerland AG
The registered company address is: Gewerbestrasse 11, 6330 Cham, Switzerland

Preface

China is at the forefront of the changing world. Until a few years ago, the world's most developed economies, concentrated in Europe and Northern America in addition to a few countries in the Asia-Pacific Region ('Western countries') on one side and China on the other, were engaged in an almost perfect share of work: Western countries were providing high-end machinery and consumer goods to the huge Chinese market, while China's cheap and hard-working labourers—the core of the 'factory of the world'—were manufacturing low-price raw materials and components for international companies as well as inexpensive daily necessities for Western consumers.

Like a company, the business model of a national economy has a limited lifespan. Introduction of market economy and opening up to the outside world provided the framework of China's economic success during the last four decades. At the same time, China's rise was linked to urbanisation—the transition from a mainly agricultural to an industrialised economy. This development model has reached its final stage. The world market is saturated with low-cost products. For a range of industries like textiles, countries in South and Southeast Asia and also in Africa nowadays provide production sites with competitive costs and acceptable quality.

China is in the course of 'reinventing itself'. Chinese companies are increasingly investing in research and development and manufacturing high-end and innovative products. In a range of industries like new energy vehicle and telecommunication, Chinese and Western companies have become direct competitors.

China's new competitiveness is coinciding with multiple global crises: COVID-19, global warming and subsequent natural disasters, and lastly the Russian-Ukrainian war. The declining share of Western countries, especially Europe, in the world population and economic power, raises doubts about their relative global significance. This uncertainty has led to questions about their future role on the global stage. China on the other hand, being aware of its growing influence, has become more self-confident and more assertive to defend its core interests. To navigate relationships with a country of 1.4 billion people striving to become a fully developed nation, which has a culture hardly understood in the Western world and is committed to upholding and advancing its own unique political system, poses a clear challenge in both the political and business arenas.

Since former US President Donald Trump imposed trade sanctions against China, Chinese-US relations have deteriorated to the worst level since decades. Politicians in the EU and its member states are increasingly viewing China as a 'strategic rival'. However, in 2022, despite a challenging political environment and lacklustre annual GDP growth rates hovering around a disappointing three per cent in China, the USA, and Europe, international trade weathered the storm. Recent data from the German Federal Office of Statistics indicate that in 2022, trade in goods between Germany and China surged by a stunning 21 per cent compared to the previous year, while trade between China and the USA increased by around five per cent, exceeding the annual GDP growth of both countries.

In our opinion, in reaction to the geopolitical development, Western companies should not seek to decouple from China, but rather enhance their China strategy and deepen their understanding of the Chinese market, in order to make more informed decisions. This book aims to contribute to this effort by analysing recent economic and political developments in China, providing insights into new opportunities and challenges, including:

- China's industry policies, in particular the Made in China 2025 (MIC25) strategy
- New globalisation projects: New Silk Road, the Asia-Pacific free economic zone 'Regional Comprehensive Economic Partnership' (RCEP)
- China's energy policy which addresses climate change and dependence on foreign sources
- Emerging market opportunities from e-commerce to manufacturing in China and market entry strategy

In addition, this book encloses an analysis of the major risks associated with investing in China and offers effective strategies to mitigate such risks.

Our approach blends research in economic science and sinology with ample experience on the ground in China, bringing together the expertise of multinational companies, small and medium-sized enterprises (SMEs), and industry associations actively engaged in China. Moreover, we have sought to depict the perspective of Chinese decision-makers, procurement managers, and customers towards European and American companies. as well as potential input from Chinese business promotion agencies and suppliers.

One of the secrets to China's success is the Confucian principle of lifelong learning. With China's significant impact on the world and its constantly evolving landscape, it is essential that the business world continuously refreshes and expands its knowledge of China.

Berlin, Germany — Tracy Dathe
Beijing, China — Volker Müller
Berlin, Germany — Marc Helmold
March 2023

Contents

About the Authors

Tracy Dathe is Professor of Business Management and Digital Transformation at the Macromedia University of Applied Sciences in Berlin, Germany. She is an experienced finance professional and expert in business intelligence. In her former capacity as CFO of a multinational medium-sized automotive supplier, she was responsible for the overall commercial management at the German headquarters, as well as for the subsidiaries in China, France, Italy, Sweden, the Czech Republic, Turkey, and the USA.

Today, in addition to her academic activities, she also supports medium-sized companies as a management advisor with the main focus on financial management, sustainability management, and intercultural communication.

Volker Müller is Senior Business Manager at the European Union Chamber of Commerce in China (retired June 2023). In this position, he supported international medical device companies to get access to the Chinese market, with a focus on regulatory affairs, public procurement, and China's healthcare reform.

Mr. Müller came to China in 1987; he has worked in Chongqing, Shanghai, Xi'an, and Beijing in the artificial intelligence and medical device industries. As General Manager and Chief Representative, he has set up subsidiaries and representative offices from scratch in different cities for both multinational companies and SMEs. Before joining the EU Chamber, he worked for a Chinese medical device manufacturer as international sales director.

He regularly gives lectures and keynote speeches at research institutes and commercial meetings, sharing his insights about China's economic development as well as chances and challenges for international companies on the Chinese market.

Marc Helmold Prof. Dr. Marc Helmold (M.B.A.) is Professor at IU International University of Applied Sciences in Berlin, Germany. He teaches Bachelor's, Master's, and M.B.A. in Sales and Pricing Management, Procurement, General Management, Strategic Management, Leadership, and Supply Chain Management.

From 1997 until 2017, he had several positions in top management positions in the automotive and railway industry. Between 1997 and 2010, he worked in several companies like Ford, Ford-Mazda Japan, Porsche, and Panasonic Automotive in managerial functions and executed lean workshops throughout the value chain.

From 2013 until 2016, he was the General Manager of Bombardier-Alstom Transportation in China and led the sourcing and marketing and sales activities. Since 2016, he is Professor and has his own consultancy. In this capacity, he improves companies in performance.

List of Abbreviations

AHK	Auslandshandelskammer, Chamber of Commerce of Germany
AI	artificial intelligence
AMP	the Advanced Manufacturing Partnership Program (a national effort of the USA to revive the domestic manufacturing industry)
ASEAN	Association of Southeast Asian Nations
BIT	bilateral investment treaty
BMWi	Bundesministerium für Wirtschaft und Klimaschutz, Federal Ministry for Economic Affairs and Energy of Germany
BMWK	Bundesministerium für Wirtschaft und Klimaschutz, Federal Ministry for Economic Affairs and Energy of Germany (former BMWi)
BRI	Belt and Road Initiative
BRUEGEL	Brussel European and Global Economic Laboratory
BTA	double taxation agreement
CAI	Comprehensive Agreement on Investment between the EU and China
CAITEC	Chinese Academy of International Trade and Economic Cooperation
CCP	the Chinese Communist Party, also known as 'CPC'
CIIE	China International Import Expo
CIPA	China International Investment Promotion Agency
CMDRF	China Medical Device Regulatory Forum
CNBW	China Netzwerk Baden-Württemberg e.V.
CNC	Computerized Numerical Control
CNOOC	China National Offshore Oil Corporation
CNPC	China National Petroleum Corporation
COCIR	European Coordination Committee of the Radiological, Electromedical and Healthcare Information Technology Industry
Comintern	the Communist International (the Third International)
CPI	consumer price index
CPC	the Communist Party of China, also known as 'CCP'
CPPCC	Chinese People's Political Consultative Conference
CPTPP	Comprehensive and Progressive Agreement for Trans-Pacific Partnership
CPS	cyber-physical system

DEPA	Digital Economy Partnership Agreement
EAC	energy attribute certificate
ECB	European Central Bank
EFTA	the European Free Trade Association
ehi	European Heating Industry
ETS	emission trading system
EU	European Union
EUCCC	European Union Chamber of Commerce in China
EU CSRD	EU Corporate Sustainability Reporting Directive
EU ETS	EU Emission Trading System
FBA	Fulfilment by Amazon warehouse
FCCC	Flanders China Chamber of Commerce
FDI	foreign direct investment
FIDIC	Fédération Internationale des Ingénieurs-Conseils, an international standard setter for consulting engineering and construction technology
FIE	foreign invested enterprise
FTA	free trade agreement
GBA	the Greater Bay Area
GDP	gross domestic product
GHG	greenhouse gas
GIZ	Gesellschaft für Internationale Zusammenarbeit (German Organisation for International Cooperation)
GMP	Good Manufacturing Practice (Medicines Manufacturing Quality Standard)
GO	Guarantee of Origin
GPA	Government Procurement Agreement
GRI	Global Reporting Initiative
GVC	global value chain
GW	gigawatt
HICP	Harmonised Index of Consumer Prices
IC	integrated circuit
ICC	the International Chamber of Commerce
IEA	International Energy Agency
IEC	International Electrotechnical Commission
IFRS	International Financial Reporting Standards
IfU	Instructions for Use
IMF	International Monetary Fund
Incoterms	International Commercial Terms
IoT	Internet of Things
IP	intellectual property
ISO	International Organization for Standardization
ISSB	International Sustainability Standards Board
JIS	Just-in-Sequence
JIT	Just-in-Time

KMT	Kuomintang (the Chinese Nationalist Party)
KPI	Key performance indicator
KQI	Key quality indicator
LNG	liquefied natural gas
MERICS	Mercator Institute for China Studies
MGI	the McKinsey Global Institute
MIC25	Made in China 2025 (a national strategic plan to develop the manufacturing sector of China)
MIIT	Ministry of Industry and Information Technology of China
MIT	Massachusetts Institute of Technology
MOFCOM	Ministry of Commerce
MoU	Memorandum of Understandings
NAFTA	North American Free Trade Agreement
NEC	New Energy Vehicles
NHC	National Health Commission (former Ministry of Health)
NHSA	National Health Security Administration
NMPA	National Medical Products Administration
NPC	National People's Congress
OECD	the Organisation for Economic Co-operation and Development
OPEC	Organization of the Petroleum Exporting Countries
PBOC	the People's Bank of China (the central bank of the People's Republic of China)
PHBS	Peking University HSBS Business School
PRC	the People's Republic of China
R&D	Research and development
RCEP	Regional Comprehensive Economic Partnership
REC	renewable energy certificate
RI	responsible investment
ROC	Republic of China
SAFE	State Administration of Foreign Exchange of China
SAR	special administrative region
SARS	severe acute respiratory syndrome
SASB	Sustainability Accounting Standards Board
SCC	Supply Chain Council
SEZ	special economic zone
Sinopec	China Petroleum & Chemical Corporation
SME	small and medium-sized enterprise
SOE	state-owned enterprise
PV	photovoltaic
TPP	Trans-Pacific Partnership
UN	United Nations
UNGA	United Nations General Assembly
USEIA	United States Energy Information Administration
USEPA	United States Environmental Protection Agency

USMCA	United States Mexico Canada Agreement
VDA	Verband der Automobilindustrie e.V. (German Automobile Industry Association)
WCED	the World Commission on Environment and Development
WTO	World Trade Organization

List of Figures

List of Tables

Introduction

1

In December 1978, under the leadership of Deng Xiaoping, the Chinese Communist Party (CCP) determined the 'Reform and Opening-Up Policy' at the Central Work Conference, the Third Plenary Session of the Eleventh Central Committee. The shift in the overall strategic focus of the Chinese policymakers towards economic growth marks the beginning of a historical process of integration of the Chinese market into the global. However, Western countries' expectation of China 'change through trade' has failed. The economic reform did not lead to a change of the political system in China.

In reaction to the global financial crisis of 2008, the most powerful industrial countries began to enforce their national strategies to stimulate the growth of the real economy. The United States launched the Advanced Manufacturing Partnership (AMP) Program to improve the global competitiveness of domestic manufacturing industries by supporting investment and innovation from industry and academia with federal government funding. Germany first proposed the governmental promotion of industrial digitalisation under the name of 'Industry 4.0' in 2013. While the Federal Ministry of Education and Research of the German government initially approved research funding of more than 470 million euros, the Federal Ministry of Economics took steps to enhance standardisation and regulations for the implementation of the innovation process. Also, France formulated a similar programme for industrial promotion in collaboration with the German Industry 4.0 called 'New Industrial France'. In Asia, Japan began to implement the 'Comprehensive Strategy for the Rebirth of Japan', covering a variety of policy packages to foster domestic economic growth in the fields of energy and environmental management, health and life sciences, agriculture, forestry and fisheries, with special focus on SMEs, while South Korea put forward 'New Power Strategy' for sustainable manufacturing.

In 2015, China called for the Chinese industrial strategy 'Made in China 2025' ('MIC25') to promote technological transformation of domestic traditional industries. The official release of 'Made in China 2025' raised immediate concerns in the United States and other Western countries. The policy would transform China from the world's largest factory of low-value products into a competitive supplier of

T. Dathe et al., *Business Opportunities and Risks in China*, Management for Professionals, https://doi.org/10.1007/978-3-031-31933-4_1

high-end equipment. Although the media reporting on the advancement of MIC25 has been quite silent since the intensified trade war between the United States and China, there is no indication that this strategy has been abandoned. In promoting domestic innovations in the above key industry sectors, the Chinese government still actively seeks cooperation with foreign institutions and business partners.

This book mainly aims to explore the opportunities and risks of economic cooperations with China and provide strategic action recommendations for European enterprises. This shall involve comprehensive analysis especially with regard to the following perspectives:

- Evolution of the Chinese political system and the cultural background.
- The special administrative regions (SAR) Hong Kong, Macao and Greater Bay Area.
- Development of infrastructure.
- Long-term economic strategy, especially MIC25.
- Internationalisation of China and its integration into the global supply chain.
- The New Silk Road and Regional Comprehensive Economic Partnership (RCEP) free-trade area.
- Energy policy: How China solves the energy dependency from overseas suppliers and renewable energies.
- Foreign trade capacities and trends.
- Major economic zones including the Yangtze River Delta, Pearl River Delta and Bohai Economic Rim.
- Consumer market potentials and trends, including the prosperity gap within China, as well as national and international competition.
- Labour market development, including regulations (minimum wage, etc.) and recruitment.
- Educational systems, including higher education and vocational training systems.
- Legislation and conventions, especially capital market and foreign exchange control systems.
- Chinese culture and business conventions.
- Positioning in a complex market, including niche markets and direct and indirect sales.
- Supply chain management, including China's role in global supply chain and claim management in China.
- Service industries in China.
- Ethical management, including ESG/CSR in a Chinese perspective.
- Risk management and strategic recommendations.
- Institutional supports and promotions for commercial activities.

2 General Information

2.1 Key Data

The People's Republic of China, usually abbreviated as China, is divided into 23 provinces, 5 autonomous regions, 4 municipalities directly under the central government and 2 special administrative regions (see Fig. 2.1 Administrative Divisions and Geographical Names of China today and Table 2.1 Administrative Divisions and Geographical Names of China).

With a total population of more than 1.4 billion people and a total land area of approximately 9.6 million square kilometres, China has 17 times the population of Germany and a geographical size almost as large as all of Europe (data source: (Statista, 2022a, 2022b, 2022c)). The longest and most important rivers of the country are the Yangtze River (长江; standard romanisation, Chángjiāng; different older romanisation, Yangtsekiang) and the Yellow River (黄河, Huáng Hé).

More than 90% of the population lives in the southern and eastern part of the country with milder climate, where the geography with flat plains and water sources facilitates the infrastructural development (see Fig. 2.1). Due to the unequal distribution of natural resources, economic development in different regions has been largely unbalanced till this day. In the past decade, the Chinese government has launched a series of development-oriented poverty reduction programmes. For example, the German automotive manufacturer Volkswagen was encouraged to build its new factory in the low-income Xinjiang Autonomous Region to create jobs to the local people. Foreign investors are offered attractive conditions and business opportunities if their projects could fit into the state development programmes.

T. Dathe et al., *Business Opportunities and Risks in China*, Management for Professionals, https://doi.org/10.1007/978-3-031-31933-4_2

Fig. 2.1 Administrative divisions and geographical names of China today. Source: https://en.wikipedia.org/wiki/File:China_administrative_claimed_included.svg

2.2 A Brief Introduction of the Chinese History

The Chinese people are very proud of their culture and the achievements of their ancestors, such as the four great inventions of ancient China: papermaking, printing, black powder and the compass. Like in other countries, nowadays, culture is based on its ancient roots. For foreign investors, understanding Chinese history is of great benefit in networking with the local business partners.

China is one of the first advanced civilisations of mankind along with Babylon, ancient Egypt and ancient India. Those earliest agrarian societies are often referred to as the cradle of civilisation. The Chinese are proud of their 5000-year-old culture, with around 3500 years, i.e. from the Shang dynasty (approx. 1570–1066 BCE), verifiably documented in writing (Keightley, 1996).

In the early Xia (2200–1600 BCE), Shang (c. 1570–1066 BCE) and Zhou (1046–256 BCE) dynasties, China was governed by a series of local rulers, who formally recognised the supreme power of the monarchical sovereign 'Son of Heaven'. Through the loss of power of the monarch Central King at the end of the Zhou dynasty, different local rulers rose to power through wars, marriages and

Table 2.1 Administrative divisions and geographical names of China

Name	Status	Population (Mio.)	Population density (per square km)
Guangxi	Autonomous region	50.2	211
Xinjiang	Autonomous region	25.9	16
Inner Mongolia	Autonomous region	24	20
Ningxia	Autonomous region	7.2	109
Tibet	Autonomous region	3.7	3
Chongqing	Municipality	32.1	389
Shanghai	Municipality	24.9	3922
Beijing	Municipality	21.9	1334
Tianjin	Municipality	13.9	1194
Guangdong	Province	126.2	700
Shandong	Province	101.7	644
Henan	Province	99.4	601
Jiangsu	Province	84.8	848
Sichuan	Province	83.7	173
Hebei	Province	74.6	393
Hunan	Province	66.5	314
Zhejiang	Province	64.7	616
Anhui	Province	61.1	436
Hubei	Province	57.5	311
Yunnan	Province	47.2	123
Jiangxi	Province	45.2	271
Liaoning	Province	42.6	290
Fujian	Province	41.6	336
Shaanxi	Province	39.6	192
Guizhou	Province	38.6	219
Shanxi	Province	34.9	223
Heilongjiang	Province	31.7	67
Gansu	Province	25	55
Jilin	Province	24	127
Taiwan[a]	Province	23.5	646
Hainan	Province	10.1	294
Qinghai	Province	5.9	9
Hong Kong	Special administrative region (SAR)	7.4	6851
Macau	Special administrative region (SAR)	0.7	20,700
Total		**1442.0**	

Data source: (National Bureau of Statistics of China, 2021; Statista, 2022a, 2022b, 2022c)
[a]Ruled by the Republic of China (see Sect. 2.2)

diplomacy. Their endeavour finally resulted in the conquest of all smaller kingdoms and founding of a unified empire by the King of Qin in 221 BCE.

To distinguish himself for his unprecedented achievement, the King of Qin invented for himself the title '秦始皇帝Qín Shǐhuángdì'—the Supreme Being First Emperor of Qin. It began the period of the Chinese Empire, and the title '皇帝huángdì' was borne by numerous successor dynasties over the next two millennia. While the famous Terracotta Army was accidentally discovered in the late twentieth century as a part of the Qin Emperor's mausoleum, his tomb remains unopened to this day. The Qin Emperor also constructed the first Great Wall of China with the purpose to protect the territory against northern nomadic peoples.

The Qin dynasty was followed by the Han dynasty (206 BCE–220 CE), to which the majority of the Chinese owe the name of their ethnicity. The Great Empire of Han was very successful both militarily and economically. During this period of Chinese history, the emergence of the Silk Road enabled an indirect trade relationship with the Roman Empire, Confucianism was adapted as the state philosophy, and Buddhism gained influence in China.

The Tang dynasty (618–907) is of similar importance to Chinese history as the Han dynasty. The Tang dynasty was characterised by cosmopolitanism through trade relations and cultural exchanges with overseas, especially with Japan and Korea. In terms of religion and philosophy, a colourful mix of Buddhism, Taoism, Confucianism as well as Islam and Christianity was observed. This period also saw the birth of the only female ruler with the title '皇帝huángdì', Empress Wu Zetian, in Chinese history.

At the end of the thirteenth century, the Mongolian army not only conquered the whole Chinese Empire but overran almost the entire Eurasian continent. The reign of the Mongol Empire in China is referred to as the Yuan dynasty (1279–1368). The Venetian trader Marco Polo wrote an interesting book about his trip to China and his encounter with the Mongol ruler Kublai Khan at that time. However, the authenticity of Marco Polo's story was later questioned by historians.

Chinese culture flourished again in the Ming dynasty (1368–1644), after the Chinese fighters managed to push back the Mongol rule. In addition to its economic success, the Ming dynasty is characterised by highly developed art disciplines such as the manufacture of porcelain and architecture. The Forbidden City in today's capital Beijing was built in the Ming dynasty. To defend the empire against the Mongols, the Ming Emperors ceaselessly reinforced and expanded the Great Wall.

The eunuch admiral Zheng He was a legend in the Ming dynasty. He was entrusted with the treasure fleet by the Ming Emperor to undertake seven expeditions to the Pacific and Indian Oceans. During the long journeys, the admiral was said to have been motivated by the chance that, as a Muslim, he could personally set foot on the holy ground of Mecca.

Today's Manchu minority from Northeast China founded China's last monarchy—the Qing dynasty (1644–1911). The Qing rulers owed their political and economic success to a skilful combination of Manchurian art of war and the Han Chinese administrative talent. Under the Qing Emperor, China resumed and expanded its territory around Xinjiang, Tibet and Mongolia (see Fig. 2.2).

Fig. 2.2 Administrative divisions and geographical names of Qing dynasty in 1911. (Translated from https://commons.wikimedia.org/wiki/File:China_1911_es.svg#/media/File:China_1911_de.svg. Partially translated from (Dathe & Helmold, 2018, S. 35–38))

The isolationism of the Qing empire and the industrialisation of the European countries and their resulting demand for free trade led to strong conflicts of interest. As a result of the lost First and Second Opium Wars, China was forced to concede to Britain the right to trade in opium, as well as to further economic concessions such as the opening of the contract ports for free trade with Great Britain, France, Russia and the United States. The resulting immense economic damage and mass poverty in China caused severe social tensions and eventually brought down the monarchy. Following the abdication of the last Emperor Pu Yi at the end of 1911, the Republic of China (ROC) was proclaimed on 1 January 1912.

In order to form a solid central government, the Chinese Nationalist Party (Kuomintang, KMT), the leading political party, waged protracted wars against the powerful warlords who ruled over large swathes of China. In 1921, the Chinese Communist Party (CCP) was founded inspired by the October Revolution in Russia and—after a period of cooperation—became a rival to KMT. Both KMT and CCP were initially supported by the Soviet Union and the Communist International (Comintern). The rivalry turned eventually into fierce military conflicts, interrupted only temporarily by the Japanese invasion during the Second World War.

In 1949, after his defeat in the civil war, Generalissimo Chiang Kai-Shek evacuated his Nationalist government to the island of Taiwan. His attempts to retake

Mainland China over the next few decades were unsuccessful. On 1 October 1949, Mao Zedong, the Chairman of the Chinese Communist Party (CCP), proclaimed the People's Republic of China (PRC). Both governments declared themselves the only true representative of China. In 1972, the People's Republic of China established diplomatic relationship with the United States and replaced the Republic of China (ROC) as China's official representative to the United Nations.

2.3 The Special Administrative Regions (SAR): Hong Kong and Macao

Hong Kong and Macao are two special administrative regions located south of Guangdong Province on both edges of the Pearl River Delta. Both SARs' per capita GDP rank among the highest in the world; they have their own legislations, currencies and customs authorities, requiring business strategies different from Mainland China. Though Hong Kong and Macao are connected with Guangdong Province by land borders, the term 'Mainland China' is generally used to describe China excluding Hong Kong, Macao and Taiwan.

Hong Kong originally refers to a 78 square kilometre island off the coast in the South China Sea, forming an ideal natural harbour. The name Hong Kong stems from the local Guangdong dialect, meaning Fragrant Harbour, in Standard Chinese (often referred to as 'Mandarin Chinese') the Chinese 香港 is romanised as Xianggang.

From the late eighteenth century, British merchants sold opium to China, balancing Britain's large trade deficit. In 1839, the Chinese imperial court started to enforce a ban on narcotics, confiscating British opium in the Pearl River Delta. The conflict escalated to the First Opium War (1839–1842), ending with a defeat of the Chinese army. In the Treaty of Nanjing, signed on 29 August 1842, Hong Kong Island was ceded to Britain.

In the Second Opium War (1856–1860), Britain occupied the Kowloon (九龙) Peninsula opposite to Hong Kong Island. In addition, in 1898, Britain forcefully leased the New Territories (新界) for 99 years, together with Hong Kong Island and Kowloon forming nowadays Hong Kong SAR, an area of 1106 square kilometre. On 19 December 1984, Great Britain and China signed an agreement, returning Hong Kong to China on 01 July 1997.

After the Second World War, Hong Kong became a manufacturing base for labour-intensive low-cost products. While Mainland China isolated itself from the Western world, relations with Hong Kong never ceased. International trading companies used Hong Kong as a springboard to sell their clients' products to Mainland China.

In 1960, Hong Kong's per capita GDP was only US$ 429, less than one third of that of the United Kingdom. Per capita GDP and subsequently expenses of manufacture rose sharply during the 1980s and 1990s (*see* Fig. 2.3). In the 1980s, as soon as Mainland China gradually allowed foreign and Hong Kong invested enterprises to establish factories on its territory, Hong Kong companies started to relocate

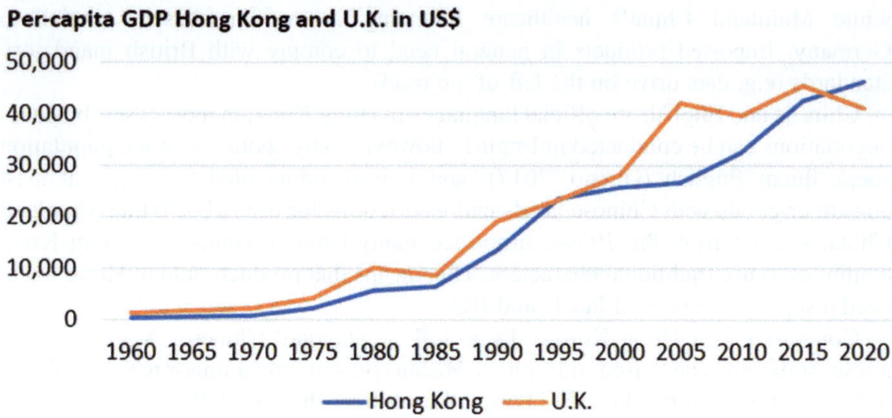

Fig. 2.3 Per capita GDP of Hong Kong and the United Kingdom in US$. Data source: Macrotrends (Macrotrends, 2022a, 2022b)

manufacture, especially to the neighbouring and most open Guangdong Province. At the end of 1997, the cumulative value of Hong Kong's direct investment in Guangdong was estimated at 48 billion US$, accounting for almost 80% of the total foreign direct investment there. Hong Kong companies and joint ventures in Guangdong Province employed about five million people (Schenk, 2008).

China's accession to the World Trade Organization (WTO) in 2001 posed a challenge to Hong Kong: restrictions for foreign investment in China were removed, doing business became much easier, most global companies started to operate directly in Mainland China instead of channelling their investment and sales via Hong Kong, and many of them relocated their China headquarters to cities like Shanghai, which are located more in the centre of China and where prices and salaries were much lower than in Hong Kong.

Hong Kong overcame these challenges by restructuring its economy. Supported by a mature legal system and a free market economy, from 1981 to 2000, employment in the service sector rose from 52% to 80% of the labour force, while manufacturing employment fell from 39% to 10% in the same period (Schenk, 2008). Today, Hong Kong is one of the most service-oriented economies in the world, with the service sector accounting for 93.4% of the GDP in 2020 (Yeung, 2022).

Considering Hong Kong as a separate economy, in 2021, Hong Kong's GDP reaches 368 billion US$, ranking 38th in the world, one place behind Malaysia and one before the 100-million inhabitants country Vietnam (World Bank, 2022). As almost all goods are imported—for SMEs, the size of the market justifies the development of a specific strategy to gain a market share in Hong Kong.

According to the 'one country, two systems' policy, Hong Kong will retain a high degree of autonomy at least until 2047. The business environment in Hong Kong is more similar to the United Kingdom than to Mainland China. For example, healthcare is financed by the government, like the British National Health Service, while Mainland China's healthcare financing is insurance-based, similar to Germany. Imported products in general need to comply with British mandatory standards (e.g. cars drive on the left of the road).

Chinese and English are official languages in Hong Kong; in most cases, business negotiations can be conducted in English; however, only about 3% of the population speak fluent English (Otieno, 2017), and it is recommended to supply at least consumer goods with Chinese labels and instructions for use (IfU). While Mainland China, starting from the 1950s, simplified many Chinese characters, Hong Kong continues to use traditional characters. This means that products sold to Hong Kong need a separate version of labels and IfUs.

Compared with Hong Kong, Macao (澳门, Standard Chinese: Aomen, Portuguese, sometimes also used in English: Macau) played only a minor role in Chinese history and economics. In 1557, Portugal took over the tiny 2.78 square kilometre island, making it the first European colony in East Asia. Land reclamation started as early as in the seventeenth century, creating the Macao Peninsula. Today, Macao has an area of almost 33 square kilometres.

Macao has a per capita GDP similar to Hong Kong; however, as the population is only around 695,000, in 2021, the GDP reached just 29.9 billion US$, ranking 101st in the world, less than Sudan (World Bank, 2022). Macao's economy heavily depends on gaming services and cross-border tourism; consequently, Macau's economy shrank severely during the Covid-19 pandemic.

In April 1987, Portugal and China reached an agreement to return Macao to China on 20 December 1999. Similar to Hong Kong, Macao is given a 50-year transition period.

Besides Chinese, Portuguese remains an official language, but only 2.3% of the population speak the language; English has replaced Portuguese as the main language in international business.

Though the 'one country, two systems' policy will be in place until 2047 and 2049, respectively, China is slowly moving to integrate the economies of Hong Kong, Macao and the most developed areas of Guangdong Province, creating new opportunities for cross-border business; see Sect. 7.3 The Greater Bay Area.

2.4 Taiwan

Taiwan is an island with an area of 35,800 square kilometres off the coast of Fujian Province, facing the Pacific Ocean. In the sixteenth century, Portuguese named the island Formosa (Beautiful Island); this name remained in common use in European languages into the twentieth century. After the First Sino-Japanese War (1894–1895), China was forced to sign the Treaty of Shimonoseki, ceding sovereignty over Taiwan to Japan. After the Second World War at the Potsdam Conference in the summer of 1945, the four victorious powers confirmed that after the defeat of Japan, Taiwan shall be returned to China. In late 1949, after the founding of the People's Republic of China (PRC), the former government of China, the Guomindang (former romanisation: Kuomintang, KMT), retreated to Taiwan, claiming that the Republic of China (ROC) still was the government of whole China. In 1972, the United Nations recognised the government in Beijing (the government of the PRC) as China's only representative to the United Nations, replacing the ROC. In the following years, most countries followed this step and established diplomatic relations with Beijing, cutting diplomatic relations with the ROC. In 1991, the KMT government in Taiwan officially ended the state of war with Mainland China, starting a phase of official contacts with the government in Beijing, followed by the establishment of strong economic links.

This leads to the current 'status quo': With exception of 14 smaller countries (status late 2022), all other states have established diplomatic relations with Mainland China, officially adhering to the 'one-China policy', but at the same time have flourishing trade relations with Taiwan (approved by the government of Mainland China) and in some cases also political or even military ties with Taiwan (strongly disapproved by Beijing).

In addition to Taiwan island, the ROC controls a few islands in the Taiwan Strait and the Jinmen (Taiwan romanisation: Kinmen) Islands that geographically belong to Fujian Province. In a broader sense, nowadays, the term 'Taiwan' is synonymous with 'Republic of China'.

In 2020, Taiwan's GDP reached 668 billion US$ (Statistics Times, 2021) ranking 21st in the world, one place behind Saudi Arabia or slightly below Central China's Hubei Province. Different from Hong Kong, Taiwan has a strong industrial sector, which contributed 36% to Taiwan's GDP in 2017 (AFM, 2020). Taiwan is one of the world's leading manufacturers of electronic components and devices, including integrated circuits, making it an important sourcing market for SMEs.

Taiwan is a free market economy; however, it has its own set of regulatory requirements, for example, sales of pharmaceutical products and medical devices need a registration with the Taiwan Food and Drug Administration, with requirements different from the mainland authorities, but similarly demanding and time-consuming.

Taiwan companies have invested heavily in Mainland China to make use of its large labour force. Until late 2021, more than 123,000 projects with a total investment volume of US$ 71.3 billion have been realised (Economic Daily, 2022). As a prominent example, the Taiwan electronics contract manufacturer Foxconn has set up 45 factories in Mainland China, including Western areas like Chongqing. In 2020, Foxconn had almost 840,000 employees in Greater China (Foxconn, 2020), thereof an estimated 800,000 on the mainland.

Provided that Covid-related travel restriction are lifted, Taiwan can easily be reached by plane from major Mainland China cities. Business visitors from most developed countries don't need a visa for Taiwan; Mainland China citizens need a special visit permit from the Taiwan authorities. Most SMEs with a subsidiary or office in Mainland China serve the Taiwan market via local distributors.

Standard Chinese is the official language in Taiwan; however, because of the relatively long phase with little interaction with Mainland China, some common technical terms (e.g. 'software') are different in Taiwan. Like in Hong Kong and

Macao, Taiwan uses traditional Chinese characters. Most companies active in China provide two sets of written material (including websites, labels and IfUs), one with simplified characters for Mainland China market and one with traditional characters for Taiwan, Hong Kong and Macao. Different from both Mainland China and Hong Kong, Taiwan uses the Wade-Giles romanisation, named after two British sinologists. The use of different romanisation schemes for Chinese characters may lead to confusion, for example, the family name 徐 is romanised Xu in Mainland China, Hsu in Taiwan and Tsui in Hong Kong.

Mainland China consumers and media may react indignantly if written company materials—even a country selection on a webpage in English language—seem to indicate that Taiwan has the status of a country. A safe way is to write 'Taiwan, China'.

When referring to their China operations (including Taiwan), many companies use the term 'Greater China', fulfilling both Mainland Chinese and Taiwan requirements.

2.5 The Minorities

English language does not distinguish between ethnic Chinese and Chinese citizens. To identify ethnic Chinese, we use the term 'Han-Chinese' (Chinese: 汉族, hanzu), a standard description in sinology. Han-Chinese account for 91.1% of the population of Mainland China. Ethnic minorities predominantly live in vast border areas of China, many of them in economically underdeveloped areas. However, rulers of two important imperial dynasties, the Mongolian Yuan dynasty (1279–1368) and the last dynasty before the founding of the Republic of China, the Manchu Qing dynasty (1644–1912), were of minority origin, leaving their mark in Chinese culture and philosophy. Nowadays, minority regions are among the most popular touristic areas in China; ethnic minorities contribute substantially to the variety of art, fashion and cuisines in China (see Table 2.2 Autonomous Regions on Provincial Level).

Table 2.2 Autonomous regions on provincial level

Ethnic group	Autonomous region	Capital	Total minority population [million][a]	10-year growth[b]
Zhuang	Guangxi	Nanning	19.57	15.6%
Uyghur	Xinjiang	Urumqi	11.77	17.0%
Hui	Ningxia	Yinchuan	11.38	7.5%
Tibetan	Tibet	Lhasa	7.06	12.4%
Mongolian	Inner Mongolia	Hohhot	6.29	5.2%

Data source: (Baidu, 2022)

[a]seventh National Census, cut-off date 01 November 2020, including ethnic minority population living outside the autonomous region

[b]Compared with the sixth National Census, 01 November 2010

During the imperial regency and the Republic of China, Han-Chinese were aware of the major minorities like Manchu (满族), Mongolians (蒙古族) and Tibetans (藏族), but there was no systematic classification of ethnicities.

Identification of an ethnic group and dissociation from others are not self-evident. An authoritative definition by the State Council and the Central Committee of the CPC states (CPC Central Committee and State Council, 2005) '1.2.1. An ethnic group is a stable community of people formed in a certain period of history. In general, an ethnic group shares common historical origins, mode of production, language, culture, customs and a sense of community. In some ethnic groups, religion also plays an important role in their formation and development process'. This means, in line with international practices, that recent immigrants from other countries don't qualify as an ethnic group.

Ethnologic research to identify ethnic minorities started in 1950 and lasted until 1989 (Wang, 2015). Fifty-four minorities were identified until 1965; the last one, the Jinuo (基诺族) in Yunnan Province, was added in 1979 (Baidu Encyclopaedia, 2022).

Ethnic minorities have the rights to territorial autonomy, and depending on the size of the minority population, autonomous areas may be established from county level up to provincial level. In the autonomous areas, the minority language is, besides Chinese, a second official language. Members of minorities can claim favourable treatment in aspects, such as civil service recruitment, university admission and (now basically abolished) family planning (Wang, 2015).

Almost all ethnic minorities in China have their own spoken language. Notable exceptions are the Manchu and Hui (回族). Though the emperor during the Qing dynasty was of Manchu origin, the ethnic Manchu were assimilated by the majority of Han-Chinese and adopted Chinese as their language. Nowadays, Manchu is a dead language like Latin in Europe. The Huis were classified as a separate ethnic group because of their Islamic belief, and their native language has always been Chinese.

Several minority languages have their own characters, for example, Mongolian and Tibetan. Uyghur uses Arabic characters, written from right to left. While in the northern neighbouring country Mongolia, in the 1940s, traditional Mongolian characters were replaced by Cyrillic, ethnic Mongolians in China still use the traditional Mongolian characters, written from top to bottom, a challenge for representation on electronic media. All minority language characters nowadays in use in China are included in the international standard Unicode (ISO/IEC 10646) and can be processed with standard office software.

Several minority languages originally had no written language; linguists created new ones based on Latin characters. For example, the written language of the largest minority, the Zhuang, was officially promulgated in 1955. Street signs and, for example, ID cards printed in minority regions are all bi-lingual (see Fig. 2.4).

For SMEs active in China, ethnicity of business partners or final customers is in general not an important factor for fine-tuning local marketing strategies. However, ethnicity may be linked to distinct, sometimes harsh, living environments. For example, many Tibetans live in altitudes of more than 3500 m; manufacturers

Fig. 2.4 Multiple languages in China. Inscription at the Yongyou Dian (Hall of Eternal Blessing) in the Lama Temple in Beijing. From left to right: Mongolian, Tibetan, Chinese and Manchu (Photo: Volker Müller)

must guarantee that their products work under low air pressure. There are rare examples that consumer taste depends on ethnicity, for instance, Han-Chinese and most other East Asian ethnicities prefer a pale, 'white' complexion; this is not the case for several minorities, for example, Mongolians.

As far as ethnic minorities have their own language, education is bi-lingual. In most cases, business people and technical personnel of ethnic minorities speak fluent Chinese. Hardly any foreign staff member in China learns the local minority language, at least not for business purposes.

Though minority languages are official languages in autonomous regions, it is legally not required to provide labels and IfUs in that language. Translation and maintenance of translated labels and IfUs is costly and—if translation is not correct—creates business risks; therefore, translation into minority languages is not recommended, except for a few niche products.

If a subsidiary in China serves neighbouring countries like Mongolia or Korea, it may be feasible to employ sales and service people of the relevant ethnic minorities in China, who speak the language of those markets.

2.6 Religions

China is a predominantly non-religious country. Figures about the number of religious believers vary widely; a study of the Gallup institute of 2017 came to the result that 47% of the population of Mainland China consider themselves as 'convinced atheists' and 23% describe themselves as 'non-religious' (bigthink, 2018).

Exact figures are difficult to obtain; only Christian churches record membership. As everywhere in the world, religion is not just a belief in supernatural gods or spirits but is interwoven with philosophy and moral guidelines. In China, the boundaries between religion and philosophy are especially blurry. In addition, different religions and philosophies co-existed for a long time, heavily influencing each other. Since ancient times, the centralised imperial court left no room for a clergy, competing for state power. This is one of the reasons for the relatively weak penetration of the traditional Chinese society by religions.

The Qing, the last imperial dynasty, was dominated by the Manchu ethnicity, most of them believing in Siberian shamanism. The emperor of China was regarded as the Son of Heaven, representing heavenly authority. Twice a year, the emperor moved in a procession from the Forbidden City through Beijing to China's most famous religious site, the Temple of Heaven, where the emperor personally prayed to heaven for good harvests. However, while the belief in heaven was truly shamanistic, the official belief of the Qing Court was Confucianism, elevating the philosophy of Confucius (551 to 479 BCE) to a religion. In modern China, Confucianism is strictly seen as a philosophy, not as a religion.

Besides shamanism and natural religions, Daoism (different spelling Taoism, Chinese: 道教) is the only native religion in China. The founder of Daoism Laozi (older romanisation, Lao Tsu; Chinese, 老子) was born around 471 BCE and—according to his followers—died at the age of 101. In the beginning, Daoism provided a philosophical explanation of the universe and moral guidelines; later generations added immortal beings and transformed Daoism into a religion. In Chinese history, Daoism was often seen as an alternative way of thinking in opposition to Confucianism. While Confucianism emphasises strict hierarchies and rituals, Daoism teaches co-existence of man and nature and individual well-being. Chinese traditional medicine and martial arts are rooted in Daoism. Today, the number of Daoist monks and believers is small, but it has a considerable influence on Chinese philosophy and spirituality.

Buddhism started to influence China in the second century BCE (Bauer, 2018). As the Himalaya formed a natural barrier between India and China, Buddhist teachings slowly found their way into China via nowadays Pakistan and Xinjiang. Chinese Buddhism incorporated older local religious beliefs, gradually extended its influence and reached its 'golden age' in the Tang dynasty (618–906). Today, Buddhism is divided into a large number of schools that co-exist without obvious conflicts. During the Tang dynasty, Buddhism reached Tibet where it absorbed many elements of the local Bon religion, forming the distinct Tibetan Lama-Buddhism. Mongolian emperors of the Yuan dynasty (1271 to 1368) brought Tibetan Buddhism back to Mongolia where Lama-Buddhism is the dominant religion until today. Later in the Qing dynasty, the Yongzheng Emperor (1722–1735) and Qianlong Emperor (1735–1795) supported Lama-Buddhism, extending its influence far beyond Tibet.

Islam reached China through two different ways: along the land-based Silk Road and via ancient maritime trading routes from the Middle East. The earliest mosque was built in 1009 by Arab traders in the eastern port city of Quanzhou, Fujian Province. Nowadays, the majority of Muslims live in the western part of China, especially in the two autonomous regions Xinjiang and Ningxia. However, there are Muslim communities in all parts of China, including Lhasa and the far northeastern provinces. Almost all Chinese Muslims are Sunni.

In the sixteenth century, Jesuit priests started to set up Christian missions in China. Large-scale proselytisation started during the First Opium War from around 1840. Christian influence spawned the Taiping Rebellion (1850–1864) against the Qing dynasty, taking an estimated 20 million lives (Britannica, 2022a, 2022b). The leader of the rebellion, Hong Xiuquan (1814–1864), believed himself to be the son of God. Later, the so-called 'Boxer Rebellion' of 1900 against foreign dominance was largely motivated by sentiments against Christian proselytisation. The rebellion ended with an international army capturing and looting Beijing (Britannica, 2022a, 2022b). Despite the violent history of Christian proselytisation, missionaries were able to establish Christian communities in most parts of China, including remote inland areas. In China, the main Christian persuasions Catholicism and Protestantism are seen as two different religions.

The five officially recognised religions in China, Daoism, Buddhism, Islam, Catholicism and Protestantism, have the status of social organisations; they are entitled to send delegates to the National Chinese People's Political Consultative Conference (CPPCC), the advisory body of the law-making National People's Congress (NPC).

Shamanist and nature religions still exist in remote minority regions of China, especially in southwestern Sichuan and Yunnan provinces as well as in Inner Mongolia.

In business life, religion plays hardly any role. In comparison with, for example, neighbouring India and Pakistan, where religious rites and doctrines heavily influence everyday life, the Chinese way of thinking is typically secular and rational. There are, of course, exceptions. For instance, products made of porcine raw material will in general not be accepted by Muslims.

Halal (Muslim) restaurants exist in almost every town in China; some universities and large companies have special counters offering halal food in their cafeterias. In recent years, vegetarian food has become popular among the young urban population. In case of doubt, before going to China for business trip, it is fully acceptable to inform the host about special dietary requirements; the Chinese side will certainly care for the visitor's needs.

2.7 Exchange Rates and Inflation

The official currency of the People's Republic of China (PRC) is renminbi yuan (ISO code: CNY). The exchange rates between euro and renminbi yuan (EUR: CNY) and US dollar and Renminbi yuan (USD: CNY) from 2010 to 2021 are summarised in Tables 2.3 and 2.4 Exchange rates USD vs. CNY from 2010 to 2021.

In economics, the term 'inflation' is used to describe a general increase in prices. Since individual prices change at different levels, inflation is typically calculated based on the weighted average price development of a basket of goods and services

Table 2.3 Exchange rates EUR vs. CNY from 2010 to 2021

EUR: CNY	2010	2011	2012	2013	2014	2015
Beginning of year	9.8238	8.8220	8.1588	8.2207	8.3491	7.5358
End of year	8.8220	8.1588	8.2207	8.3491	7.5358	7.0608
Average of year	**9.9419**	**8.9953**	**8.1052**	**8.1648**	**8.1864**	**6.9755**
EUR: CNY	**2016**	**2017**	**2018**	**2019**	**2020**	**2021**
Beginning of year	7.0608	7.3202	7.8338	7.8751	7.8205	8.0225
End of year	7.3202	7.8044	7.8751	7.8205	8.0225	7.1947
Average of year	**7.3511**	**7.6290**	**7.8081**	**7.7355**	**8.2637**	**7.6298**

Data source: European Central Bank (European Central Bank, 2022a, 2022b)

Table 2.4 Exchange rates USD vs. CNY from 2010 to 2021

USD: CNY	2010	2011	2012	2013	2014	2015
Beginning of year	6.8259	6.6000	6.2939	6.2301	6.0537	6.2046
End of year	6.6000	6.2939	6.2301	6.0537	6.2046	6.4778
Average of year	**6.7698**	**6.4630**	**6.3866**	**6.1478**	**6.1620**	**6.2824**
EUR: CNY	**2016**	**2017**	**2018**	**2019**	**2020**	**2021**
Beginning of year	6.4778	6.9430	6.5063	6.8755	6.9618	6.5250
End of year	6.9430	6.5063	6.8755	6.9618	6.5250	6.3726
Average of year	**6.6394**	**6.7576**	**6.6090**	**6.9081**	**6.9042**	**6.4508**

Data source: Federal Reserve System (Federalreserve.gov, 2022)

used by primary consumers. The said prices are tracked as a price index over several time periods to measure consumer price inflation. For example, the European Central Bank (ECB) has set a specific consumer price index (CPI) called 'Harmonised Index of Consumer Prices (HICP)' to measure the inflation in the euro area (European Central Bank, 2022a, 2022b).

According to the prevailing opinion of economists, a moderate and stable inflation level is favourable. High inflation, i.e. when the nominal prices of most goods and services rise rapidly, will erode the real value of money and have severely destructive effects on the real economy. Deflation (= negative inflation), on the other hand, is likely to weaken the economy because the consumers will postpone consumption due to anticipated future price decrease and investors will be reluctant to invest in the future of the business.

The European Central Bank, whose main objective is to maintain price stability, aims for 2% annual inflation over the medium term (European Central Bank, 2022a, 2022b).

In the previous decade, China's inflation rate has been moderate. Notably, China appears to have managed to control inflation during the ongoing Covid-19 crisis and the Russia-Ukraine crisis that have caused high inflation in the Western countries (see Fig. 2.5).

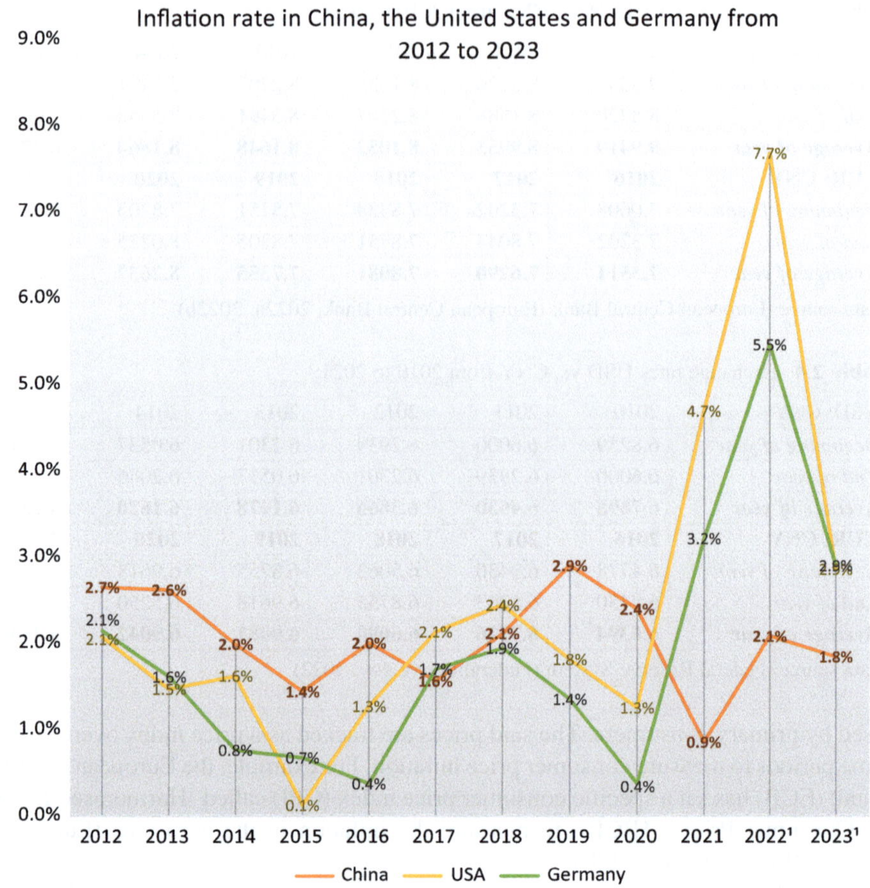

Fig. 2.5 Inflation rate in China from 2012 to 2023. Data source: (Statista, 2022a, 2022b, 2022c) based on survey by IMF. *Forecast data

References

AFM. (2020). *Taiwan economy: GDP, growth, Investments. Asia Fund Managers (AFM).* Retrieved Oct 05, 2022, from https://www.asiafundmanagers.com/gbr/taiwan-economy-2019/.

Baidu. (2022). *How many ethnic groups exceed 10 million people? Statistic data arrived.* Retrieved Oct 05, 2022, from https://baijiahao.baidu.com/s?id=1733671264344651569.

Baidu Encyclopaedia. (2022). *The Chinese Nation (in Chinese).* Retrieved Oct 05, 2022, from https://baike.baidu.com/item/中华民族/1186

Bauer, W. (2018). *Geschichte der chinesischen Philosophie (in German).* BECK Publishing House.

bigthink. (2018). *China and Europe stand out on world map of atheism.* Retrieved Oct 05, 2022, from https://bigthink.com/strange-maps/china-and-europe-stand-out-on-world-map-of-atheism/

Britannica. (2022a). *Boxer Rebellion.* Retrieved Oct 07, 2022, from https://www.britannica.com/event/Boxer-Rebellion

Britannica. (2022b). *Taiping Rebellion*. Retrieved Oct 07, 2022, from https://www.britannica.com/event/Taiping-Rebellion

CPC Central Committee and State Council. (2005). *The decision on further strengthening ethnic work and accelerating economic and social development of ethnic minorities and minority regions (in Chinese)*. Zhengzhou VIOS foreign investment service center. Retrieved Oct 05, 2022, from https://www.waizi.org.cn/law/4965.html

Dathe, T., & Helmold, M. (2018). *Erfolgreich im Chinageschäft: Strategien und Handlungsempfehlungen für kleinere und mittlere Unternehmen (KMU)*. Springer Gabler.

Economic Daily. (2022). *Taiwan's Economic Growth depends on the Trade between the two Sides of the Taiwan Strait (in Chinese)*. Von. Retrieved Oct 08, 2022, from https://baijiahao.baidu.com/s?id=1741810377582946171

European Central Bank. (2022a). *Euro foreign exchange reference rates*. By European Central Bank. Retrieved Oct 05, 2022, from https://www.ecb.europa.eu/stats/policy_and_exchange_rates/euro_reference_exchange_rates/html/index.en.html

European Central Bank. (2022b). *What is inflation? By Educational explainers*. Retrieved Oct 05, 2022, from https://www.ecb.europa.eu/ecb/educational/explainers/tell-me-more/html/what_is_inflation.en.html

Federalreserve.gov. (2022, Aug 22). *Foreign Exchange Rates - H.10*. Federal Reserve. Retrieved Oct 05, 2022, from https://www.federalreserve.gov/datadownload/

Foxconn. (2020). *CSR Report 2020, 2. Employees. Von*. Retrieved Oct 08, 2022, from https://www.foxconn.com/s3/reports/CSR CSR報告書/英文/2020/Employees.pdf.

Keightley, D. (Autumn 1996). *Art, ancestors, and the origins of writing in China*. Representations, S. No. 56, Special Issue: The New Erudition., 68–95.

Macrotrends. (2022a). *Hong Kong GDP Per Capita 1960–2022*. Retrieved Oct 05, 2022, from https://www.macrotrends.net/countries/HKG/hong-kong/gdp-per-capita

Macrotrends. (2022b). *U.K. GDP Per Capita 1960–2022*. Retrieved Oct 05, 2022, from https://www.macrotrends.net/countries/GBR/united-kingdom/gdp-per-capita

National Bureau of Statistics of China. (2021, May 11). *Communiqué of the Seventh National Population Census (No. 3)*. Population by Region: http://www.stats.gov.cn/english/PressRelease/202105/t20210510_1817188.html.

Otieno, M. O. (2017). *What languages are spoken in Hong Kong? WorldAtlas*. Retrieved Oct 08, 2022, from https://www.worldatlas.com/articles/what-languages-are-spoken-in-hong-kong.html

Schenk, C. R. (2008). *Economic history of Hong Kong*. Economic History Association. Retrieved Oct 08, 2022, from https://eh.net/encyclopedia/economic-history-of-hong-kong/

Statistics Times. (2021). *List of Countries by GDP (Nominal)*. Retrieved Oct 08, 2022, from https://statisticstimes.com/economy/countries-by-gdp.php

Statista. (2022a, April). *China: Inflationsrate von 1981 bis 2021 und Prognosen bis 2027*. Inflationsrate von 1980 bis 2021 und Prognosen bis 2027; Inflation rate from 1987 to 2027. Retrieved Oct 08, 2022, from https://de.statista.com/statistik/daten/studie/167115/umfrage/inflationsrate-in-china/; https://de.statista.com/statistik/daten/studie/165718/umfrage/inflationsrate-in-den-usa/; https://www.statista.com/statistics/375207/inflation-rate-in-germany/

Statista. (2022b). *Cities with the highest population density worldwide in 2021*. (in inhabitants per square km). Retrieved Oct 05, 2022, from https://www.statista.com/statistics/1237290/cities-highest-population-density/

Statista. (2022c, April). *Germany: Total population from 2017 to 2027*. Economy & Politics›International. Retrieved Oct 08, 2022, from https://www.statista.com/statistics/624170/total-population-of-germany/

Wang, L. (2015). *The identification of minorities in China*. University of Hawai'i. Retrieved Oct 05, 2022, from https://blog.hawaii.edu/aplpj/files/2015/09/APLPJ_16_2_Wang.pdf

World Bank. (2022). *Gross domestic product 2021. World development indicators database*. Retrieved Oct 04, 2022, from https://databankfiles.worldbank.org/data/download/GDP.pdf

Yeung, C. (2022). *Economic and trade information on Hong Kong*. The Hong Kong Trade Development Council (HKTDC). Retrieved Oct 05, 2022, from https://research.hktdc.com/en/article/MzIwNjkzNTY5

3 The Enormous Pace of Infrastructural Development

3.1 Structural Change: From International Aid Recipient to a High-Tech Nation

In December 1978, under the leadership of Deng Xiaoping, the Chinese Communist Party (CCP) determined the 'Reform and Opening-Up Policy' at the Central Work Conference, the Third Plenary Session of the Eleventh Central Committee. The shift in the overall strategic focus of the Chinese policymakers towards economic growth marks the beginning of a historical process of integration of the Chinese market into the global economy (China (Hainan) Reform and Development Research Institute, n.d.). Later on, Deng was widely addressed by the Chinese media as the 'architect of socialism with Chinese characteristics' combining socialist ideology with elements of market economics.

At the time, China's infrastructure was significantly lacking compared to that of developed countries. Infrastructure refers to a country's basic structures for transportation, energy and water supplies, communication as well as medical and educational services, etc., encompassing both physical facilities and effective management organisations. Infrastructure plays a crucial role in a country's economic development. The well-developed transportation and communication networks facilitate the effective coordination and cost-efficient movement of goods and people; reliable water and energy supply systems for electricity, gasoline and natural gas are indispensable for industrial production.

On the brink of an economic collapse, China was in dire need of both financial resources and management expertise to improve its infrastructure. The successful cooperation with the World Bank has fuelled China's historical economic reform. Founded in 1945, the World Bank is an intergovernmental financial institution known as one of the three major institutions for the coordination of international economic affairs (the other two are the International Monetary Fund (IMF) and the World Trade Organization (WTO)). Shortly after a personal meeting between Deng Xiaoping and Robert McNamara, the President of the World Bank, China officially resumed its legal seat in the World Bank (Reformdata.org, 2005). As of 30 June

T. Dathe et al., *Business Opportunities and Risks in China*, Management for Professionals, https://doi.org/10.1007/978-3-031-31933-4_3

2021, the World Bank has provided approximately US$ 65.67 billion cumulative lending to China for the support of 438 development projects in the vast fields of transportation, energy supply, industrial and urban development, food and agriculture, education, public health, environmental and natural resource management, financial sector, information technology, etc. (The World Bank Office, Beijing, 2021). Remarkably, the World Bank mainly invested in the infrastructural projects—precisely the fields the private investors are usually reluctant to enter.

The World Bank was an important source of foreign investment to China in the early stage of the economic reform. It provided China with the urgently needed funds which were in short supply, both as direct fund provider and as guardian for private capital investment. In support of the implementation of the loan projects, the World Bank arranged numerous training programmes to the Chinese cooperation partners, covering both general knowledge on project management under market economy and technical assistance. The training activities soon expanded to a wide range of areas such as macroeconomics, industrial development and agricultural poverty alleviation. In addition, the central ministries and governments at all levels established numerous World Bank project offices to optimise the efficient and close interorganisational interactions. Some cadres who received international policy and business trainings in the early days have become recognised talents in the fields of economy, diplomacy or science and technology and are currently playing an important role in the society.

Since the beginning of market liberalisation, China's GDP growth has continuously averaged more than 9% per year. In 2021, the annual GDP exceeded 43 times that of 1978 (see Fig. 3.1). According to the World Bank's global absolute poverty standard of US$ 1.9 per person per day, China has lifted more than 800 million people out of poverty in the past 40 years, making up nearly 75% of the global poverty reduction in the same period. In addition, the overall population are now provided with significantly improved access to health, education and other social services (The World Bank Group, 2021) (The State Council of the People's Republic of China, 2022).

While the early interactions with the international financial institutions mainly revolved around helping China with the design of economic reform strategies, improving international project management and obtaining funds to overcome development bottlenecks, a two-way relationship has emerged in the later stages: while China absorbs international expertise in dealing with its key challenges in economic development, its own experiences in return strengthen the ability of the international institutions to help other developing countries (The World Bank, 2019). More recently, China's role has evolved from a beneficiary to a unique mix of major donor, shareholder, aid recipient and collaborator. By the end of 2021, China overtook Japan as the second largest contributor to the system of development banks, providing USD $ 66 billion annually of the total of US$ 200 billion subsidised loans to developing countries in need (Reuters, 2021).

Measured by nominal GDP, China has become the world's second largest economy and undisputed export champion since 2010 (IMF, 2022; UNCTAD, 2021). As 'the world's factory', China largely relied on resource-intensive

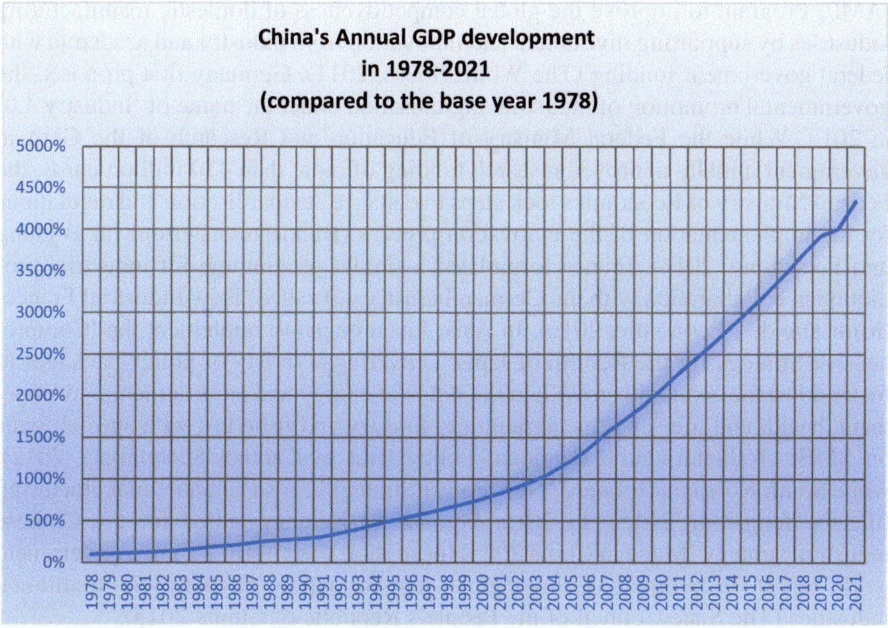

Fig. 3.1 China's annual GDP development from 1978 to 2021. Data source: The World Bank (World Bank, 2022)

manufacturing for exports with low-paid labour on its earlier economic path. However, the rapid rise in the costs of production factors such as land, labour, natural resources and environment exploitation is now constraining the previous development patterns, slowing down productivity and diminishing returns on investment. Above all, severe environmental pollution and exploding living expenses threaten to exacerbate social tensions.

In order to restore the healthy economic, environmental and social balances, the state government has put various strategies in place to counteract the negative legacies of the past decades by shifting the economy from low-cost production towards high-end manufacturing and services. One of the government's most prominent long-term strategies in the pursuit of upgrading the nation's manufacturing industrial system is known as 'Made in China 2025' (see Sect. 3.2). Today, the country is home to complete supply chains in large areas of industry sectors and, with its progressive innovations, enjoys the reputation of a high-tech nation.

3.2 Made in China 2025 (MIC25)

In reaction to the global financial crisis of 2008, the most powerful industrial countries began to enforce their national strategies to stimulate the growth of the real economy. The United States launched the Advanced Manufacturing Partnership

(AMP) Program to improve the global competitiveness of domestic manufacturing industries by supporting investment and innovation from industry and academia with federal government funding (The White House, 2011). Germany first proposed the governmental promotion of industrial digitalisation under the name of 'Industry 4.0' in 2013. While the Federal Ministry of Education and Research of the German government initially approved research funding of more than 470 million euros, the Federal Ministry of Economics took steps to enhance standardisation and regulations for the implementation of the innovation process (Bundesministerium für Bildung und Forschung, 2016). France formulated a similar programme for industrial promotion in collaboration with the German Industry 4.0 called 'New Industrial France' (Ministère de l'Économie, 2016). In Asia, Japan began to implement the 'Comprehensive Strategy for the Rebirth of Japan', covering a variety of policy packages to foster domestic economic growth in the fields of energy and environmental management, health and life sciences, agriculture, forestry and fisheries, with special focus on SMEs (Naikaku-kanbō (National Policy Unit of Cabinet Secretariat), 2012), while South Korea put forward 'New Power Strategy' for sustainable manufacturing (finance.ifeng.com, 2015). In 2015, Premier Li Keqiang called for the Chinese industrial strategy 'Made in China 2025' (or in short form 'MIC25') in a government work report to promote technological transformation of domestic traditional industries (The State Council of the People's Republic of China, 2015).

Being both the national future vision of the manufacturing industry with similar technical focus in the same time period, China's MIC25 is often compared with Germany's Industry 4.0. The term 'Industry 4.0', coined by a group of technology strategists for the German government, stands for industrial modernisation characterised by a deep integration of information technologies, such as the Internet of Things (IoT) and artificial intelligence (AI) technologies, into cyber-physical systems (CPS) to achieve machine self-organisation ('smart factory'). The choice of the term suggests a comparable importance of the current driven development as the most significant cutting-edge technologies in human industrial history known as 'industrial revolutions' (see Fig. 3.2 The concept of Industry 4.0).

To the Chinese experts, however, while Germany is generally seen in the stage of development from Industry 3.0 to Industry 4.0, China has yet to close the gap to Industry 3.0 before they could reach out for 4.0. The current shortcomings of the Chinese manufacturing industries were summarised as follows (finance.ifeng.com, 2015; The State Council of the People's Republic of China, 2015):

- Lack of innovation: dependency on foreign technologies and import of high-end equipment.
- Inadequate product image: national brands of quality products unknown to international markets.
- Inadequate resource and energy utilisation efficiency and pollution.
- Imperfect industrial structure: lack of high-end equipment and services.
- Inadequate digitalisation and depth of integration of industrialisation.
- Insufficient industrial internationalisation and global collaborations.

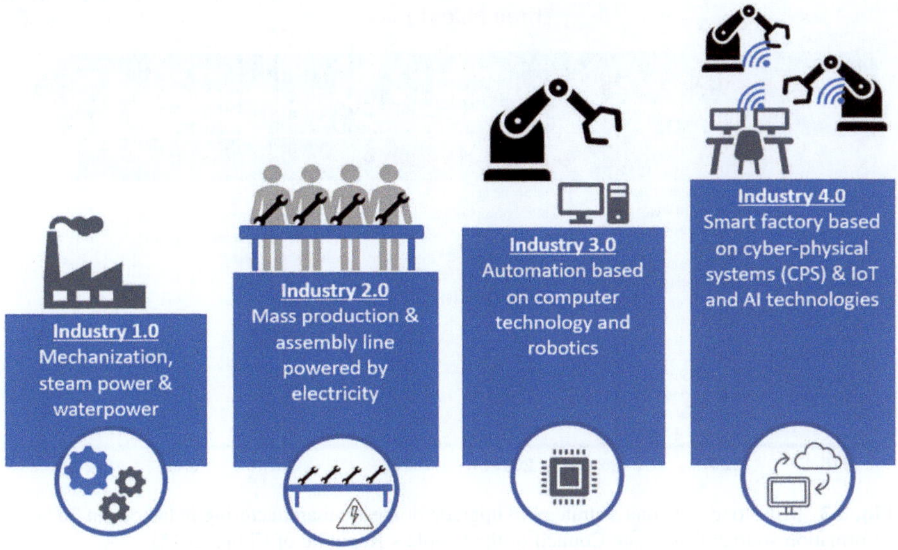

Fig. 3.2 The concept of Industry 4.0: from Industry 1.0 to Industry 4.0

'Made in China 2025' is an action plan for the first 10 years of China's ambitious roadmap on its way to overcome the above shortcomings, in order to transform into a world-leading industrial nation within three decades. A strong manufacturing industry is considered the basis of economic prosperity and effective national security. In interpretation of some domestic experts, the plan implies that China should rise as a major manufacturing power by 2025 and, subsequently, catch up with Germany and Japan to become a global manufacturing power by 2035 (finance.ifeng.com, 2015).

In the long-term overall strategy to upgrade domestic manufacturing industries, China defined the objectives with three milestones as follows (see Fig. 3.3):

- The first step ('Made in China 2025'): to become a major manufacturing power in 10 years' time. This step was divided into two intervals:
  By 2020,
  - To master a number of core technologies in key areas.
  - To achieve competitiveness in beneficial business sectors through improved product quality.
  - To enhance digitalisation and networking technologies in smart manufacturing processes.
  - To significantly improve the efficiency of energy and material consumption and reduce waste disposal.

  By 2025,
  - To achieve overall improvement of product quality.
  - To significantly expand the innovation capacity.
  - To improve labour productivity.
  - To advance the integration of industrialisation and digitalisation.

Fig. 3.3 Milestone of China's strategy to upgrade domestic manufacturing industries in 30 years. Information source: (The State Council of the People's Republic of China, 2015)

  - To improve the efficiency of energy and material consumption and reduce waste disposal in accordance with the advanced international standards.
  - To enhance strong international competitiveness through the creation of a group of multinational companies and forming industrial clusters in beneficial economic sectors.
- The second step: to become a global manufacturing power by 2035, including:
  - To achieve breakthroughs in product development in key economic sectors.
  - To enhance global leadership in innovation capacities.
  - To achieve fully realised industrialisation.
- The third step: to become a leading manufacturing superpower by 2049 (the 100th anniversary of the founding of the People's Republic of China), including:
  - To establish a global innovation leadership.
  - To achieve significant overall competitive advantages.
  - To build world-leading technology and industry systems.

To optimally bundle the governmental efforts, MIC25 defined ten core industries for the design of promotional programmes through state funding (see Fig. 3.4):

1. *New generation of information technology (IT) industry, including:*
   - *Integrated circuits and special equipment*—to increase manufacturing capacity for integrated circuit design, intellectual property (IP) cores and design tools, universal chips relevant to national information/network security and the electronic control in machine industry, high-density packaging and three-dimensional (3D) micro-assembly technology.
   - *Information and communication equipment*—core technologies such as new computing techniques, broadband internet connections, advanced storage,

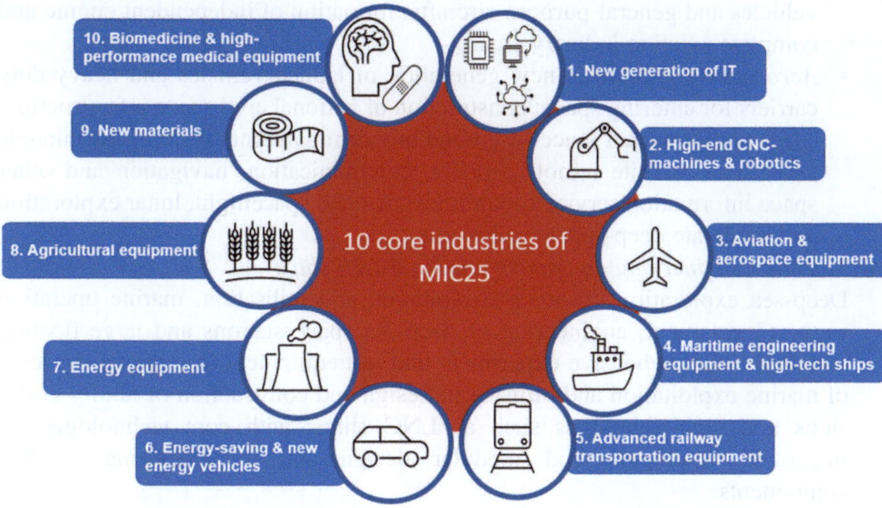

Fig. 3.4 The ten core industries defined in Made in China 2025 (MIC25). Information source: (The State Council of the People's Republic of China, 2015)

systematic security assurance, 5G technology, core routing and exchange technology, intelligent optical transmission technology, future web design and architecture, development of quantum computing and neural networks, research and development of high-end servers, innovative intelligent terminals, new-generation base stations and further equipment for network security.

- *Operating systems and industrial software*—industrial infrastructural systems such as operating systems for industrial design and data security, high-end industrial software such as intelligent design and simulation tools, manufacturing IoT, industrial big data processing, high-end industrial platform software and application software in key areas and to set standards for industrial software integration and security assessment.

2. *High-end CNC machines and robotics*
   - *High-end CNC machines*—cutting-edge technologies and equipment for CNC manufacturing and additive manufacturing to improve reliability and accuracy retention, including key components such as servo motors, bearings, gratings and key application software.
   - *Robotics*—industrial robots for automotive, machinery, electronics, dangerous goods manufacturing, national defence, chemical industry, light industry and specialised service robots for medical and healthcare, family services, education and entertainment.
3. *Aviation and aerospace equipment*
   - *Aviation equipment*—development of large aircraft and wide-body passenger aircraft; international collaboration for heavy-duty helicopters; industrialisation of trunk and regional aircraft, helicopters, unmanned aerial

vehicles and general-purpose aircrafts; formation of independent engine and complete aviation industry chain.

- *Aerospace equipment*—new generation of launch vehicles and heavy-duty carriers for entering space; construction of national civil space infrastructure, space platforms and space-to-ground broadband internet systems, sustainable and stable satellite remote sensing, communication, navigation and other space information service capabilities; manned spaceflight, lunar exploration and moderate deep-space exploration.

4. *Maritime engineering equipment and high-tech ships*
   Deep-sea exploration, resource exploitation and utilisation, marine operation support equipment; engineering of deep-sea space stations and large floating structures; comprehensive experiment and test equipment to improve the level of marine exploitation and utilisation; design and construction of luxury cruise ships and high-tech ships such as LNG ships, with core technologies of integrated, intelligent and modular design and manufacturing of key components
5. *Advanced railway transportation equipment*
   Application of new materials, new technologies and new processes; systematic safety assurance, energy conservation and environmental protection; digital, intelligent and networked technologies; lightweight and modular product families; high-speed and heavy-duty rail transit equipment systems with overall solutions throughout the entire life cycle of the systems
6. *Energy-saving and new energy vehicles*
   Further development of electric vehicles and fuel cell vehicles; core technologies for low-carbon, information-based and intelligence automobiles; engineering and industrialisation of core technologies such as power batteries, drive motors, high-efficiency internal combustion engines, advanced transmissions, lightweight materials and intelligent control; formation of a complete industrial system and innovation system from key components to complete vehicles; promotion of national brands for energy-saving and new energy vehicles with advanced international standards
7. *Energy equipment*
   Industrialisation and application of large-scale, high-efficiency and ultra-clean coal-fired power units; extension of manufacturing level of super-capacity hydropower units, nuclear power units and heavy-duty gas turbines; development of new energy and renewable energy equipment, advanced energy storage devices, power transmission and transformation for smart grids and user terminals; industrialisation of key components and materials such as high-power electrical and electronic devices and high-temperature superconducting materials
8. *Agricultural equipment*
   Advanced agricultural machinery and equipment used in the main production processes of grain, cotton, oil, sugar and other bulk grains and strategic commercial crops, such as breeding, farming, planting, management, harvesting, transportation and storage; large-scale tractors and their compound work

equipment; high-end agricultural equipment such as large complex harvesters with key components; capacities for data collection, intelligent decision-making and precise operations of agricultural machinery and equipment; formation of information-based overall solutions for agricultural production

9. *New materials*
   Special metal functional materials, high-performance structural materials, functional polymer materials, special inorganic non-metallic materials and advanced composite materials; research and development of new materials such as advanced melting, solidification moulding, vapour deposition, profile processing and efficient synthesis; basic research and system construction to overcome bottlenecks of industrial production; special new materials for military and civilian use; integration of military and civilian development in the new material industry; in consideration of impact of disruptive new materials on traditional materials, investment and development of strategic cutting-edge materials such as superconducting materials, nanomaterials and graphene- and bio-based materials; upgrading of basic materials
10. *Biomedicine and high-performance medical equipment*
   New chemical drugs, traditional Chinese medicines and biotech drugs for major diseases, with focus on new processes and new target chemical drugs, antibody drugs, antibody-conjugated drugs, new structural protein and peptide drugs, new vaccines and innovative traditional Chinese medicine with outstanding clinical advantages and personalised medicine; innovation and industrialisation of medical devices, with focus on high-performance diagnosis and treatment equipment such as imaging equipment and medical robots; high-value medical consumables such as fully degradable vascular stents; mobile medical products such as wearables and remote diagnosis and treatment devices; breakthroughs and applications of new technologies such as biological 3D printing and induced pluripotent stem cells.

The official release of ‘Made in China 2025’ raised immediate concerns in the United States and other Western countries. The policy would transform China from the world’s largest factory of low-value products into a competitive supplier of high-end equipment.

In the past, the West outsourced the labour- and material-intensive production to China to benefit from the price advantage of the local resources and labour, allowing themselves to focus on technical innovations with significantly higher returns. By reducing its reliance on foreign technology, China would eventually change this business model and sustainably limit the profits of foreign investors. Furthermore, as an industrial superpower with a vast domestic market, China would inevitably shake the dominance of the West and expectedly change the world order under the Western leadership.

Not surprisingly, the United States has used MIC25 to accuse China of non-market behaviours, particularly with regard to government subsidies, and to impose sanctions on Chinese companies by raising additional tariffs on numerous product categories and placing firms from sensitive industry sectors on the Entity List to restrict their international business activities.

Although the media reporting on the advancement of MIC25 has been quite silent since the intensified trade war between the United States and China, there is no indication that this strategy has been abandoned. In promoting domestic innovations in the above key industry sectors, the Chinese government still actively seeks cooperation with foreign institutions and business partners. In numerous business sectors, the Chinese companies have made great progress in building domestic brands for quality products, for example, Geely (automotive), BYD (electric automobile and rechargeable batteries), Fuyao (car glass), DJI (Da-Jiang Innovations, commercial unmanned aerial vehicles (drones)), Huawei (telecommunication equipment and consumer electronics), Lenovo (personal computers), Haier (home appliances) and ERKE (sportswear).

3.3 State Regulations and State-Owned Enterprises (SOEs)

The state regulations play a dominant role in China's business environment. Since the beginning of the economic reform in 1978, the Chinese government constantly takes a 'learning-by-doing' approach to test the compatibility of new policies on a small scale in isolated economic zones before they are expanded to the rest of the economy. This approach helps the government to optimise the trade-offs between the liberalisation and internalisation of the economy and combating external financial risks (MERICS, 2019).

Because of its political system, the state-owned enterprises (SOEs) that represent the socialist public ownership may always stay the leading force to drive China's national economy. However, since the beginning of the economic reform in 1978 (see Sect. 3.1), the organisational structure of SOEs has changed fundamentally. It took almost two decades for the SOEs to gradually undergo complex strategic adjustments to transform from carriers of the planned economy to modern business entities in the global market economy (Yu, 2020). Even today, the Chinese SOEs still owe their economic power to their financial and regulatory advantages due to their proximity to the national policymakers. At the same time, with the faster growth of privately owned enterprises (POEs) and a controlled privatisation process, the share of SOEs in China's economy continuously declines (Bruegle.org, 2021).

Historically, since the founding of the People's Republic of China in 1949, SOEs have been a central element of China's economic system. However, after decades of strategic preference of ideological to economic goals, many SOEs became bloated and inefficient. In the 1990s, during the painful reform process that was to benefit the country in a long run, many unprofitable SOEs were closed, resulting in mass unemployment and economic upheaval. In 2020–2022, China launched a successful reform project for SOEs, aiming to modernise the organisations by streamlining their operations and shifting the focus on innovation, technology and sustainability.

In contrast to Western criticism, the Chinese don't view state-owned enterprises (SOEs) and private-owned enterprises (POEs) as isolated opposing forces but

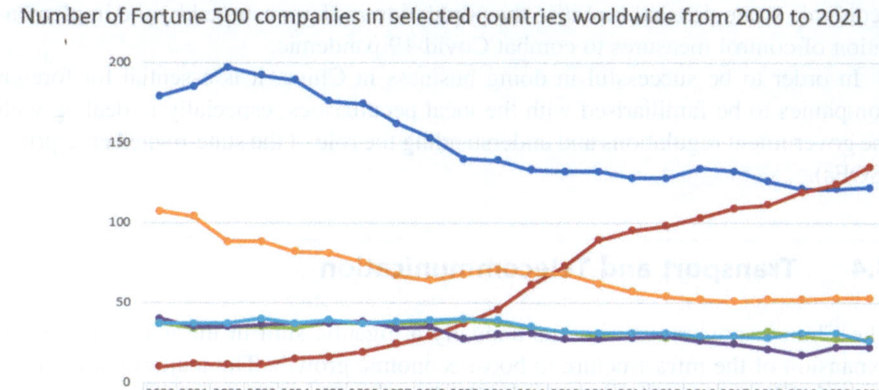

	2000	2001	2002	2003	2004	2005	2006	2007	2008	2009	2010	2011	2012	2013	2014	2015	2016	2017	2018	2019	2020	2021
United States	179	185	197	192	189	176	174	162	153	140	139	133	132	132	128	128	134	132	126	121	121	122
China	10	12	11	11	15	16	19	24	29	37	46	61	73	89	95	98	103	109	111	119	124	135
Germany	37	34	35	35	34	37	37	37	37	39	37	34	32	29	28	28	28	29	32	29	27	27
United Kingdom	40	35	35	36	37	37	38	34	35	27	30	31	27	27	28	29	26	24	21	17	22	22
France	37	37	37	40	37	39	37	38	39	40	39	35	32	31	31	31	29	29	28	31	31	26
Japan	107	104	88	88	82	81	75	67	64	68	71	68	68	62	57	54	52	51	52	52	53	53

Fig. 3.5 Number of Fortune 500 companies in selected countries from 2000 to 2021. Data source: (Statista, 2022)

interconnected entities. In their Yin und Yan philosophy, SOEs are portrayed as the locomotive of the national economy that improves the business environment for POEs. The development of POEs, in turn, would foster the growth of SOEs.

A further criticism against the publicly listed SOEs is the potential for conflict of interest, with concerns that they may prioritise the needs of the state and the people over the profit motives of shareholders. To address this criticism, China has implemented various regulations aimed at enhancing corporate governance transparency and promoting responsiveness to market pressure.

Due to the large size and the financial capacity of the Chinese state-owned enterprises (SOEs), their business activities have an enormous impact on the market. In the past, they have contributed significantly to China's economic growth, both domestically and internationally.

Cooperation with the state-owned enterprises (SOEs) bears lucrative opportunities to business partners. On the other hand, the inequality in economic power may easily lead to dependency. The overwhelming influence of SOEs is sometimes criticised by foreign think tanks for lack of competitive neutrality compared to the privately owned enterprises (POEs) which in turn could affect the market mechanisms (Bruegle.org, 2021).

According to the American multinational business magazine *Fortune*, the number of Chinese companies among the worldwide 500 largest companies (the annual 'Fortune 500' list by revenue) rose from 10 in year 2000 to 135 in year 2021, with the majority of those being SOEs (see Fig. 3.5). In 2020 and 2021, China has more Fortune 500 companies than the United States. Some of the main reasons for China's faster economic growth could be seen in China's ability to carry out long-term economic strategies and mobilise the population as demonstrated by the implementation of control measures to combat Covid-19 pandemic.

In order to be successful in doing business in China, it is essential for foreign companies to be familiarised with the local peculiarities, especially in dealing with the government regulations and understanding the role of the state-owned enterprises (SOEs).

3.4 Transport and Telecommunication

The Chinese government invests annually a gigantic sum in the maintenance and expansion of the infrastructure to boost economic growth. The major investment in favour of the industrialisation process lies in the traffic and transportation sectors, as well in the energy supply (Dathe & Helmold, 2018).

The Chinese government constantly invests in the transportation network. As per 2020, China's railway lines cover nearly 150,000 kilometres, ranking second in the world after the United States; the road network exceeds five million kilometres, ranking third in the world after the United States and India. A well-developed transport infrastructure enables efficient passenger and cargo (see Table 3.1 The capacity of transportation lines in China from 2017 to 2020, Table 3.2 The cargo turnover in China from 2017 to 2020 and Table 3.3 Passenger traffic in China from 2017 to 2020).

In addition, China also has the worldwide longest railway line for passenger transportation by high-speed trains (speed >250 km/h). The network has already

Table 3.1 The capacity of transportation lines in China from 2017 to 2020

Total length of transport line (in thousand km)	2017	2018	2019	2020
Railway	127.0	131.7	139.9	146.3
Roads	4773.5	4846.5	5012.5	5198.1
Motorway	136.4	142.6	149.6	161.0
Inland waterway	127.0	127.1	127.3	127.7
Regular flight routes	7843.0	8379.8	9482.2	9426.3
Oil and gas pipelines	119.3	122.3	126.6	134.1

Data source: (National Bureau of Statistics of China, 2022a, 2022b)

Table 3.2 The cargo turnover in China from 2017 to 2020

Cargo turnover (in billion ton-kilometres)	2017	2018	2019	2020
Railway	2696	2882	3018	3051
Roads	6677	7125	5964	6017
Waterway	9861	9905	10,396	10,583
Aviation	24	26	26	24

Data source: (National Bureau of Statistics of China, 2022a, 2022b)

Table 3.3 Passenger traffic in China from 2017 to 2020

Passenger traffic (in billion travelled kilometres)	2017	2018	2019	2020[a]
Railway	1346	1415	1471	827
Streets	977	928	886	464
Waterway	8	8	8	3
Aviation	951	1701	1171	631

Data source: (National Bureau of Statistics of China, 2022a, 2022b)
[a]A clear declination of passenger traffic since the beginning of the Covid-19 pandemic can be observed

been expanded to over 40,000 km and connects 93% of all Chinese cities with more than 500,000 inhabitants (Xinhua Network, 2022).

To facilitate the ticketing process for mass passenger transportation services, China has launched the 12,306 Railway Internet Ticketing System (https://www.12306.cn/en/index.html) which fully supports e-tickets for all high-speed train and intercity train connections since April 2020. Since 2021, China National Railway Group also provides online processing functions on the railway freight e-commerce platform. Meanwhile, around 7000 companies have registered on the online platform, initiating some 200,000 electronic waybills. That means that 97% of all transport orders have been processed online. The online platforms not only improve the efficiency of transactions but also help fight the Covid-19 pandemic by limiting interpersonal contacts (Xinhua Network, 2022).

Furthermore, the communication infrastructure has improved rapidly (see *Fehler! Verweisquelle konnte nicht gefunden werden.*). The increasing technical capacities for data communication are important prerequisites for future technologies based on the digitalisation of industrial processes. For the manufacturing companies, there is a trend towards networking machines and human operators in forms of machine-to-machine (M2M), person-to-person (P2P) and machine-to-person (M2P) communication. The integrated communication accelerates the production steps through automation. This increases both the production efficiency and quality and subsequently reduces the transaction costs. This kind of automation of production by means of networks of value-added participants is often discussed under the term 'smart manufacturing'. The automatic computerised decision-making process based on modern dynamic machine learning techniques is referred to as artificial intelligence (AI) (Dathe & Helmold, 2018).

The courier service in China plays an important role in the delivery of goods, especially in e-commerce. Documents and smaller packages are often delivered within a few hours within the same city (see Table 3.4 China's telecommunication capacity and courier service from 2017 to 2020). The mopeds of the courier services on the streets of Chinese cities have become indispensable. On demand, small packages are often delivered within a few hours within the same city.

The sophisticated transport and telecommunication networks, paired with the far-reaching industrialisation with relatively stable energy supplies, enable the

Table 3.4 China's telecommunication capacity and courier service from 2017 to 2020

Communication capacities	2017	2018	2019	2020
Express courier service (in million)	40,056	50,710	63,523	83,358
Package delivery (in million)	27	24	21	20
Internet participants (in million)	772	829	904	989
Internet penetration rate (in %)	55.8	59.6	64.5	70.4
Mobile phone users (in million)	1417	1566	1601	1594
Internet broadband terminals (in million)	776	868	916	946

Data source: (National Bureau of Statistics of China, 2022a, 2022b)

rapid growth of e-commerce during the Covid-19 pandemic and cement China a central hub of the global economy.

3.5 Innovation Policy

The McKinsey Global Institute (MGI), the business and economic research institution of the global management consulting firm McKinsey & Company, classifies innovation activities in four categories ('innovation archetypes'):

- Efficiency-driven.
- Customer-focused.
- Engineering-based.
- Science-based.

According to a recent study by McKinsey & Company, Chinese manufacturers are shifting their strategic focus from refining production processes and expand cost leadership to boost profit innovation of technologies and product design (McKinsey, 2021).

To achieve the strategic goal of innovation self-sufficiency, the Chinese government has continuously introduced new policies in the past decades to intensify R&D spendings and improve the competitiveness of the domestic manufacturing industry by pooling nationwide resources (see Fig. 3.6 Internal R&D spending in China from 2012 to 2021).

The Fourteenth Five-Year Plan for the National Economic and Social Development of the Chinese government ('14th Five-Year Plan') defined the following core scientific and technological research fields of strategic importance for national security (Government of China, 2021):

- *Artificial intelligence*, such as development of special chips; building platforms for open-source algorithm such as deep learning frameworks; decision-making techniques; audio, visual, graphic information processing; natural language recognition; etc.

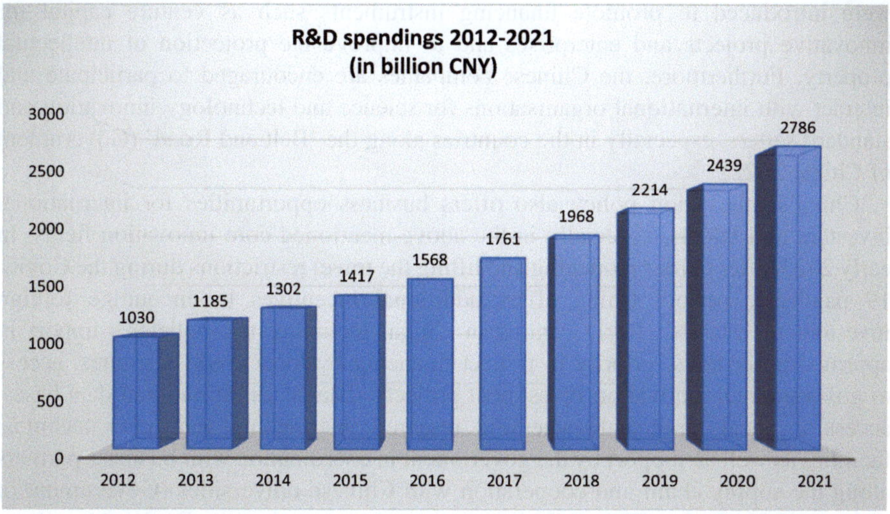

Fig. 3.6 Internal R&D spending in China from 2012 to 2021. Source: (National Bureau of Statistics of China, 2022a, 2022b)

- *Quantum information technology*, including quantum space communication, development of quantum computer prototypes and practical products, precision measurement technology based on quantum computing, etc.
- *Integrated circuits (ICs)*, including IC design tools, development of target equipment and materials, IGBT and MEMS processing technologies, upgrading memory technologies, etc.
- *Brain science and brain-inspired technologies*, such as brain cognitive principle analysis, brain mesoscopic neural connection visualisation, brain-inspired computing and brain-computer fusion technology, etc.
- *Gene technique and biotechnology*, especially genomics, genetic breeding, innovative vaccine, non-invasive diagnosis, antibody drug research, biosafety, etc.
- *Life and health sciences and technologies*, such as basic research on pathogenesis of cancer and cardiovascular, respiratory and metabolic diseases, active health intervention technology, regenerative medicine, microbiome, prevention and control of major infectious diseases and major chronic non-infectious diseases.
- *Deep-space, deep-sea and polar exploration*, including basic science research, Mars orbiting and other interstellar exploration, reusable space transportation systems, exploration equipment, three-dimensional observation systems, etc.

Guided by the national strategic policies, the Chinese government promotes innovation in the target fields of science and technology with tax incentives and government funding. Scientists and entrepreneurs are increasingly involved in the decision-making process for national strategy. Special fundings for technology-based small- and medium-sized enterprise (SMEs) projects were integrated in the '14th Five-Year Plan' to support the founders and founding incubators. New policies were introduced to promote financing instruments such as venture capital for innovative projects and enterprises and to improve the protection of intellectual property. Furthermore, the Chinese companies are encouraged to participate and interact with international organisations for science and technology innovation and standard setters, especially in the countries along the 'Belt and Road' (Government of China, 2022).

China's innovation policy also offers business opportunities for international investors and talents, especially in the above-mentioned core innovation fields. In early 2023, after border reopening and lifting the travel restrictions during the Covid-19 pandemic period, China offers additional incentives to encourage foreign investors to establish R&D centres in China, including tax policies, support in approval procedures, priority in project financing by local credit institutes, access to governmental innovation investment projects, data access at national data bases, access to local large-scale scientific research instruments and other technical facilities as well as support by the government in coordination with business partners along the supply chain and cooperation with Chinese universities (Government of China, 2023). As the CEO of German automotive manufacturer BMW, Mr. Oliver Zipse stated in early 2023, 'A lot of things happening in the tech world are starting in China, and then are being extended to the world'. China is actively encouraging the establishment of R&D centres within its borders, and many multinational companies are taking advantage of this opportunity (Xinhua News Agency, 2023).

References

BRUEGEL.Org. (2021, February). *China's state-owned enterprises and competitive neutrality*. Policy Contribution Issue n°05/21 by Alicia García-Herrero and Gary Ng. Retrieved Jan 23, 2023, from https://www.bruegel.org/sites/default/files/wp-content/uploads/2021/02/PC-05-2021.pdf

Bundesministerium für Bildung und Forschung. (2016, Jan 21). *Industrie 4.0. Forschung/Digitale Wirthschaft und Gesellschaft*. Retrieved Jan 23, 2023, from https://www.bmbf.de/bmbf/de/forschung/digitale-wirtschaft-und-gesellschaft/industrie-4-0/industrie-4-0.html

China (Hainan) Reform and Development Research Institute. (n.d.). *China's Reform and Opening-up Database*. www.chinareform.org.cn. Retrieved Jan 23, 2023, from http://www.reformdata.org/records/1978.shtml

Dathe, T., & Helmold, M. (2018). *Erfolgreich im Chinageschäft: Strategien und Handlungsempfehlungen für kleinere und mittlere Unternehmen (KMU)*. Springer Gabler Verlag.

finance.ifeng.com. (2015, Mar 11). *Li Keqiang's trump card: Made in China 2025*. Retrieved Jan 25, 2023, from https://finance.ifeng.com/a/20150311/13545234_0.shtml

Government of China. (2021, Mar 13). 中华人民共和国国民经济和社会发展第十四个五年规划和2035年远景目标纲要. Xinhua News Agency. Retrieved Jan 26, 2023, from http://www.gov.cn/xinwen/2021-03/13/content_5592681.htm

Government of China. (2022, Sep 05). 科技部 财政部关于印发《企业技术创新能力提升行动方案(2022—2023年)》的通知. Ministry of Science and Technology and ministry of Finance. Retrieved Jan 26, 2023, from http://www.gov.cn/zhengce/zhengceku/2022-08/15/content_5705464.htm

Government of China. (2023, Jan 18). 国务院办公厅转发商务部科技部关于. Office of the State Council. Retrieved Jan 26, 2023, from http://www.gov.cn/zhengce/content/2023-01/18/content_5737692.htm

IMF. (2022, April). *World economic and financial surveys*. World Economic Outlook Database. Retrieved Jan 31, 2023, from https://www.imf.org/en/Publications/WEO/weo-database/2022/April/select-country-group

McKinsey. (2021, Sep 16). *China's digital R&D imperative*. McKinsey & Company. Retrieved Dec 31, 2022, from https://www.mckinsey.com/business-functions/operations/our-insights/chinas-digital-r-and-d-imperative

MERICS. (2019, Jun 19). *China's caution about loosening cross-border capital flows*. Mercator institute for China studies. Retrieved Dec 30, 2022, from https://merics.org/en/report/chinas-caution-about-loosening-cross-border-capital-flows

Ministère de l'Économie. (2016, Jun 30). *New industrial France: Building France's industrial future*. Ministry for Economy and Finance. Retrieved Dec 31, 2022, from https://www.economie.gouv.fr/files/files/PDF/web-dp-indus-ang.pdf

Naikaku-kanbō (National Policy Unit of Cabinet Secretariat). (2012, Aug 08). *Rebirth of Japan: A comprehensive strategy*. Cabinet Decision–July 31, 2012. Retrieved Dec 28, 2022, from https://www.cas.go.jp/jp/seisaku/npu/pdf/20120821/20120821_en.pdf

National Bureau of Statistics of China. (2022a). *Annual data*. Retrieved Dec 31, 2022, from https://data.stats.gov.cn/easyquery.htm?cn=C01

National Bureau of Statistics of China. (2022b, Feb 28). *Share of clean energy consumption in total energy consumption 2017–2021*. Statistical Communiqué of the People's Republic of China on National Economic and Social Development in 2021. Retrieved Dec 1, 2022, from http://www.stats.gov.cn/tjsj/zxfb/202202/t20220227_1827960.html

Reformdata.org. (2005, July 31). *World Bank and China's reform and opening*. China reform information database. Retrieved Dec 31, 2022, from http://www.reformdata.org/2005/0731/19611.shtml.

Reuters. (2021, Nov 18). *Report shows China's growing clout at World Bank, global institutions. Andrea Shalal*. Retrieved Dec 31, 2022, from https://www.reuters.com/business/finance/report-shows-chinas-growing-clout-world-bank-global-institutions-2021-11-18/

Statista. (2022, Aug 05). *Number of fortune 500 companies worldwide 2000-2021, by country. Statista research department, Survey by Qlik*. Retrieved Dec 31, 2022, from https://www.statista.com/statistics/1204099/number-fortune-500-companies-worldwide-country/

The State Council of the People's Republic of China. (2015, May 08). *Notice of the state council on printing and distributing "made in China 2025"*. Guo Fa [2015] No. 28. Retrieved Dec 28, 2022, from http://www.gov.cn/zhengce/content/2015-05/19/content_9784.htm

The State Council of the People's Republic of China. (2022, Apr 02). *The Ministry of Finance, the National Research Center and the World Bank jointly released a research report–China's poverty reduction achievements provide reference for the world*. Retrieved Dec 28, 2022, from http://www.gov.cn/xinwen/2022-04/02/content_5683094.htm

The White House. (2011, Jun 24). *President Obama launches advanced manufacturing partnership*. Office of the Press Secretary. Retrieved Dec 30, 2022, from https://obamawhitehouse.archives.gov/the-press-office/2011/06/24/president-obama-launches-advanced-manufacturing-partnership

The World Bank. (2019, Nov 11). *China–Country Partnership Framework for the Period FY2020–2025*. Retrieved Dec 28, 2022, from https://documents.worldbank.org/en/publication/documents-reports/documentdetail/902781575573489712/china-country-partnership-framework-for-the-period-fy2020-2025

The World Bank. (2022, July 20). *GDP growth (annual %)–China*. World Bank national accounts data, and OECD National Accounts data files. Retrieved Dec 31, 2022, from https://data.worldbank.org/indicator/NY.GDP.MKTP.KD.ZG?locations=CN

The World Bank Group. (2021, July). *Facts and figures*. The World Bank Office. Retrieved Dec 31, 2022, from https://thedocs.worldbank.org/en/doc/4758e6e0b19b63c0d5f0319e364b9ab4-0070012021/original/f-fs-fy21-en.pdf

The World Bank Office, Beijing. (2021, July). *The World Bank Group in China. Facts and figures*. Retrieved Dec 31, 2022, from https://thedocs.worldbank.org/en/doc/4758e6e0b19b63c0d5f0319e364b9ab4-0070012021/original/f-fs-fy21-en.pdf

UNCTAD. (2021, Apr 27). *China: The rise of a trade titan*. Retrieved Dec 28, 2022, from https://unctad.org/news/china-rise-trade-titan

Xinhua Network. (2022, July 11). *Extraordinary decade of changes: The leading model of China's high-speed rail*. Retrieved Dec 28, 2022, from http://www.news.cn/politics/2022-07/11/c_1128821004.htm

Xinhua News Agency. (2023, Jan 13). *Int'l companies confident in China's innovation vitality*. Von Belt and Road Portal. Retrieved Feb 20, 2023, from https://eng.yidaiyilu.gov.cn/qwyw/rdxw/302051.htm

Yu. (2020). *On the status and function of the state-owned economy in China's economy and society*. CORE/ China Academic Journal Electronic Publishing House. Retrieved Dec 30, 2022, from https://core.ac.uk/download/pdf/343508295.pdf

Internationalisation of China

4

4.1 Integration in Global Value Chain (GVC): Twenty Years of WTO

Since the introduction of 'Reform and Opening-Up Policy' in 1978, China has improved the efficiency of economic operations by taking over advanced management practices from international cooperation partners, such as the competitive bidding system, the engineer supervision system and the owner responsibility system of the World Bank. For example, the Beijing-Tianjin-Tangshan Expressway financed with World Bank loans, the first inter-provincial highway project of 142.7 km in accordance with modern standards, reformed China's highway construction management system by adopting the internationally accepted FIDIC terms as contract glossary, introducing contract management practice and facilitating a monitoring mechanism (Reformdata.org, 2005).

In the mid-1990s, a trend towards globalisation emerged mainly owed to rapid advancement of cost-effective information and communication technologies, as well as global transport logistics (Dathe & Helmold, 2018). China's integration into global economy is formally marked by its accession to the multilateral trading system of the World Trade Organization (WTO) after 15 years' endeavour.

The World Trade Organization (WTO) founded in 1995 is an international organisation for global market liberalisation. It provides a system of trade rules and settles trade disputes between the member governments. Since 29 July 2016, the WTO represents 164 member states with 98% of total world trade volume (WTO.org, 2022a, 2022b). The People's Republic of China became the 143rd WTO member on 11 December 2001 (WTO.org, 2001).

In July 2015, China also joined the OECD Development Centre as a non-OECD member state to collaborate on global policy solutions to stimulate economic growth and improve living standards in developing countries, deepening China's integration in the world economy (OECD, 2018).

The Chinese economy has received an enormous boost from the globalisation process, especially after two decades of free market access through participation in

T. Dathe et al., *Business Opportunities and Risks in China*, Management for Professionals, https://doi.org/10.1007/978-3-031-31933-4_4

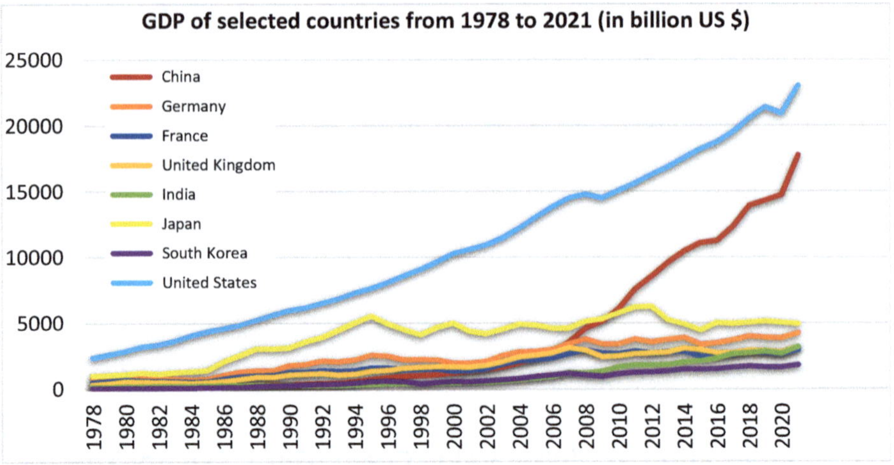

Fig. 4.1 GDP of selected countries from 1978 to 2021. Data source: The World Bank (The World Bank, 2022a, 2022b)

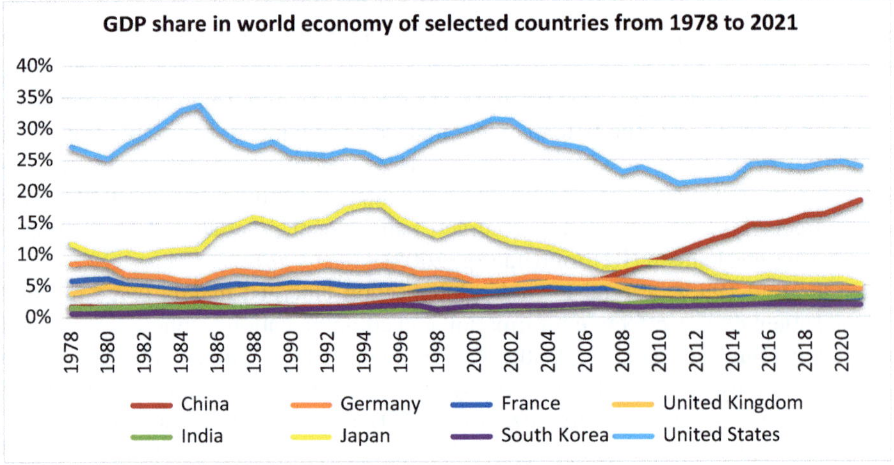

Fig. 4.2 GDP share in world economy of selected countries from 1978 to 2021. Data source: The World Bank (The World Bank, 2022a, 2022b)

the WTO. The share of Mainland China's gross domestic product (GDP) in world economy has risen from 4% in 2001 to over 18% in 2021 (see Figs. 4.1 and 4.2). Since 2010, China has overtaken Japan as the second largest national economy (data source: (The World Bank, 2022a, 2022b)). By the end of May 2022, China has entered effective bilateral investment treaties (BITs) with 108 countries and double taxation agreements (BTAs) with 112 countries and regions (including tax arrangements between the Mainland and Hong Kong, Macao and Taiwan) (Ministry of Commerce of the People's Republic of China, 2022).

Table 4.1 WTO members with the highest number of dispute cases as respondent

	Countries/economic unions	As complainant	As respondent	As third party
1	United States	124	156	172
2	European Union (formerly EC)	110	91	216
3	China	22	49	192
4	India	24	32	177
5	Canada	40	23	170
6	Argentina	21	22	66
7	Korea, Republic of	21	19	139
8	Australia	11	17	117
9	Brazil	34	17	164
10	Japan	28	16	225
11	Indonesia	12	15	47
12	Mexico	25	15	112
13	Chile	10	13	48
14	Türkiye (formerly Turkey)	6	12	106
15	Russian Federation	8	11	97

Data source: (WTO.org, 2022a, 2022b)

China's accession poses an unprecedented challenge for the World Trade Organization (WTO) that nobody expected 20 years ago. For the first time, WTO is dealing with a socialist country with such enormous economic impact (BRUEGEL, 2019). Although the Chinese central government has abolished more than 2300 laws and regulations, and local governments more than 190,000 to embrace market economy, it sticks firmly to the 'socialist market economy system'. Those who hoped for 'change through trade'—that China would eventually give up its political system—ended in disappointment (Handelsblatt, 2021).

While the Western politicians repeatedly lament government subsidies and distortions of competition in favour of state-owned companies in China, some Western economists concede that China's state economy also strengthens the resilience of the world economy. For example, China was able to stabilise its economy effectively by pumping huge sums into the market during the collapse of the international financial system in 2008–2009. The political system also empowers the Chinese government to take strong anti-pandemic measures to combat the Covid-19 crisis (Tagesschau, 2021; UNCTAD, 2021).

Discontent over China's alleged breaches of fair-trade rules has grown in the Western media, although the definition and admissibility of the main charge of state aid are likely to continue to undergo years of debate at the WTO headquarters in Geneva. Based on the allegations, the former US President Donald Trump imposed $300 billion punitive tariffs on Chinese exports which are currently maintained by his successor Joe Biden. Apparently, China is not the only country suspected of violating trade rules (see Table 4.1 WTO members with the highest number of dispute cases as respondent). China's economic power is increasingly viewed as a political challenge by the established industrial nations. As more Western analysts are convinced that China could overtake the United States as the largest economy as early as 2028, the potential hostility is mounting (Handelsblatt, 2021).

In summary, China's integration in the global value chain (GVC) has enabled the economy to expand rapidly. At present, China has developed industrialisation of many manufacturing sectors, including precision instruments, industrial machinery, computer and smartphones, solar panels, battery production, etc. The economic development over the past four decades helped China to lift more than 800 million people out of poverty, more than anywhere else in the same period (see Sect. 3.1) (UNCTAD, 2021).

However, the rise of China as a global economic power has triggered geopolitical tensions with the United States and its allies. The shift of their national policies could curb exports from China in the future and end or even reverse the ongoing globalisation process, which in turn could jeopardise the current living standards of all countries in the world. To counter the geopolitical challenges, President Xi Jinping of the People's Republic of China (PRC) repeatedly emphasised a new strategy in his recent speeches, making the domestic market the main body of future economic development, while remaining accessible to the world market (Xinhua Net, 2020).

Furthermore, the Chinese economy is challenged by the negative demographical development and the increasing labour costs in the domestic market that erode China's global competitiveness. It is observed that some industry sectors are being relocated from China to lower-wage countries like Vietnam and South Asia. On the other hand, there is an intrinsic motivation of the Chinese market participants to conquer more profitable sections of the global value chain (GVC) such as technical innovations for efficient production processes based on automation (AI) and robotics and such in fulfilment of the overall rising demand for social and ecological performance (Tagesschau, 2021; UNCTAD, 2021).

4.2 New Trends in China's Opening-Up Policy

Around 1949, the year of the foundation of the People's Republic of China, most Western companies retreated from China. The Soviet Union supported China to build infrastructure and heavy industry, trying to duplicate their own development model. However, in the late 1950s, ideological differences lead to a deterioration of the relation between the two countries; in 1960, the Soviet Union recalled all its technical experts from China, joint projects were completely cancelled, and the trade between China and the Soviet Union as well as most Eastern European countries came to a hold. For almost two decades, China followed a policy of self-sufficiency. In December 1978, the CPC adopted Deng Xiaoping's new policy of economic reforms and China's opening-up to the outside world. During the 1980s, multinational companies started to invest in China, mostly in the mandatory form of joint ventures. After China's accession to the WTO in December 2001, most limitations to China's international trade and in investment were lifted; subsequently, a large number of multinational companies and SMEs established trade relations and set up subsidiaries in China.

The openness of an economy depends on many factors; its comprehensive result can be measured in terms of free flow of goods, capital and people. On the highest level, President Xi Jinping's report to the 20th party congress of the CPC states: 'On the journey ahead, we must firmly adhere to the following major principles: ... Remaining committed to deepening reform and opening up' (Shanghai Observer, 2022).

Trade is one of the main drivers of Chinas economic growth. Since 2020, China is the world's largest trader. In 2021, China's trade reached 6.9 trillion US$ (China.org, 2022). In the same year, China's exports amounted to approximately 19% of its GDP (Statista, 2022a, 2022b), more than the GDP of the United Kingdom. Trade in services reached 0.80 trillion US$, 11.5% of its total trade, but only about half of the trade in service's share in total global trade. In the future, China's trade in services is expected to grow faster than trade in goods. Cross-border e-commerce increased tenfold from 2017 to 2021 and reached 0.30 trillion US$. Given the popularity of e-commerce in domestic consumption in China, cross-border e-commerce is a promising sector for growth.

In 2021, China exported 3.36 trillion US$ worth of goods, a trade surplus of 0.67 trillion US$ or almost 25% of the value of the imported goods (2.69 trillion US$). The trade surplus stems almost exclusively from trade with North America and the EU, causing dissatisfaction in the national governments in those regions. As one measure to increase imports, since 2018, China is holding the annual China International Import Expo (CIIE) exports. Every year, the Expo is visited by Chinese high-level procurement departments; the CIIE has developed as one promising channel for international companies to launch business development in China.

While international brands have a good reputation among Chinese consumers and companies, China's public procurement market prefers domestic products. According to China's Government Procurement Law, public procurement agencies shall buy products made in China, 'unless products, projects and services are not available in China or not available under reasonable commercial conditions' (Baidu, 2022b). A way to ensure mutual access to government markets would be China's accession to the Agreement on Government Procurement (GPA) under the framework of the WTO. China applied to join the GPA as early as 2007; however, approval to China's accession needs unanimous approval by all current 48 members (the EU counting as one member). Negotiations about China's accession protocol—laying down the precise terms of China's accession—are ongoing, but there is no timeline when the process will be completed.

To a large extent, China's trade surplus is caused by huge investment of European and North American companies in China, manufacturing in China for China, instead of importing goods. Investment by foreign enterprises in China is allowed in all sectors, unless restricted in a negative list. The 2021 version of the negative list has 31 items—two less than the 2020 version—in which foreign investment is either completely forbidden or only possible with a Chinese joint venture partner (NDRC, 2021). For example, investment in hospitals is only possible in cooperation with a

Chinese partner company. As a tendency, the number of restricted industries is gradually reduced. Notably, from 2018 to 2020, China lifted all restrictions to ownership in automobile manufacture. A different shorter negative list (27 instead of 31 restricted industries) applies to experimental free-trade zones (Government of the PRC, 2021). The WTO agreement allows emerging economies to protect certain sectors of its economy for a transitional period. As China's industry becomes more and more competitive, further shortening of the negative lists is expected.

Free exchange of personnel is an important factor for economic openness. For FIE, it is straightforward to send qualified employees to China or employ foreign nationals in China. Foreign nationals with special skills can establish their private-owned SME or micro-enterprise in China. Chinese labour law and social security regulations treat foreign employees equal. However, the threshold for foreign nationals to obtain an unlimited residence permit is still high. In March 2020, the Ministry of Justice had published a draft regulation on granting permanent residence permit for foreign nationals for public consultation, which would have made it considerably easier to obtain a permanent residence permit (Observer Net, 2020). However, after negative feedback from the public, this regulation has not come into force. Therefore, a fundamental change of the current policy cannot be expected. In the coming years, China needs to create jobs for a large number of unqualified youths; hence, the job market will not be opened for low-qualified workers.

As in the past, China is going to further open up special regions of China, then evaluate the result and possibly roll out successful policies on a national level. One prominent example is a new free-trade zone, covering the whole of Hainan Province with ten million inhabitants (see Sect. 14.1).

4.3 The New Silk Road

Trade between Europe and China has a history of more than 2000 years, beginning at the time of the Roman Empire and the Chinese Han dynasty (206 BCE–220 CE). The trading routes were not just one single road but formed a vast network, crisscrossing Central Asia with side roads to India and the Middle East. From the late nineteenth century, this trade network was retrospectively named 'Silk Road' referring to one of ancient China's most important export products. In addition, starting from around the tenth century, Chinese traders established maritime trade links with Southeast Asia. During the Ming dynasty (1368 to 1644), China became an important seafarer nation, establishing settlements in many Southeast Asian countries.

The following, last imperial dynasty of China, the Qing dynasty (1644 to 1912), had its roots in the landlocked Manchuria (Northeast China) and isolated China from the world. When, in the 1980s, China started to introduce a market economy and open up after 300 years of isolation, the newly founded Chinese companies had hardly any knowledge of international markets and focused on the huge domestic Chinese market.

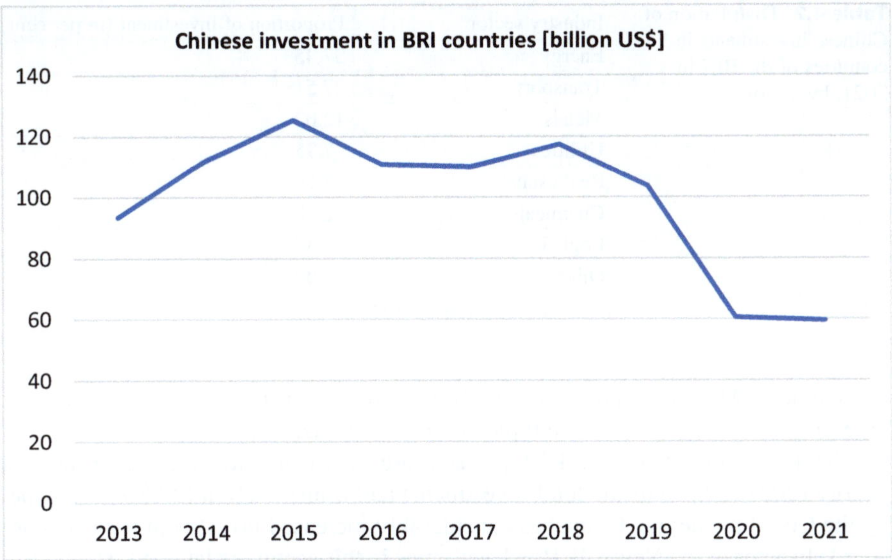

Fig. 4.3 Chinese investment in BRI countries [billion US$]. Data source: (Statista, 2022a, 2022b)

To accelerate China's internationalisation of the economy, on 07 September 2013, President Xi Jinping announced the establishment of the New Silk Road Economic Corridor (Baidu Encyclopedia, 2022a) and, on 03 October 2013, of the twenty-first Century Maritime Silk Road. In line with the Chinese abbreviation (一带一路), in English, the combination of the new land born and maritime silk roads has been named 'Belt and Road Initiative' (BRI or B&R).

Similar to its ancient predecessor, the New Silk Road is not a monolithic scheme, but a broad umbrella under which a wide range of different forms of cooperations are subsumed. Huge infrastructure projects have gained most attention, but, for example, China also promotes cultural exchange with BRI partner countries and invests in education, offering grants especially designed for university students from BRI countries.

In March 2022, according to Chinese sources, memorandum of understandings (MoU) have been signed with 147 countries; however, 7 of them have not published a confirmation of signing a full MoU (Nedopil Wang, 2022). The BRI has a considerable overlap with other trade agreements, for example, the RCEP free-trade agreement.

From 2013 to June 2022, cumulative BRI engagement amounts to 932 billion US $, about 561 billion US$ in construction contracts and US$371 billion in non-financial investments (Nedopil Wang, 2022). After a steep increase after announcing the BRI, China's investment in BRI countries was basically stable in the years from 2015 to 2019 and dropped during the Covid pandemic (see Fig. 4.3 Chinese investment in BRI countries [billion US$]). In addition to the effect of the pandemic, China is now more carefully reviewing the effect and sustainability of its

Table 4.2 Distribution of Chinese investments in countries of the BRI in 2021, by sector

Industry sector	Proportion of investment (in per cent)
Energy	37.45
Transport	27.51
Metals	12.02
Utilities	7.75
Real estate	5.76
Chemicals	2.50
Logistics	2.37
Other	3.00

Data source: (Statista, 2022a, 2022b)

engagement. Most BRI projects have been launched in developing countries and emerging economies, which are typically high-risk markets.

The important sectors of BRI projects are classical infrastructure projects in energy (2021: 37.5% of the total investment) and transportation (27.5%). Spawned by the Covid pandemic, China has considerably increased investment in healthcare. As a subsector of the New Silk Road, activities in this sector are labelled 'Health Silk Road'. From 2020 to 2021, healthcare-related investment in BRI countries grew by 246% to 450 million US$; however, this is still less than 1% of the total BRI investment in 2021 (Table 4.2).

The regional focuses of BRI investment are East/Southeast Asia and the Middle East. Investment within the BRI is not mono-directional. Until 2020, 27,000 enterprises from BRI countries have made their presence in China with a cumulative actual investment of about 60 billion US$ (MOFCOM, 2021).

There are basically three ways how non-Chinese companies can benefit from the BRI:

- Utilising newly constructed infrastructure.
- Serving new or growing markets spawned by the construction of new infrastructure.
- Direct participation in BRI-related projects.

As a prominent example, the China-Europe freight train network provides a new option for shipment from and to China, offering a compromise between fast but very expensive air transport and cheap but very slow sea freight. Most freight trains pass the Chinese-Kazakhstan boarder at Khorgos (霍尔果斯, standard Chinese romanisation: Huoerguosi). The town Khorgos was just founded in 2014 and has now 65,000 permanent inhabitants; it is the Chinese town closest to Europe. Within the city lies a tax-free area, offering lowest prices of many European products in China. As a result, Khorgos has become a magnet for inner-Chinese tourism.

An example outside China is the China-Pakistan Economic Corridor. Until a few years ago, power cuts were frequent in Pakistan, deterring investment. After China's investment in electricity generation and the seaport in Gwadar, Pakistan has become a new centre of textile industry, benefiting from low labour cost and the proximity to Middle East markets.

Direct participation in BRI projects is challenging for Western companies. Many invitations for tenders are released not in China but in the partner countries. These are mostly developing or smaller emerging markets, where international companies, especially SMEs, may not be present. A second option is to participate in BRI project via China; this means in general cooperation with a Chinese partner company or acting as a subcontractor. A survey in 2020 shows that mainly large multinational companies have been able to participate in BRI tenders in China (European Chamber, 2020), while SMEs often lack information and channels to suitable business partners in China. However, a majority of companies report an improvement of fairness and access to and transparency of BRI tenders. If this tendency continues, chances for SMEs to participate in BRI projects via China will increase.

4.4 The RCEP Free-Trade Area

A free-trade area is a region without or with reduced trade barriers among member states. The trade between the member states of a free-trade agreement (FTA) is mostly duty-free, while tariffs on imports from non-members are set individually by each member (WTO, n.d.). The worldwide most influential free-trade areas include EFTA (the European Free Trade Association), TPP/CPTPP (Trans-Pacific Partnership/Comprehensive and Progressive Agreement for Trans-Pacific Partnership) and NAFTA/USMCA (North American Free Trade Agreement/United States-Mexico--Canada Agreement).

On 15 November 2020, China signed the multilateral free-trade agreement Regional Comprehensive Economic Partnership (RCEP) with 14 Asia-Pacific countries. These include the ten ASEAN (the Association of Southeast Asian Nations) countries Brunei, Cambodia, Indonesia, Laos, Malaysia, Myanmar, the Philippines, Singapore, Thailand and Vietnam, as well as the Western allies Australia and New Zealand, Japan and South Korea. India, another large economy in the Asia-Pacific region, withdrew from the deal in November 2019 amid concerns about the potential impact on certain economic sectors, for example, removing trade barriers would create a risk that industrial goods from China and dairy products from Australia and New Zealand crowd out domestic suppliers.

Due to the regional population growth and China's economic rise, the RCEP community is believed to have shifted the centre of the world economy towards the Asia-Pacific region. The new agreement currently covers around 30% of world trade volume (see Fig. 4.4), 30% of global gross domestic product and with 2.2 billion people 30% of the world population. For comparison: The European Union covers around 33% of world trade.

The focus is on economic integration in the Asia-Pacific region, particularly in promoting economic and technical cooperations for the economically weak member states, in order to achieve a balanced regional development. In consideration of different economic capacities and political systems of the member states, RCEP set

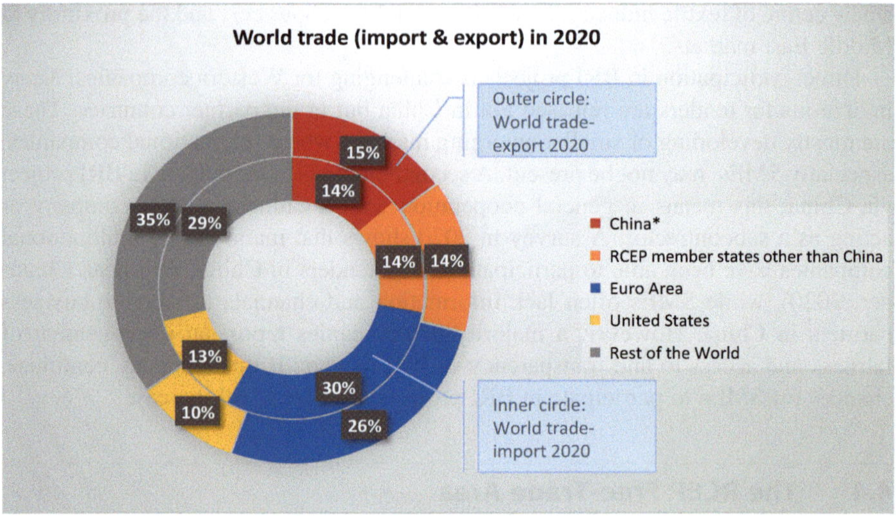

Fig. 4.4 Shares of RCEP member states in world trade as of 2020. Data source: The World Bank (World Bank, 2022a, 2022b). *China: including Mainland China (PRC), Hong Kong SAR and Macao SAR

lower standards for environmental protection and labour rights than the CPTPP (Comprehensive and Progressive Agreement for Trans-Pacific Partnership).

The RCEP Agreement came to effect on 1 January 2022 (The State Council of the People's Republic of China, 2022). Customs duties for more than 90% of the goods traded in the RCEP region will be gradually eliminated to zero, and a large part of the service sector will be made accessible to the member states; barriers for investment by member state companies will be lifted. In the future, exporters will be able to trade with all RCEP members with a single certificate of origin. This simplification will largely cut down time and money consumption for cross-border supply chain transactions. The agreement also sets requirements regarding e-commerce, telecommunications, copyright, etc. According to calculations by international think tanks, the RCEP is likely to increase the export growth of the member countries by 10.4% above the initial value in 2025.

The RCEP Agreement weakens the market position of non-member states and thus poses major economic challenges especially to the EU and the United States. With a 1.4 billion population and the world's fastest-growing economy, China plays an essential role in the global market. The country is an important sales target country for many European industrial companies. The German car manufacturer VW, for example, sells around 40% of the vehicles it produces worldwide in China (see Table 4.3 Volkswagen passenger car deliveries to customers by market in 2021). For the German car manufacturers Volkswagen, Daimler and BMW, the competitors Toyota, Honda, Nissan, Hyundai and Kia now possess a significant advantage in the Chinese market, thanks to their duty-free status as RCEP community members. However, companies from non-member states could also participate

Table 4.3 Volkswagen passenger car deliveries to customers by market in 2021

	Deliveries (units)	Share in total deliveries
Europe/other markets	**3,698,882**	**43,0%**
Western Europe	**2,761,568**	**32,1%**
Of which: Germany	959,748	11,1%
France	238,366	2,8%
United Kingdom	422,594	4,9%
Italy	248,414	2,9%
Spain	220,148	2,6%
Central and Eastern Europe	**624,815**	**7,3%**
Of which: Czech Republic	114,250	1,3%
Russia	204,772	2,4%
Poland	120,831	1,4%
Other markets	**312,499**	**3.6%**
Of which: Turkey	121,885	1.4%
South Africa	72,847	0.8%
North America	**876,558**	**10.2%**
Of which: United States	647,521	7.5%
Canada	98,829	1.1%
Mexico	130,208	1.5%
South America	**436,852**	**5.1%**
Of which: Brazil	311,519	3.6%
Argentina	56,186	0.7%
Asia-Pacific	**3,598,455**	**41.8%**
Of which: China	*3,301,444*	*38.3%*
India	52,481	0.6%
Japan	65,549	0.8%
Worldwide	**8,610,747**	**100.0%**

Data source: (Volkswagen, 2021)

in the free trade by producing in the RCEP free-trade area. Thus, foreign manufacturers, such as the automotive companies BMW, Mercedes and Tesla, need to have production facilities in China to secure duty-free access to the entire RCEP market.

A well-considered reaction by the European policymakers to RCEP is desirable, as it will have a lasting impact on the economic future of the EU member states, since the huge Chinese market is almost irreplaceable worldwide.

4.5 CPTPP and DEPA

In order to expand the economic and military influence of the United States in Asia to counteract on the growing power of China, the former US President Barack Obama initiated the Trans-Pacific Partnership (TPP)—a multilateral free-trade agreement with Asian countries without China. However, his successor President Donald Trump soon after withdrew from this strategic project in favour of bilateral trade agreements. In 2017, after the retreat of the United States, Japan took over the leadership of the free-trade agreement, known thereafter as the Comprehensive and Progressive Agreement for Trans-Pacific Partnership (CPTPP). Many states are at the same time members of RCEP and CPTPP, such as Japan, Vietnam, Singapore, Brunei, Malaysia, Australia and New Zealand (Helmold & Dathe, 2020).

Without the participation of the United States, Comprehensive and Progressive Agreement for Trans-Pacific Partnership (CPTPP) has loss significant influence compared to TPP. On 16 September 2021, China formally applied to join the CPTPP and promised to launch reforms to meet the high standards and to provide extensive market access to member states with commercial interests (Ministry of Commerce of the People's Republic of China, 2022).

To intensify the international digital economic cooperations, China formally applied to join the Digital Economy Partnership Agreement (DEPA) on 1 November 2021. DEPA initiated by Chile, New Zealand and Singapore is a new type of trade agreement designed to facilitate trade and cooperations for the digital economy (Asian Trade Centre, 2020). China aims at the promotion of innovation and sustainable development through global digital economic cooperations with the member states (Ministry of Commerce of the People's Republic of China, 2022).

References

Asian Trade Center. (2020, Jan 28). *Unpacking the digital economy partnership agreement (DEPA)*. Deborah Elms. Retrieved Oct 24, 2022, from https://asiantradecenter.org/talkingtrade/unpacking-the-digital-economy-partnership-agreement-depa

Baidu Encyclopedia. (2022a). *One Belt one Road (in Chinese)*. Retrieved Oct 13, 2022, from https://baike.baidu.com/item/一带一路/13132427

Baidu Encyclopedia. (2022b). *The government procurement law of the PRC (in Chinese)*. Retrieved Oct 23, 2022, from https://baike.baidu.com/item/中华人民共和国政府采购法/1469008

Bruegel. (2019, Jun 12). *China's participation in the WTO has been anything but smooth, as its self-proclaimed socialist market economy system has alienated its trading partner*. André Sapir & Petros Mavroidis. https://www.bruegel.org/working-paper/china-and-world-trade-organisation-towards-better-fit.

China.org. (2022). *Infographic: China's foreign trade development in past decade*. Retrieved Oct 23, 2022, from http://www.china.org.cn/business/2022-06/02/content_78250362.htm

Dathe, T., & Helmold, M. (2018). *Erfolgreich im Chinageschäft: Strategien und Handlungsempfehlungen für kleinere und mittlere Unternehmen (KMU)*. Springer Gabler Verlag.

European Chamber. (2020). *The road less travelled, European involvement in China's belt and road initiative: by European Union (EU) Chamber of Commerce in China*. Retrieved Oct 19, 2022, from https://www.europeanchamber.com.cn/en/publications-archive/762/The_Road_Less_Travelled_European_Involvement_in_China_s_Belt_and_Road_Initiative

Government of the PRC. (2021). *Special administration of investment of foreign enterprises in free trade zones (Negative List) (in Chinese)*. Retrieved Oct 23, 2022, from http://www.gov.cn/zhengce/zhengceku/2021-12/28/5664887/files/95c06b40d81e470baf3b720216fefc46.pdf

Handelsblatt. (2021, Dec 10). *Welthandelsorganisation: 20 Jahre in der WTO: Wie China vom Hoffnungsträger zur Bedrohung wurde*. Von Torsten Riecke; Dana Heide. Retrieved Oct

24, 2022, from https://www.handelsblatt.com/politik/international/welthandelsorganisation-20-jahre-in-der-wto-wie-china-vom-hoffnungstraeger-zur-bedrohung-wurde/27878530.html

Helmold, M., & Dathe, T. (2020, Nov 20). *Europa braucht auf RCEP eine Antwort*. Springer Professional. Retrieved Oct 24, 2022, from https://www.springerprofessional.de/wirtschaftspolitik/globalisierung/europa-braucht-auf-rcep-eine-antwort/18597834

Ministry of Commerce of the People's Republic of China. (2022, Sep). *Invest in China*. Integration of international rules. Retrieved Oct 24, 2022, from https://fdi.mofcom.gov.cn/come-newzonghe.html?parentId=124

MOFCOM. (2021). *8th anniversary of the "Belt and Road" initiative*. Retrieved Oct 16, 2022, from http://english.mofcom.gov.cn/article/relevantnewsforpc/onebeltandoneroad/202111/20211103219229.shtml

NDRC. (2021). *Special Administration of Investment of Foreign Enterprises (Negative List) (in Chinese)*. Retrieved Oct 23, 2022, from https://www.ndrc.gov.cn/xxgk/zcfb/fzggwl/202112/P020211227540591870254.pdf

Nedopil Wang Christoph. (2022). *Shanghai, Green Finance & Development Center, FISF Fudan University. Brief: China Belt and Road Initiative (BRI) Investment Report H1 2022*. Retrieved Oct 16, 2022, from https://greenfdc.org/china-belt-and-road-initiative-bri-investment-report-h1-2022

Observer Net. (2020). *The Ministry of Justice publishes the draft 'Administrative Provisions for Unlimited Residence Permits for Foreigners' for public consultation (in Chinese)*. Retrieved Oct 22, 2022, from https://baijiahao.baidu.com/s?id=1659674039985385245

OECD. (2018, March). *Active with the people's republic of China*. Retrieved Oct 24, 2022, from https://www.oecd.org/china/active-with-china.pdf

Reformdata.org. (2005, July 31). *World Bank and China's Reform and Opening*. China Reform Information Database. Retrieved Oct 24, 2022, from http://www.reformdata.org/2005/0731/19611.shtml

Shanghai Observer. (2022). *Chinese–English comparison: Bilingual important expressions from the report to the 20th party congress*. Retrieved Oct 22, 2022, from https://export.shobserver.com/baijiahao/html/540677.html

Statista. (2022a). *Share of exports in gross domestic product (GDP) in China from 2011 to 2021*. Retrieved Oct 23, 2022, from https://www.statista.com/statistics/256591/share-of-chinas-exports-in-gross-domestic-product

Statista. (2022b). *Distribution of Chinese investments in countries of the Belt and Road Initiative (BRI) in 2021, by sector*. Retrieved Oct 19, 2022, from https://www.statista.com/statistics/1228706/china-belt-and-road-initiative-investment-distribution-by-industrial-sector/

Tagesschau. (2021, Dec 11). *Welthandel: Chinas Aufstieg zum Hightech-Land*. Astrid Freyeisen. Retrieved Oct 24, 2022, from https://www.tagesschau.de/wirtschaft/china-wto-welthandel-101.html

The State Council of the People's Republic of China. (2022, Jan 01). *RCEP comes into effect on first day of 2022*. Xinhua. Retrieved Oct 24, 2022, from https://english.www.gov.cn/statecouncil/ministries/202201/01/content_WS61cf9521c6d09c94e48a3037.html

The World Bank. (2022a, July 20). *GDP (current US$)*. World Bank national accounts data, and OECD National Accounts data files. Retrieved Oct 24, 2022, from https://data.worldbank.org/indicator/NY.GDP.MKTP.CD

The World Bank. (2022b, July 20). *GDP growth (annual %)–China*. World Bank national accounts data, and OECD National Accounts data files. Retrieved Oct 24, 2022, from https://data.worldbank.org/indicator/NY.GDP.MKTP.KD.ZG?locations=CN

UNCTAD. (2021, Apr 27). *China: The rise of a trade titan*. https://unctad.org/news/china-rise-trade-titan.

Volkswagen. (2021). *Volkswagen Group deliveries*. Volkswagen Aktiengesellschaft Group Management Report (Annual Report 2021). Retrieved Oct 24, 2022, from https://annualreport2021.volkswagenag.com/group-management-report/business-development/deliveries.html

WTO. (n.d.). *Glossary Term: Free trade area.* World Trade Organization. Retrieved Oct 24, 2022, from https://www.wto.org/english/thewto_e/glossary_e/free_trade_area_e.htm
WTO.org. (2001). *Accessions: China.* World Trade Organization. Retrieved Oct 24, 2022, from https://www.wto.org/english/thewto_e/acc_e/a1_chine_e.htm
WTO.org. (2022a, Aug 24). *Disputes by member.* World Trade Organization. Retrieved Oct 24, 2022, from https://www.wto.org/english/tratop_e/dispu_e/dispu_by_country_e.htm
WTO.org. (2022b). *What is the WTO?* World Trade Organization. Retrieved Oct 24, 2022, from https://www.wto.org/english/thewto_e/whatis_e/tif_e/org6_e.htm
Xinhua Net. (2020, Sep 05). *Understanding the "big cycle" and "double cycle" in Xi Jinping's important speeches.* Retrieved Oct 24, 2022, from http://www.xinhuanet.com/politics/xxjxs/2020-09/05/c_1126455277.htm

5 Energy Supply

5.1 Energy Dependency and Energy Policies

According to previous empirical studies, energy is responsible for at least half the industrial growth in a modern economy while accounting for around 10% of total production costs (Barney & Franzi, 2002). Rapid economic growth usually goes hand in hand with an increasing demand for energy. Without proper energy policies in place, a supply shortage can soon become a bottleneck for a fast-growing manufacturing industry. The current Russia-Ukraine war has thrown the global energy market into turmoil. The subsequent energy crisis in Europe due to exploding prices made clear that energy is not only a key input factor for sustainable economic growth but also a vital resource of daily life and a key factor for social stability.

In the early 1970s, the industrialised countries were heavily dependent on fossil fuels from overseas. In 1973, the Organization of the Petroleum Exporting Countries (OPEC) imposed an oil embargo against the United States and later also the Netherlands, Portugal, South Africa, etc. in retaliation for their support of Israel in the Arab-Israeli War. The OPEC nations banned oil export to the targeted countries and at the same time reduced their own oil production. Due to the declining production of the US and European oil corporations (the 'Seven Sisters') and the free capital flow of US dollar in the international exchange, an exorbitant upward oil price spiral triggered a catastrophic hyperinflation in the United States and its allied countries. This event was later referred to as the 'first oil crisis' or the 'first oil shock' (U.S. Department of State, n.d.).

Although the first oil crisis could finally be solved with diplomacy, the industrial countries had determined to develop common energy policies in order to effectively secure energy supply and prevent foreign suppliers from using 'energy weapons' to achieve their political goals in the future. The International Energy Agency (IEA) was founded in Paris in November 1974 to deal with a wide range of issues relating to energy security—reliable, affordable and sustainable access to all energy sources—through international energy cooperations. Today, the IEA has 31 member states and in addition entertains collaboration with 10 non-member states through the

T. Dathe et al., *Business Opportunities and Risks in China*, Management for Professionals, https://doi.org/10.1007/978-3-031-31933-4_5

association programme, coordinating in total about 75% of global energy consumption (IEA, 2022a, 2022b, 2022c).

China became an association country to the International Energy Agency (IEA) in November 2015 to cooperate with other nations on energy issues over the global intergovernmental platform of IEA. According to IEA, China's energy section has been focusing on electricity, natural gas as well as cleaner and more efficient energy technologies to support its transition towards a knowledge-based economic model (IEA, 2019).

Due to its increasing industrialisation, China's dependency on energy imports, especially oil and gas, grows steadily. Aware of the potential risk of energy dependency, Chinese policymakers have long implemented the economic strategy shift from 'growth at any cost' to 'sustainable, energy-secure growth' (Li & Clark II, 2019) to increase self-sufficiency. As of 2021, China has reached an energy self-sufficiency rate of more than 80%, mainly due to the rising domestic energy production. Overall, the Chinese government has improved the energy self-sufficiency by promoting domestic innovations and production of clean and renewable energy technologies (e.g. heavy industry based on hydrogen, biofuel and carbon capture and utilisation) while increasing energy use efficiency (The State Council of the People's Republic of China, 2022; Reuters, 2022).

Due to the size of its economy, China plays a key role in the worldwide combat against global warming by limiting emission of greenhouse gases. According to a recent analysis of Royal Dutch Shell, China will reach peak emission in 2030 and achieve carbon neutrality in 2060 (The State Council of the People's Republic of China, 2022; Reuters, 2022).

The fundamental content of China's long-term energy policy has been summarised in a white paper by the State Council of the People's Republic of China on 26 December 2007 as (China Daily, 2007):

- *Energy savings*: The energy efficiency should be continuously improved by adjusting industrial structure, innovating energy-saving technologies, promoting energy-saving products and improving energy management.
- *Focus on domestic production*: The constantly growing demand for energy demand should primarily be covered by expanding domestic energy supply in order to increase energy security.
- *Diversification of energy sources*: The domestic energy structure should be optimised by combining a controlled expansion of coal production, intensification of electricity generation, acceleration of oil and natural gas production, increase in coalbed methane as well as construction of nuclear power plants and energetic promotion of renewable energies such as hydroelectric power.
- *Technical innovation*: The sustainable development of energy industry should be enhanced with technical improvement based on domestic innovations and complementary imported technologies.
- *Environment protection*: Resource-saving and environment-friendly technologies should contribute to a sustainable energy solution.

- *International cooperations*: In complementation to domestic energy innovation and production, cooperation with the International Energy Agency and other countries should be strengthened to ensure national and international energy security.

China's energy strategy holds a wide range of business opportunities for private sectors, for example, as innovation partnerships in the energy sector. The emphasis on energy security in China's foreign policy ensures the manufacturers' confidence in the long-term energy availability.

5.2 Energy Consumption and Environmental Protection

5.2.1 Total Consumption

China's continuous investment in innovative technologies for low-emission, high-efficiency, clean and renewable energy use has borne fruit in the past. Figure 5.1 indicates that China's energy efficiency has improved significantly, as the increase of energy consumption has lagged well behind the positive GDP development in the previous decade.

Being the 'world's factory' and the most populous country in the world, China is unsurprisingly the largest energy consumer worldwide (in 2021, 25% of total global energy consumption (enerdata.net, 2022a, 2022b)) and of greenhouse gas (GHG) emission (30.6% in 2020, (Statista, 2020)). Greenhouse gases are the gases that trap

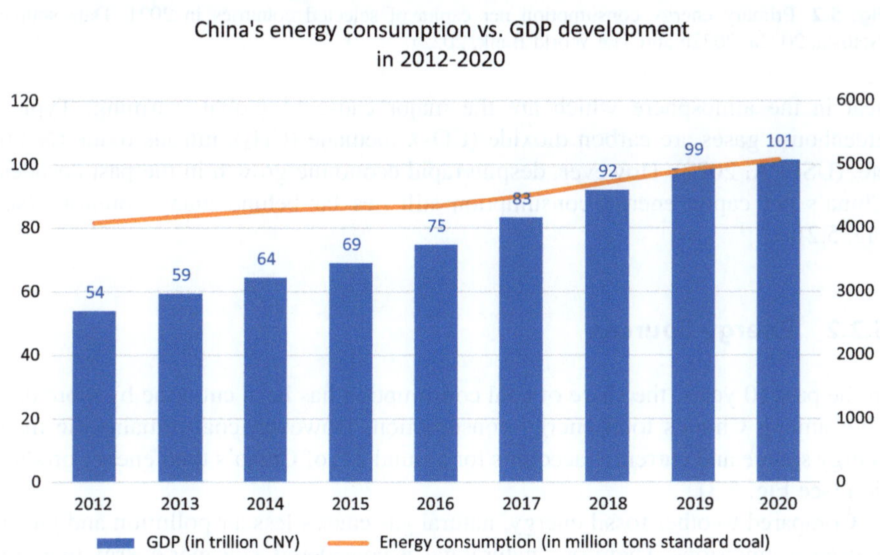

Fig. 5.1 China's energy consumption vs. GDP development from 2012 to 2020. Data source: (National Bureau of Statistics of China, 2022)

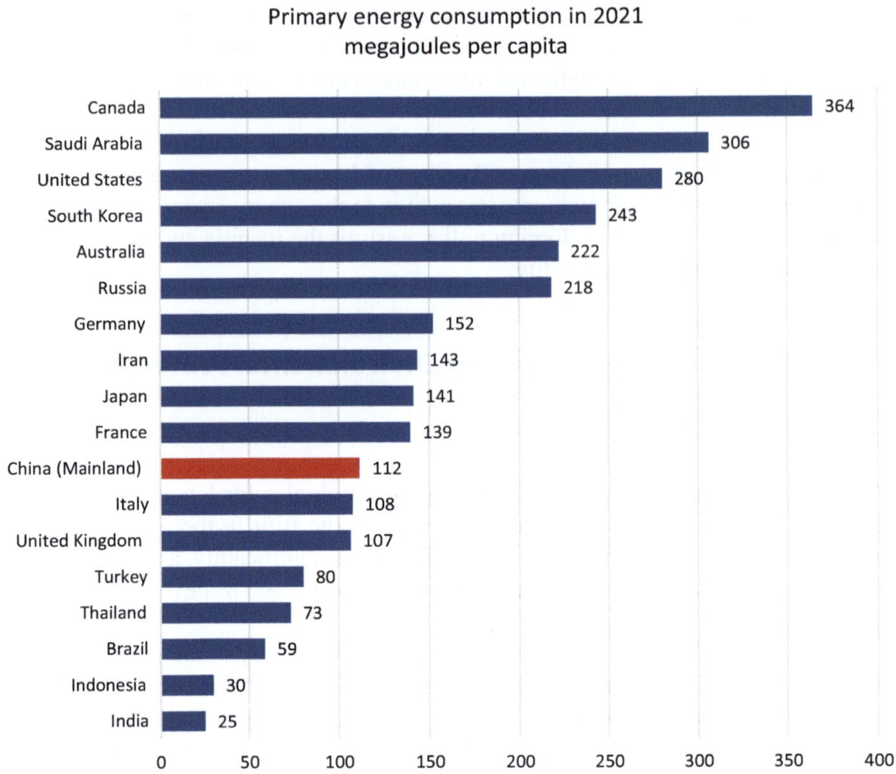

Fig. 5.2 Primary energy consumption per capita of selected countries in 2021. Data source: (Statista, 2022a, 2022b and The World Bank, 2022)

heat in the atmosphere which are the major cause of global warming. Typical greenhouse gases are carbon dioxide (CO_2), methane (CH_4), nitrous oxide (N_2O), etc. (USEPA, 2022). However, despite rapid economic growth in the past decades, China's per capita energy consumption still lies far behind many countries (see Fig. 5.2).

5.2.2 Energy Sources

In the past 10 years, the share of coal consumption has been cut done by more than 10% among China's total energy consumption. However, coal remains the main energy source and currently accounts for around 2/3 of China's total energy production (see Fig. 5.3).

Compared to other fossil energy, natural gas causes less air pollution and greenhouse gas emissions. Therefore, natural gas is considered a cleaner energy than, for example, petroleum (USEIA, 2021). In the past, natural gas has continuously replaced petroleum in overall consumption. As a result of technical innovations,

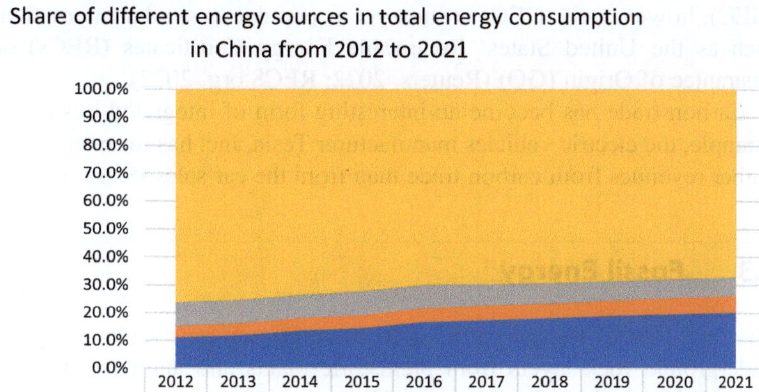

	2012	2013	2014	2015	2016	2017	2018	2019	2020	2021
Coal	76.2%	75.4%	73.5%	72.2%	69.8%	69.6%	69.2%	68.5%	67.6%	67.0%
Petroleum	8.5%	8.4%	8.3%	8.5%	8.3%	7.6%	7.2%	6.9%	6.8%	6.6%
Natural gas	4.1%	4.4%	4.7%	4.8%	5.2%	5.4%	5.4%	5.6%	6.0%	6.1%
Primary electricity and others	11.2%	11.8%	13.5%	14.5%	16.7%	17.4%	18.2%	19.0%	19.6%	20.3%

Primary electricity and others ■ Natural gas ■ Petroleum ■ Coal

Fig. 5.3 Distribution of energy sources in total consumption in China from 2012 to 2021. Data source: (National Bureau of Statistics of China, 2022)

such as electric vehicles and photovoltaic products, as well as the promotion of clean energies, the share of electricity has doubled over a period of 10 years (see Fig. 5.3).

5.2.3 Carbon Trade

Carbon trade is a market instrument aimed to reduce overall emission of carbon dioxide or other greenhouse gases. Emission trade systems are designed according to a 'cap-and-trade' model. As a rule, the emitters are assigned a set limit of permitted emissions (cap). They may sell the unused quota or buy additional permission the set limit is exceeded. Emission trade adds costs to additional pollution and, as a result, creates incentives for the emitters to reduce emissions.

In Europe, the EU Emissions Trading System (EU ETS) has been in operation since 2005. At present, carbon marketplaces have been introduced in 45 countries including in Canada, Japan, New Zealand, South Korea, Switzerland, the United States, etc. The Chinese Emissions Trading Scheme is the worldwide largest carbon trade market. It was launched in July 2021 after prior testing since 2013. Uniquely, China's scheme uses intensity of emissions (the amount of emissions per unit of energy generated) instead of absolute amounts of allowed emissions as in the emission trade systems of other countries (European Commission, 2022; nature, 2021).

Renewable energy certificates (RECs) are commonly also known as green tags. With the help of energy attribute certificates (EACs), the attributes of electricity generated from renewable energy sources can be traced and traded as nominal negative emissions. The Chinese EACs are named as Green Electricity Certificate

(GEC); however, the GECs are not yet as popular as similar international schemes such as the United States' Renewable Energy Certificates (RECs) or the EU's Guarantee of Origin (GO) (Reuters, 2022; RECS.org, 2022).

Carbon trade has become an interesting form of integrated business model. For example, the electric vehicles manufacturer Tesla, Inc. has for many years generated higher revenues from carbon trade than from the car sales (Stern.de, 2021).

5.3 Fossil Energy

The term 'fossil energy' is used to describe non-renewable energies formed in underground rock layers from prehistoric plants and animals, including coal, oil and natural gas (U.S. Department of Energy, n.d.).

5.3.1 Coal

China is by far the largest coal producer in the world. The market demand of around 4 billion tons per year is mainly covered by domestic production. At the same time, China is also the world's largest coal importer, although imports account for only about 7% of the total market supply (see Fig. 5.4 and Table 5.1 China's coal dependency rate from 2012 to 2019).

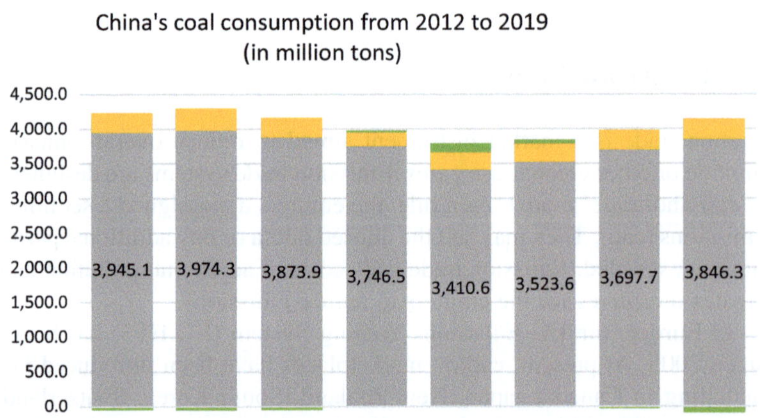

	2012	2013	2014	2015	2016	2017	2018	2019
Change of inventory	-37.7	-43.7	-41.1	25.5	127.6	48.4	-26.4	-84.7
Export	-9.3	-7.5	-5.7	-5.3	-8.8	-8.1	-4.9	-6.0
Import	288.4	327.0	291.2	204.1	255.6	270.9	282.1	299.8
Domestic production	3,945.1	3,974.3	3,873.9	3,746.5	3,410.6	3,523.6	3,697.7	3,846.3

Domestic production · Import · Export · Change of inventory

Fig. 5.4 China's coal consumption from 2012 to 2019. Data source: (National Bureau of Statistics of China, 2022)

Table 5.1 China's coal dependency rate from 2012 to 2019

In million tons	2012	2013	2014	2015	2016	2017	2018	2019
Total consumption	**4186.5**	**4250.2**	**4118.3**	**3970.7**	**3784.9**	**3834.8**	**3948.5**	**4055.4**
Domestic production	3945.1	3974.3	3873.9	3746.5	3410.6	3523.6	3697.7	3846.3
Import	288.4	327.0	291.2	204.1	255.6	270.9	282.1	299.8
Dependency rate	7%	8%	7%	5%	7%	7%	7%	7%

Data source: (National Bureau of Statistics of China, 2022)

In China, coals are divided into two main categories based on their properties: steam coal and coking coal (also known as metallurgical coal). While steam coal is used to generate heat or steam, for example, in power plants, steam train locomotives or combustion boilers, coking coal is primarily used to produce coke for steelmaking (China Energy Network, 2021).

Due to high inland transportation costs, some power plants in Chinese coastal areas source up to 60 to 70% of their steam coal consumption from oversees to benefit from large price advantages. Coal import is often used to stabilise the local coal market, especially to cover summer peak and winter storage. To prevent a systematic oversupply and protect domestic production, China has tightened coal import restrictions since 2017. As of end 2020, China's most important countries of origin of steam coal imports are Indonesia (61%), Australia (23%), Russia (10%), the Philippines (3%) and Mongolia (2%) (China Energy Network, 2021).

The reserves and the production of high-quality coking coal in China are quite limited. With growing domestic steel production and the trend towards large-scale blast furnaces in steel mills to meet increasing quality requirements, the demand for coking coal imports rises constantly. As of 2020, the main exporters of coking coal to China are Mongolia (45%), Australia (41.4%), Russia (7%) and Canada (4%) (China Energy Network, 2021).

According to a recent analysis by the International Energy Agency (IEA), the global economic recovery from the Covid-19 pandemic shock and the rising natural gas prices have increased the use of coal for power generation. In 2021, China's coal demand reached all-time high of 4230 million tons, followed by India at 1053 million tons (IEA, 2022a, 2022b, 2022c). Besides, the EU's ban on Russian coal imports due to the Russia-Ukraine conflict will force the European countries to turn to suppliers in the Asia-Pacific region, pushing up the regional prices. The geopolitical development may reshape China's coal import structure in the near future.

5.3.2 Oil and Gas

China's domestic oil and gas market is dominated by three state-owned enterprises (SOEs): China National Petroleum Corporation (CNPC), China Petroleum & Chemical Corporation (Sinopec) and China National Offshore Oil Corporation (CNOOC). CNPC and Sinopec ranked #4 and #5 on the Fortune Global 500 list in 2021 (Fortune, 2022).

Despite rising investment by domestic suppliers in oil and gas exploitation and exploration, China remains highly dependent on imports. As the world's largest crude oil importer, China imported around 513 million tons oil for a total consumption of 726 million tons in 2021, with an import dependency rate of over 70% (The State Council of the People's Republic of China, 2022), similar as in the previous years (see Fig. 5.5 and Table 5.2 China's crude oil dependency rate from 2012 to 2019).

Since the turn of the millennium, some major oil-producing countries including Iran, Venezuela and Russia are increasingly subject to external economic coercive

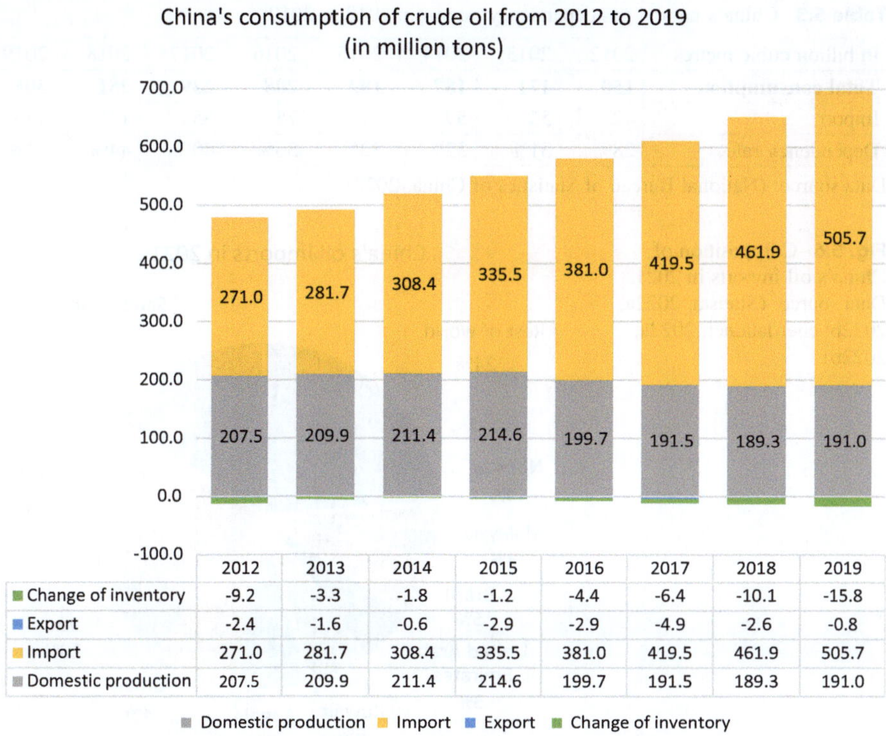

Fig. 5.5 China's crude oil consumption from 2012 to 2019. Data source: (National Bureau of Statistics of China, 2022)

Table 5.2 China's crude oil dependency rate from 2012 to 2019

In million tons	2012	2013	2014	2015	2016	2017	2018	2019
Total consumption	**466.8**	**486.7**	**517.4**	**545.9**	**573.3**	**599.7**	**638.5**	**680.1**
Import	271.0	281.7	308.4	335.5	381.0	419.5	461.9	505.7
Dependency rate	58%	58%	60%	61%	66%	70%	72%	74%

Data source: (National Bureau of Statistics of China, 2022)

measures. For example, the United States imposed long-lasting sanctions on Iran since 2018, or the EU recently banned on Russian oil since the begin of Russia-Ukraine military conflict. Those sanctions in forms of trade suspensions, financial freezes, import embargoes, etc. eventually result in the oil supply of the targeted countries being restricted from entering international trade and financial markets.

The above sanctions have two opposing effects on China's oil imports: On the one hand, they push up the oil price at the global market and increase the overall import costs over time. On the other hand, the sanctioned countries are forced to offer large discounts for oil sales to non-Western countries like China or India so that

Table 5.3 China's natural gas dependency rate from 2012 to 2019

In billion cubic metres	2012	2013	2014	2015	2016	2017	2018	2019
Total consumption	**150**	**171**	**187**	**193**	**208**	**239**	**281**	**306**
Import	42	53	59	61	75	95	125	133
Dependency rate	28%	31%	32%	32%	36%	40%	44%	44%

Data source: (National Bureau of Statistics of China, 2022)

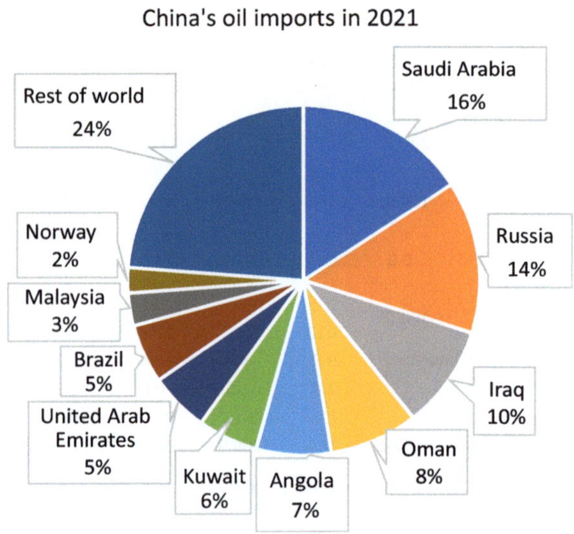

Fig. 5.6 Composition of China's oil imports in 2021. Data source: (Statista, 2022a, 2022b; enerdata.net, 2022a, 2022b)

those could benefit from immediate price advantages in at least short term (PHBS, 2022).

In the global combat against climate change, natural gas has become a widely favoured transitional energy source because it produces much less greenhouse gases than other fossil fuels, including coal and oil. From 2012 to 2019, China's gas consumption has doubled (see Table 5.3 China's natural gas dependency rate from 2012 to 2019). At the same time, the dependency rate on gas imports rose from 28.1% in 2012 to 46.1% in 2021. Liquefied natural gas (LNG) accounts for 65.9% and pipeline gas 34.1% of the gas imports (The State Council of the People's Republic of China, 2022).

At present, China is the worldwide largest LNG importer (Energy Information Adminstration, 2022). By late 2022, a total of 24 LNG receiving terminals were put into operation, with total receiving capacity of around 94 million tons per year. In addition, gas storage facilities are also on the rise and will reach approximately 14.7 billion cubic metres by the end of 2021 with further ambitious underground storage build-out in plan (The State Council of the People's Republic of China, 2022).

In the past, China has been dealing with the uncertainty at the global oil and gas market with careful diversification and independent foreign policies (see Figs. 5.6 and 5.7).

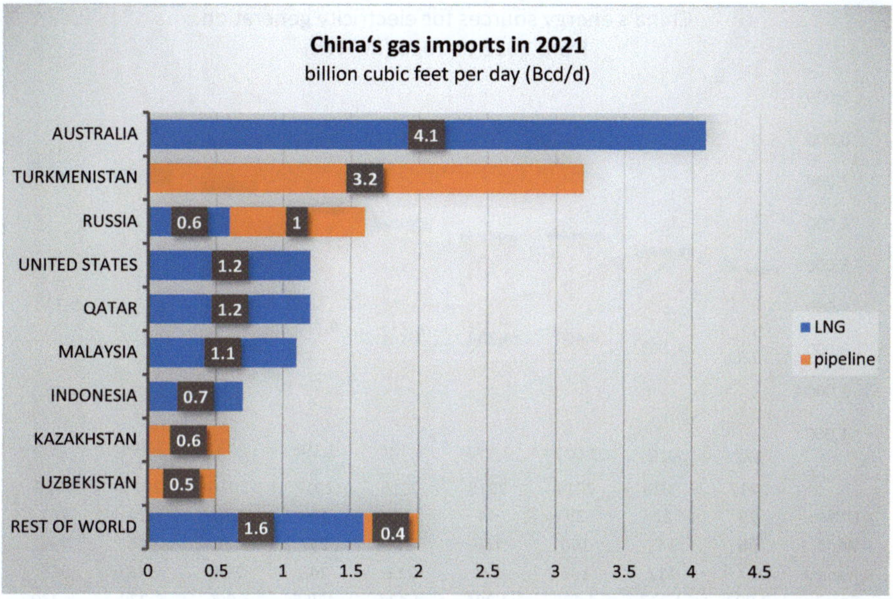

Fig. 5.7 Composition of China's gas imports in 2021. Data source: (Energy Information Adminstration, 2022)

5.4 Electricity and Renewable Energies

China's energy consumption is being increasingly covered by primary electricity (see Fig. 5.3). According to Royal Dutch Shell, China may raise the electricity share in total energy generation from today's 20% to 60% in the future to meet the carbon net zero goal by 2060 (Reuters, 2022). The electricity in China is almost exclusively generated by domestic providers.

In the recent years, China's promotion of clean, low-carbon, safe and efficient energy system has achieved remarkable results. In 2021, the share of renewables in China's total energy consumption has been steadily increasing in the past and reached 17.6% of the total energy supply (The State Council of PRC, 2022). In comparison, renewable energy sources accounted for 19.7% of total energy consumption in Germany (The Federal Government of Germany, 2022) and 12.2% in the United States for the same year (U.S. Energy Information Adminstration, 2022).

At present, China is home to the world's top 10 suppliers of solar photovoltaic (PV) manufacturing equipment, providing more than 80% of the world's solar panels of all manufacturing stages such as polysilicon, ingots, wafers, cells and module. By the end of 2020, China's solar capacity has reached 23 GW, while the installed solar panels have reached 1500 km^2, equivalent to the total area of Greater London (IEA, 2022a, 2022b, 2022c). From 2012 to 2020, the share of wind power

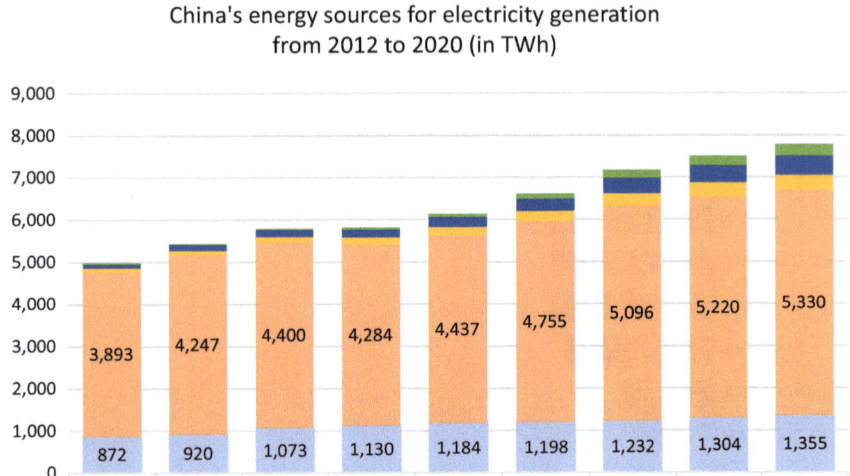

	2012	2013	2014	2015	2016	2017	2018	2019	2020
Others	29	12	29	44	62	107	178	224	261
Wind	96	141	160	186	237	297	366	406	466
Nuclear	97	112	133	171	213	248	294	348	366
Fossil	3,893	4,247	4,400	4,284	4,437	4,755	5,096	5,220	5,330
Hydro	872	920	1,073	1,130	1,184	1,198	1,232	1,304	1,355

Hydro Fossil Nuclear Wind Others

Fig. 5.8 China's energy sources for electricity generation from 2012 to 2020. Data source: (National Bureau of Statistics of China, 2022)

and nuclear power in electricity generation rose from around 2% to 6% and from 2% to almost 5%, respectively. Hydropower, another important form of renewable energy, has remained above 17% of electricity supply despite the rapid rise in power consumption (see Fig. 5.8). However, recent severe droughts have sparked global concerns about the future of hydropower.

According to a recent report by Royal Dutch Shell, China has made a major contribution to global energy sustainability as the leading producer of renewable energies and manufacturer and the largest user market of electric vehicles. With increasing installed capacity and rapidly falling costs, power generation from solar energy has long become profitable without government subsidies. In addition, the government continuously improves the adaptability of power systems to the grid connection and shore supply to enable large-scale consumption of wind and solar power generation. China aims to achieve a total installed capacity of wind power and solar power of more than 1.2 billion kilowatts by 2030 and net zero emission by 2060 (The State Council of China, 2022; The State Council of China, 2022).

References

Barney, F., & Franzi, P. (2002). *The future of energy from future dilemmas: Options to 2050 for Australia's population, technology, resources and environment.* CSIRO Sustainable Ecosystems, pp. 157–189.

China Daily. (2007, Dec 26). *White paper "China's energy status and policies" released (full text).* The State Council. Retrieved Oct 31, 2022, from http://www.chinadaily.com.cn/hqzg/2007-12/26/content_6349998_3.htm

China Energy Network. (2021, Jan 08). *China doesn't lack of coal, so why import? Thermal coal and coking coal have different purposes.* Zhang Lei; Ran Ze. Retrieved Oct 28, 2022, from https://www.china5e.com/news/news-1107722-1.html

enerdata.net. (2022a, Jan 17). *China's crude oil imports in 2021 declined by 5.4% to 513 Mt.* Retrieved Oct 28, 2022, from https://www.enerdata.net/publications/daily-energy-news/chinas-crude-oil-imports-2021-declined-54-513-mt.html

enerdata.net. (2022b). *Total energy consumption.* By world energy & climate statistics–Yearbook 2022. Retrieved Oct 31, 2022, from https://yearbook.enerdata.net/total-energy/world-consumption-statistics.html

European Commission. (2022). *International carbon market.* Retrieved Oct 28, 2022, from https://ec.europa.eu/clima/eu-action/eu-emissions-trading-system-eu-ets/international-carbon-market_en

Fortune. (2022). *The top 10. Global 500.* Retrieved Aug 29, 2022, from https://fortune.com/global500/

IEA. (2019). *China: Key energy statistics.* Retrieved Oct 31, 2022, from https://www.iea.org/countries/china

IEA. (2022a). *China currently dominates global solar PV supply chains.* Retrieved Oct 31, 2022, from https://www.iea.org/reports/solar-pv-global-supply-chains/executive-summary

IEA. (2022b, July). *Coal market update–July 2022.* International energy agency. Retrieved Oct 31, 2022, from https://www.iea.org/reports/coal-market-update-july-2022/demand

IEA. (2022c, May 10). *History: From oil security to steering the world toward secure and sustainable energy transitions.* Retrieved Oct 31, 2022, from https://www.iea.org/about/history

Li, X., & Clark, W. W., II. (2019). *Climate preservation in urban communities case studies.* Elsevier.

National Bureau of Statistics of China. (2022). *Annual data.* Retrieved Oct 28, 2022, from https://data.stats.gov.cn/easyquery.htm?cn=C01

nature. (2021, July 20). *China launches world's largest carbon market: But is it ambitious enough? Bianca Nogrady.* Retrieved Oct 28, 2022, from https://www.nature.com/articles/d41586-021-01989-7

PHBS. (2022, Apr 11). *The changing trend of international oil market and China's oil import trade.* Liu Shuhan. Retrieved Oct 28, 2022, from https://thinktank.phbs.pku.edu.cn/2022/zhuantibaogao_0413/66.html

RECS.org. (2022). *Public information.* RECS energy certificate association. Retrieved Oct 28, 2022, from https://recs.org/public-information/

Reuters. (2022, Jan 17). *Shell says electricity to meet 60% of China's energy use by 2060.* Retrieved Oct 29, 2022, from https://www.reuters.com/business/energy/shell-says-electricity-meet-60-chinas-energy-use-by-2060-2022-01-17/

Statista. (2020). *Distribution of fossil fuel CO2 emissions worldwide in 2020, by select country.* Retrieved Oct 29, 2022, from https://www.statista.com/statistics/271748/the-largest-emitters-of-co2-in-the-world/

Statista. (2022a, May 27). *Main suppliers of crude oil to China in 2020 and 2021 (in million metric tons).* Retrieved Oct 29, 2022, from https://www.statista.com/statistics/1310953/oil-imports-by-country-china/

Statista. (2022b). *Primary energy consumption worldwide in 2021, by country*. Energy & Environment. Retrieved Oct 29, 2022, from https://www.statista.com/statistics/263455/primary-energy-consumption-of-selected-countries/

Stern.de. (2021, Feb 08). *Teslas geheime Geldmaschine: Der Gewinn kommt nicht aus dem Verkauf von autos*. Daniel Bakir. Retrieved Nov 02, 2022, from https://www.stern.de/wirtschaft/news/tesla-und-die-geheime-geldmaschine%2D%2Dder-gewinn-stammt-nicht-aus-dem-autoverkauf-30358900.html

The Federal Government of Germany. (2022, Aug 16). *Klimafreundliche und krisensichere Energieversorgung*. Energie und Klimaschutz. Retrieved Oct 29, 2022, from https://www.bundesregierung.de/breg-de/themen/klimaschutz/energieversorgung-sicherheit-2040098

The State Council of China. (2022, May 14). *About promoting new energy in the new era*. Implementation plan for high-quality development. Retrieved Nov 02, 2022, from http://www.gov.cn/zhengce/content/2022-05/30/content_5693013.htm

The State Council of PRC. (2022, Feb 15). *Nation more energy self-sufficient*. Retrieved Nov 04, 2022, from http://english.www.gov.cn/news/topnews/202202/15/content_WS620ae42cc6d09c94e48a50dc.html

The State Council of the People's Republic of China. (2022, Feb 15). *Nation more energy self-sufficient*. Retrieved Nov 02, 2022, from http://english.www.gov.cn/news/topnews/202202/15/content_WS620ae42cc6d09c94e48a50dc.html

The World Bank. (2022). *Population, total*. DataBank. https://data.worldbank.org/indicator/SP.POP.TOTL

U.S. Department of Energy. (n.d.). *Energy sources: fossil*. Retrieved Nov 04, 2022, from https://www.energy.gov/science-innovation/energy-sources/fossil

U.S. Department of State. (n.d.). *Oil Embargo, 1973–1974*. Von Office of the historian. Retrieved Nov 04, 2022, from https://history.state.gov/milestones/1969-1976/oil-embargo

U.S. EIA. (2022, May 02). *As of 2021, China imports more liquefied natural gas than any other country*. U.S. Energy Information Administration. Retrieved Nov 04, 2022, from https://www.eia.gov/todayinenergy/detail.php?id=52258

U.S. Energy Information Administration. (2022, May 13). *How much of U.S. energy consumption and electricity generation comes from renewable energy sources?* Retrieved Nov 04, 2022, from https://www.eia.gov/tools/faqs/faq.php?id=92&t=4

USEIA. (2021, Dec). *Natural gas explained: Natural gas and the environment*. U.S. Energy Information Administration. Retrieved Nov 04, 2022, from https://www.eia.gov/energyexplained/natural-gas/natural-gas-and-the-environment.php

USEPA. (2022, May 16). *Overview of greenhouse gases*. United States environmental protection agency. Retrieved Nov 04, 2022, from https://www.epa.gov/ghgemissions/overview-greenhouse-gases#overview

6 Market Opportunities

6.1 Overall Development of Chinese Economy

In recent years, the Chinese economy has faced a series of internal challenges such as unfavourable demographical development, structural slowdown in productivity growth, environmental pollution and excessive leverage of large real estate developers. In order to ensure successive upgrading of China's economy in the global value chain, the Chinese government has introduced various macroeconomic policies, such as promoting domestic innovations with government support and reducing dependency on foreign trade by boosting domestic consumption and increasing disposable income of private households through increasing progression of taxation to reduce income tax burden for low- und medium-income households.

Given its size, China's economic development has a huge impact on global trade. Vice versa, the major events in the global supply chain are also most influential impulses for China's national economy. For example, the current COVID-19 pandemic outbreaks and subsequent regional shutdowns, global inflation and energy price shocks caused by the war in Ukraine have all inevitably become headwinds slowing down the Chinese economy.

Over the past decade, China has achieved a stable strong GDP growth rate with a moderate deceleration in the recent years. After the impact of the pandemic outbreak in 2020, China has largely recovered in 2021, achieving a real GDP growth (calculated based on stable prices) of 8.1%. However, amid increasing uncertainty about the Chinese government's strict pandemic control measures, current geopolitical challenges posed by the war in Ukraine and tensions with Taiwan, experts have downgraded their forecast for China's economic growth in 2022 to 3% in 2022 (see Fig. 6.1) (World Bank, 2022a, b) (CNBC, 2022).

From 2012 to 2021, Chinese government spending has steadily contributed approximately 16% to the total GDP. This includes expenditures for public services to the society and subsidised goods and services provided to households, both

T. Dathe et al., *Business Opportunities and Risks in China*, Management for Professionals, https://doi.org/10.1007/978-3-031-31933-4_6

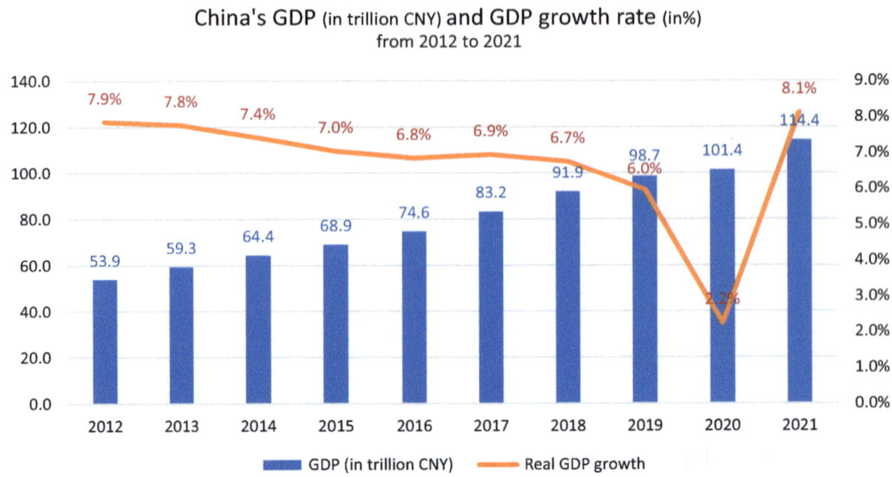

Fig. 6.1 China's GDP development from 2012 to 2021. Data source: (National Bureau of Statistics of China, 2022a, b, c, d) (World Bank, 2022a, b)

calculated as the difference between the value of output goods and services and the income obtained by the government. Business investment accounting for the largest share in GDP is calculated as the acquisition value of fixed assets necessary for enterprises to provide goods and services at the market, less the fixed asset disposal. The share of personal consumption expenditure of Chinese residents increased from 35% in 2012 to 38% 2021, while the nominal amount rose from 19.1 trillion yuan in 2012 to 43.9 trillion yuan by 130%, indicating even larger potential of a huge consumer market (see Fig. 6.2).

6.2 Foreign Trade

At present, China is the world's largest exporter and the second largest importer after the United States. China's current zero-Covid strategy appears to have been effective in containing the spread of the virus within the country's territory. While avoiding excessive death toll, the economy achieved slight growth in 2020 followed by a steep rise of more than 21% in 2021. During 2021, the total import and export of goods and services reached 39.1 trillion yuan, equivalent to US $ 6.1 trillion, while the fast-growing economic interactions along the 'Belt and Road' accounted for almost 30% of the total foreign trade volume (see Fig. 6.3) (National Bureau of Statistics of China, 2022a, b, c, d). However, there are some doubts about the long-term economic effects of China's strict anti-pandemic measures, since factories' shutdowns are expected to cause severe disruptions in the global supply chain and local economy.

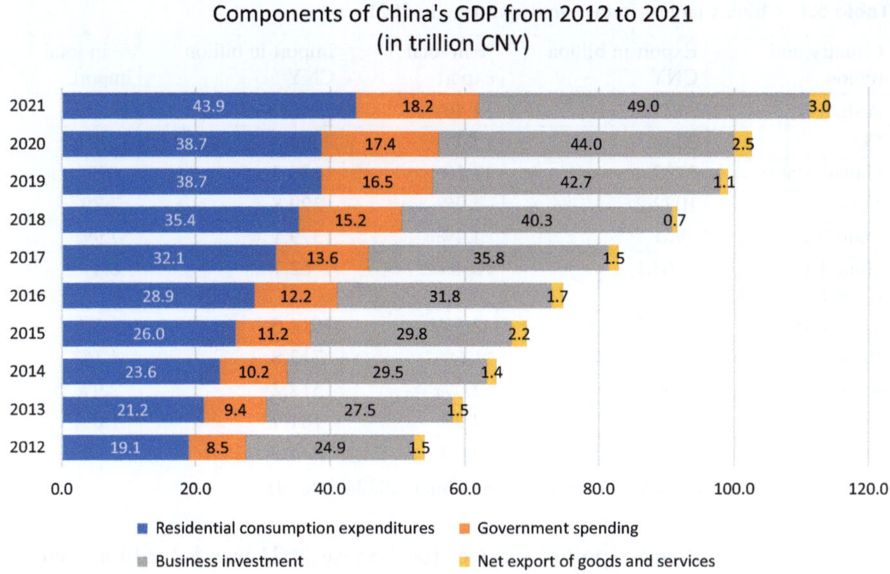

Fig. 6.2 Components of China's GDP (by expenditure method) from 2012 to 2021. Data source: (National Bureau of Statistics of China, 2022a, b, c, d)

Fig. 6.3 China's foreign trade balance from 2012 to 2021. Data source: (National Bureau of Statistics of China, 2022a, b, c, d)

Table 6.1 China's largest foreign trade partners in 2021

Country and region	Export in billion CNY	% in total export	Import in billion CNY	% in total import
ASEAN	3125.5	14.4%	2548.9	14.7%
EU	3348.3	15.4%	2002.8	11.5%
United States	3722.4	17.1%	1160.3	6.7%
Japan	1072.2	4.9%	1329.8	7.7%
South Korea	961.7	4.4%	1379.1	7.9%
Hong Kong (China)	2264.1	10.4%	62.7	0.4%
Taiwan (China)	506.3	2.3%	1614.6	9.3%
Brazil	346.4	1.6%	713.8	4.1%
Russia	436.4	2.0%	512.2	2.9%
India	630.2	2.9%	181.9	1.0%
South Africa	136.5	0.6%	214.7	1.2%

Data source: (National Bureau of Statistics of China, 2022a, b, c, d)

The total import and export of services for the year 2021 was 5.3 trillion yuan, an increase of 16% over the previous year. Among them, service exports were 2.5 trillion yuan, an increase of over 31%; service imports were 2.8 trillion yuan, an increase almost 5%. The foreign trade balance for service import and export was 211 billion yuan deficit (National Bureau of Statistics of China, 2022a, b, c, d).

Over the past decade, the share of export business in the total gross domestic product has declined from 24% in 2012 to 19% in 2021. This indicates an increasing independence of the Chinese economy through a greater focus on the local market (see Fig. 6.3).

The most important foreign trade partner for China is the Association of Southeast Asian Nations (ASEAN), which accounts for over 14% of both total import and total export in 2021, followed by the European Union (EU), accounting for 15% of exports and more than 11% of imports. The United States is also one of the largest trading partners, making up 17% of exports and just under 7 of imports (see Table 6.1).

The most important export commodities from China are electronics including automatic data processing equipment including spare parts (e.g. desktops, laptops, tablets, servers, etc.), integrated circuits, cellular phones, textile including fabrics and clothing as well as plastic and steel products (see Table 6.2 China's foreign trade in 2021: types of export commodities).

The most important import commodities for China are high-end integrated circuits. Partially due to the ongoing trade war with the United States, there is a bottleneck with the lithography machine and chemical materials for the production of high-end chips in China. Besides, there is also a high demand for the import of

Table 6.2 China's foreign trade in 2021: types of export commodities

Description	Quantity	Unit	In billion CNY
Steel	67	Million tons	529
Textile (yarns, fabrics and other products)	–		938
Clothing and accessories	–		1100
Shoes	8732	Million pairs	310
Furniture including spare parts	–		477
Bags and suitcases	2	Million tons	180
Toys	–		298
Plastic products	–		640
Integrated circuits	310,700	Million units	993
Automatic data processing equipment including spare parts	–		1649
Cellular phones	954	Million units	945
Digital display	1424	Million units	179
Automobile including chassis	2120	Thousand units	223

Data source: (National Bureau of Statistics of China, 2022a, b, c, d)

Table 6.3 China's foreign trade in 2021: types of import commodities

Description	Quantity	Unit	In billion CNY
Soybeans	97	Million tons	346
Edible vegetable oil	10	Million tons	71
Iron ore	1124	Million tons	1194
Coal and lignite	323	Million tons	232
Crude oil	513	Million tons	1662
Refined oil	27	Million tons	108
Natural gas	121	Million tons	360
Polymer plastic	34	Million tons	395
Mechanical pulp	30	Million tons	130
Steel	14	Million tons	121
Unwrought copper and copper products	6	Million tons	339
Integrated circuits	635,500	Million units	2794
Automobile including chassis	940	Thousand units	349

Data source: (National Bureau of Statistics of China, 2022a, b, c, d)

energy (e.g. petroleum, national gas, coal), raw material for metal production (e.g. iron ore, copper and steel), automobile and agricultural products (especially soybeans and edible vegetable oil) (see Table 6.3 China's foreign trade in 2021: types of import commodities).

The market potential in China has increasingly attracted investments from overseas. In 2021, the total foreign direct investment (FDI) excluding banking, securities and insurance fields has reached 1149.4 billion yuan or US$ 173.5 billion, of which

Table 6.4 Foreign direct investments (FDIs) in China in year 2021 (Excluding banking, financial services and insurance)

Business sector	No. of enterprises	Total amount in billion CNY
Agriculture, forestry, animal husbandry and fishery	491	6
Manufacturing	4455	222
Supply industry: Electricity, heat, gas, water production, etc.	465	25
Transportation, warehousing and postal service	693	35
Data transmission, software and other IT services	4053	135
Wholesale and retail trade	13,379	110
Real estate	1125	157
Leasing and rental	9290	219
Repairs and other residential services	522	3
Others	13,170	239
Total	**47,643**	**1149**

Data source: (National Bureau of Statistics of China, 2022a, b, c, d)

346.9 billion yuan or US$ 52.2 were invested in high-tech industries (see Table 6.4 Foreign Direct Investments (FDIs) in China in Year 2021).

6.3 Consumer Market

6.3.1 Consumer Income and Consumption Expenditure

Along with the continuously improving average per capita disposable income of residents of China, the purchasing power of the stable middle class has increased significantly over the past years. To many foreign companies, China has become one of the most important consumer markets worldwide.

In Fig. 6.4, the population is divided into five income groups with equal share (20%) of the total population, arranged in ascending order: lower-income group, lower-middle-income group, middle-income group, upper-middle-income group and high-income group. From 2015 to 2021, the average per capita disposable income of the upper 20% income group has increased enormously by 57%. In other words, more than 288 million residents achieved a disposable income of over 85,836 RMB (equal to US$ 13,663) in 2021. In comparison, according to the data of the German Federal Office of Statistics, the current average per capita disposable income and receipts for a total population of 84.1 million in Germany is around € 21,555, with an average private consumption expenditure of € 14,681 per person per year (Statistisches Bundesamt, 2022a, b). Given the size of the Chinese population and in consideration of the relatively low living expenses, there are few alternatives to the Chinese consumer market.

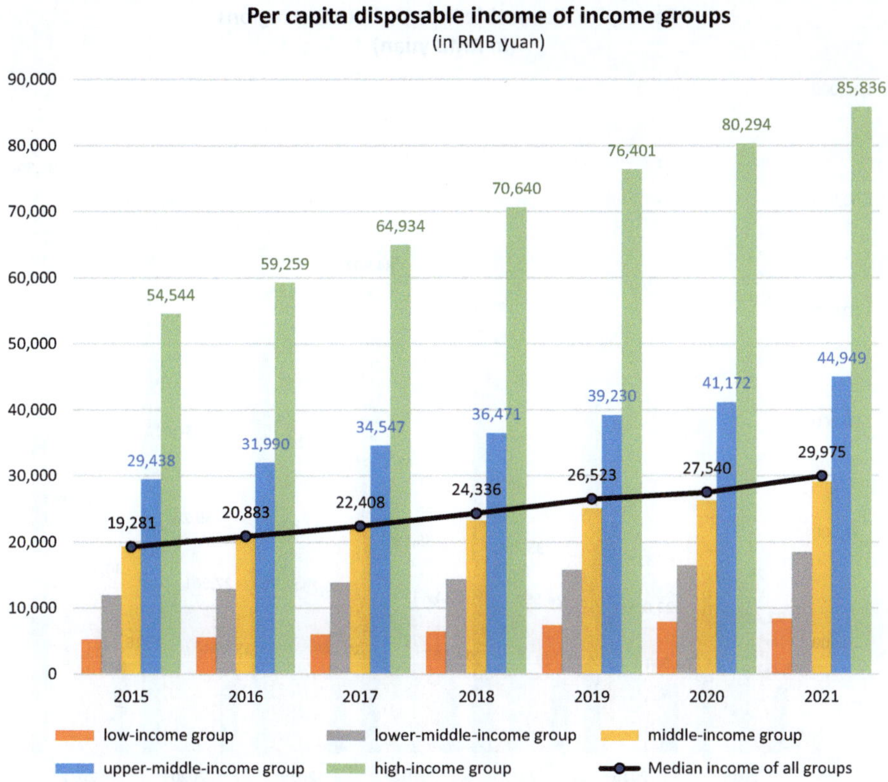

Fig. 6.4 Average disposable income per capita in China from 2015 to 2021. Data source: (National Bureau of Statistics of China, 2022a, b, c, d)

For 2015 to 2021, the share of urban population in China's total population has increased from 57 to 65% (National Bureau of Statistics of China, 2022a, b, c, d). In general, the average income of the Chinese urban regions is significantly higher than that of the rural population, although the income gap has been reduced successively. In 2021, the average per capita disposable income of the upper 20% of the urban population (around 183 million people) was 102,596 RMB (equal to US$ 16,330 or € 15,904). However, the average income of top 20% population in the rural regions was only 42% of the high-income group in the urban regions in the same year (see Figs. 6.5 and 6.6).

The large income gap implies that a market augmentation separating the individual income groups in urban and rural areas is important to most providers targeting the Chinese consumer market.

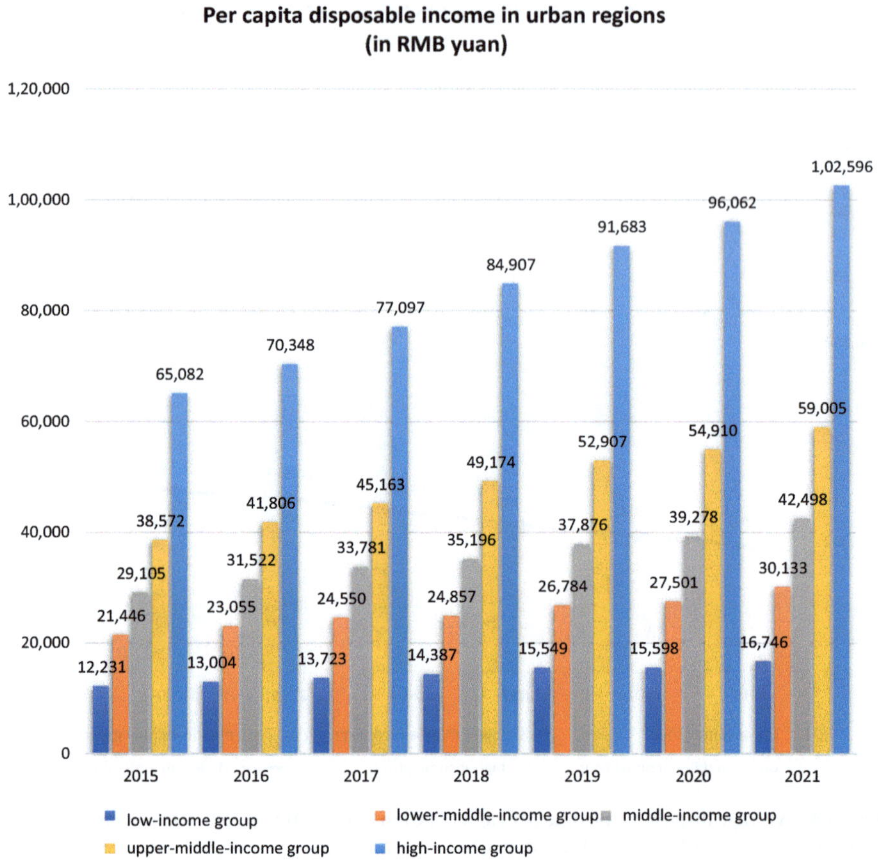

Fig. 6.5 Average disposable income per capita in Chinese urban regions from 2015 to 2021. Data source: (National Bureau of Statistics of China, 2022a, b, c, d)

Despite the Covid-19 pandemic, the per capita consumption expenditure of the Chinese residents in 2021 reached 24,100 yuan, an increase of 12.6% over the previous year after deducting the price factor (National Bureau of Statistics of China, 2022a, b, c, d). Due to the large income gap between urban and rural residents, the average consumption spending in rural areas was only about half as much as that in urban areas in 2021. The per capita consumption expenditure of urban residents was 30,307 yuan, an increase of 12.2% over the previous year, or 11.1% in real terms after deducting price factors; the per capita consumption expenditure of rural residents was 15,916 yuan, an increase of 16.1%, or 15.3% in real terms (see Fig. 6.7).

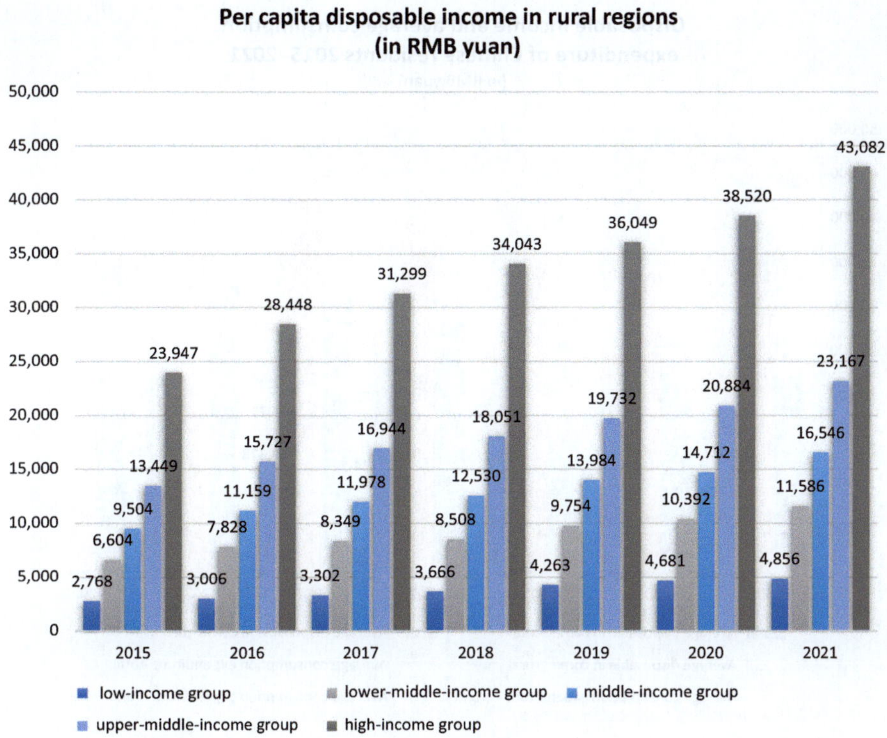

Fig. 6.6 Average disposable income per capita in Chinese rural regions from 2015 to 2021. Data source: (National Bureau of Statistics of China, 2022a, b, c, d)

Among the total consumption expenditure, the largest amounts were spent on food, alcohol and tobacco (7718 yuan and 30% of total spending), accommodation (5641 yuan and 23% of total spending), traffic and communication (3156 yuan and 13% of total spending) and education and entertainment (2599 yuan and 11% of total spending) (see Figs. 6.8 and 6.9). Like in most countries in the world, the Engel coefficient—the food share in consumption expenditure—was lower (28.6%) in higher-income urban areas and higher (32.7%) in lower-income rural areas (National Bureau of Statistics of China, 2022a, b, c, d). On the other hand, the urban residents must spend a larger share of their disposable income on accommodations (24.4 compared to 20.8% in rural areas) (National Bureau of Statistics of China, 2022a, b, c, d).

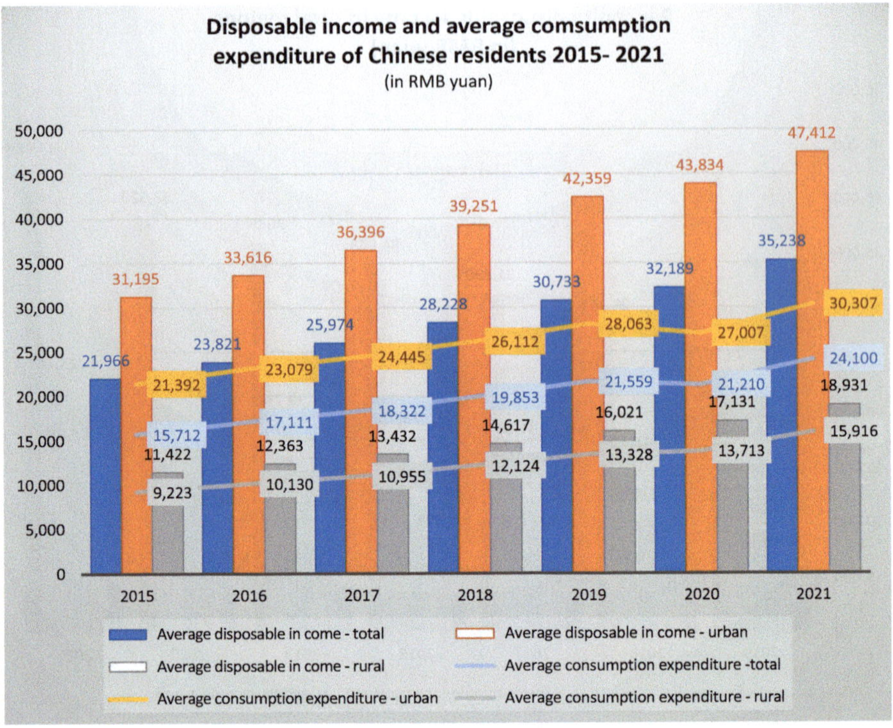

Fig. 6.7 Disposable income vs. consumption expenditure of Chinese residents from 2015 to 2021. Data source: (National Bureau of Statistics of China, 2022a, b, c, d)

6.3.2 Retail Market: Market Size and Stability

In 2021, the total retail sales of consumer goods in China reached 44,082 billion yuan, equal to US$ 6834 billion or € 5778 billion. Overall, 86% of the sales revenues of consumer goods retailing was achieved in urban regions and 14% in rural regions. Divided by consumption types, the retail sales of goods were 39,393 billion yuan (equal to US$ 6107 billion or € 5163 billion), and the service revenues were 4690 billion yuan (equal to US$ 727 billion or € 615 billion) (National Bureau of Statistics of China, 2022a, b, c, d).

By the end of 2021, 301.5 million passenger vehicles were registered in China, including 262.5 million private motor vehicles (of which 167.4 million private sedan cars) and 7.3 million tricycles and low-speed trucks (National Bureau of Statistics of China, 2022a, b, c, d).

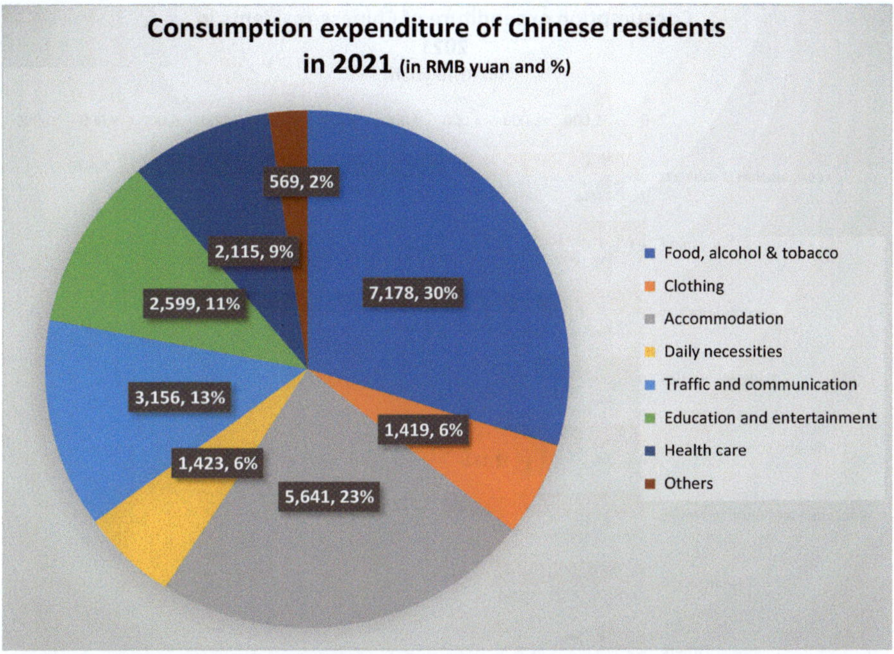

Fig. 6.8 Consumption expenditure of Chinese residents in 2021. Data source: (National Bureau of Statistics of China, 2022a, b, c, d)

Despite its dependency on energy imports, China has avoided an energy crisis by diversifying the import sources (see Chap. 5). Compared to the countries currently involved in an energy crisis due to the sanctions imposed on Russia for the Ukraine war, China like India has maintained a moderate inflation rate by adapting a neutral position in the conflict (see Fig. 6.10). At present, the Chinese politics seems to be helpful in maintaining the stability at the consumer market. Of course, it is important to closely monitor the trade war between the United States and China to stay aware of the potential risks (see Chapter 16).

Given its size, it is difficult to find a consumer market that can substitute the large Chinese market.

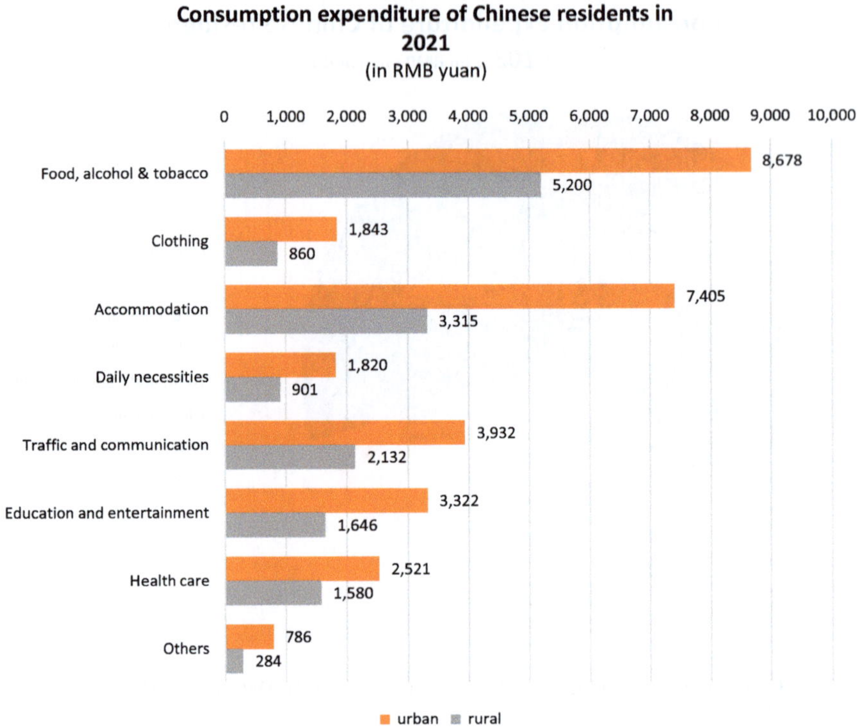

Fig. 6.9 Average consumptions of Chinese citizens in urban and rural regions in 2021. Data source: (National Bureau of Statistics of China, 2022a, b, c, d)

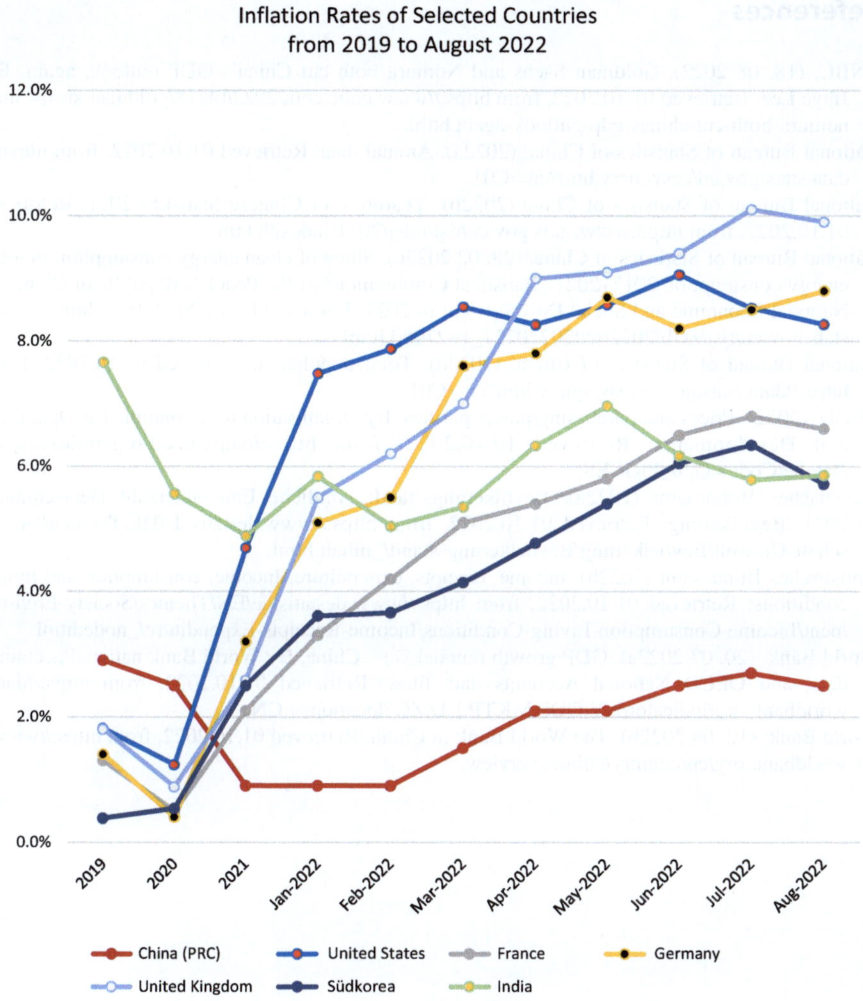

Fig. 6.10 Inflation rates of selected countries from 2019 to August 2022. Data source: OECD (OECD, 2022)

References

CNBC. (18. 08 2022). Goldman Sachs and Nomura both cut China's GDP outlook, again. By Jihye Lee: Retrieved 01.10.2022, from https://www.cnbc.com/2022/08/18/goldman-sachs-and-nomura-both-cut-chinas-gdp-outlook-again.html.

National Bureau of Statistics of China. (2022a). Annual data. Retrieved 01.10.2022, from https://data.stats.gov.cn/easyquery.htm?cn=C01.

National Bureau of Statistics of China (2022b). Yearbook of Chinese Statistics 2021. Retrieved 01.10.2022, from http://www.stats.gov.cn/tjsj/ndsj/2021/indexch.htm.

National Bureau of Statistics of China. (28. 02 2022c). Share of clean energy consumption in total energy consumption 2017–2021. Statistical Communiqué of the People's Republic of China on National Economic and Social Development in 2021: Retrieved 01.10.2022, from http://www.stats.gov.cn/tjsj/zxfb/202202/t20220227_1827960.html.

National Bureau of Statistics of China. (2022d). Total population. Retrieved 01.10.2022, from https://data.stats.gov.cn/easyquery.htm?cn=C01.

OECD. (2022). Prices and purchasing power parities. By Organisation for Economic Co-Operation and Developments: Retrieved 10.10.2022, from https://stats.oecd.org/Index.aspx?DataSetCode=G20_PRICES.

Statistisches Bundesamt (2022a). Bevölkerungsstand: Amtliche Einwohnerzahl Deutschlands 2021. Bevölkerung: Retrieved 01.10.2022, from https://www.destatis.de/DE/Themen/Gesellschaft-Umwelt/Bevoelkerung/Bevoelkerungsstand/_inhalt.html.

Statistisches Bundesamt (2022b). Income, receipts, expenditure. Income, consumption and living conditions: Retrieved 01.10.2022, from https://www.destatis.de/EN/Themes/Society-Environment/Income-Consumption-Living-Conditions/Income-Receipts-Expenditure/_node.html.

World Bank. (20. 07 2022a). GDP growth (annual %)—China. By World Bank national accounts data, and OECD National Accounts data files.: Retrieved 01.10.2022, from https://data.worldbank.org/indicator/NY.GDP.MKTP.KD.ZG?locations=CN.

World Bank. (12. 04 2022b). The World Bank in China. Retrieved 01.10.2022, from https://www.worldbank.org/en/country/china/overview.

7 Economic Hubs

7.1 Major Economic Zones

In China, the designated economic zones are major urban agglomerations with the potential to lead regional development as economic engines. The term 'economic zone' is not to be confused with 'special economic zone' (SEZ) which stands for regions with special economic policies and favourable conditions to attract foreign investment.

The most comprehensive infrastructure for industrial activities can be found in three major economic zones: the Yangtze River Delta Region, the Pearl River Delta Economic Zone and Greater Bay Area (GBA) and the Bohai Economic Rim. For foreign companies, these are often the best sales as well as procurement markets.

7.1.1 Yangtze River Delta

The Yangtze River Delta Region is an economic hub in Eastern China with a total area of 358,000 square kilometres, characterised by a high degree of industrialisation in a variety of business sectors such as automotive, railway, aviation, electronics and mechanical engineering industries and steel production. This region covers the metropolis Shanghai and the high-income provinces Jiangsu, Zhejiang as well as Anhui, including more than 20 large economically developed cities such as Nanjing, Wuxi, Changzhou, Suzhou, Ningbo and Wenzhou. Innovation is fuelled by the creation of the special economic zone Pilot Free Trade Zone of Shanghai Lingang, the Yangtze River Delta ecological development zone with 2300 square kilometres and a comprehensive transportation network. This region has attracted many international manufacturers such as Bosch, Siemens, Yazaki, Mitsubishi, etc. (Xinhua, 2019).

T. Dathe et al., *Business Opportunities and Risks in China*, Management for Professionals, https://doi.org/10.1007/978-3-031-31933-4_7

7.1.2 Pearl River Delta Economic Zone

The Pearl River Delta Economic Zone is the economic engine of the coastal province Guangdong in South China, next to the special administrative regions (SARs) Hong Kong and Macao. It consists of the urban areas in Guangzhou, Shenzhen, Dongguan, Zhuhai, Foshan, Zhongshan, Jiangmen and parts of Huizhou and Zhaoqing. In 2021, the gross domestic product (GDP) of the nine cities exceeded 10 trillion yuan, with Guangzhou, Shenzhen, Dongguan and Foshan each reaching a GDP over 1 trillion yuan (The People's Government of Guangdong Province, 2022).

To ensure smooth flows of workforce, logistics, capital and information within the economic zone, the Guangdong Provincial Government has launched numerous infrastructural projects. Today, the Pearl River Delta cultivates some worldwide competitive innovation and manufacturing clusters, especially in the fields of information technology and electronics, automotive, smart home appliances, robotics and petrochemicals. In addition, the construction and textile industries also play an important role in the local economy.

The development of the Pearl River Delta has largely benefited from investment from Hong Kong and Macao. In 2019, in addition to the Pearl Delta Economic Zone, the State Council of China announced the 'Development Plan Outline for the Guangdong-Hong Kong-Macao Greater Bay Area' (The Government of Hong Kong, 2019) to further promote the economic integration of Guangdong, Hong Kong and Macao (see Sect. 7.3).

7.1.3 Bohai Economic Rim

The Bohai Economic Rim encompasses the northern regions surrounding the Bohai Sea, including the capital city Beijing, the municipality Tianjin, the Province Hebei, the Shandong Peninsula and the central and southern areas of Liaoning Province. In comparison to the Yangtze River Delta and Pearl River Delta, there are much larger regional differences within the Bohai Economic Rim, so that this economic zone is further divided into three secondary economic zones: the Beijing-Tianjin-Hebei Zone, the Shandong Peninsula Zone and the Liaodong Peninsula Zone.

The Bohai Rim region is the major base for China's heavy industry and chemical industry. The research institutions and universities of the region have cultivated a quarter of national talents for scientific research and technical innovations. There are clusters for aviation, shipbuilding, railway, automotive and electronics industries (The State Council of the P.R.C., 2010).

Due to the geographical proximity to Japan and South Korea, many business collaborations with those two countries are concentrated in the Bohai Region, especially in the seaport city of Qingdao, the economic centre of Shandong Province. Qingdao and the adjacent cities in the eastern part of Shandong Province are home to many heavy-industry multinational corporations such as Kawasaki Heavy Industries (KHI), Siemens and Bombardier. The said MNCs often collaborate with local manufacturers. For example, Bombardier operates in joint ventures with the Chinese railway vehicle manufacturer CRRC Qingdao Sifang Locomotive & Rolling Stock Co. Ltd. to provide rail transportation products.

7.2 Special Economic Zones and Free-Trade Zones

In December 1978, the Third Plenary Session of the 11th Central Committee of the CPC decided to replace China's strictly planned economy by a market economy and to open up the isolated country to the outside world. There was not any experience within or outside China how to implement such a fundamental reform. China used a trial-and-error approach to test the feasibility of new policies in small areas and—if proven successful—roll out such reforms on a nationwide scale. The following year, 1979, four special economic zones (SEZ) were established in Shenzhen, Zhuhai, Shantou (all in Guangzhou Province) and Xiamen (Fujian Province). Foreign investment and establishment of Chinese private enterprises were first allowed in these SEZs. Especially Shenzhen bordering Hong Kong became a unique success story. The town Shenzhen was founded just in 1979 with a population of 30,000. In 2022, Shenzhen's population reached 17.5 million. Since 2018, Shenzhen's GDP exceeds that of Hong Kong.

In the 1980s, Shanghai, the only noteworthy industrial centre when founding of the People's Republic, was in danger of falling behind the successful southern Chinese cities. In 1992, the answer was the designation of a special economic zone in Pudong district, the formerly mainly agricultural eastern part of Shanghai. Already in 2010, Shanghai harbour in Pudong exceeded Singapore to become the one with the highest turnover of goods in the world. Consequently, Pudong became the most important port of entry for products imported to China, with many foreign invested trading companies founding their China headquarters in Pudong. In addition, Pudong became the financial centre of China. The city district of Pudong has now almost 5.7 million inhabitants, many of them highly qualified talent that moved to Shanghai from other parts of the country.

After China's accession to the WTO, the whole territory of China opened up; subsequently, the advantages of the early SEZs dwindled. To further boost foreign investment and international trade, China's central government established free-trade zones (FTZs)—their full official name: 'China (province/municipality) Pilot Free Trade Zone'. The first one was founded in September 2013 in Shanghai Pudong. Until late 2022, all 4 municipalities directly under the central government, 1 autonomous region (Guangxi in southwestern China) and 16 of 23 provinces have established FTZs (FDI China, 2022). With the exception of Hainan (see below), each FTZ covers an area of about 120 km^2. Named by the province or municipality where the FTZ is located, each FTZ consists of several disjunct areas. In the case of provinces (except Sichuan and Shanxi, two cities each), every FTZ is spread over three different cities (see Table 7.1 Free-trade Zones on National Level, Approved by the State Council). For example, in the southeastern province of Fujian, the FTZ covers three different areas in the provincial capital Fuzhou as well as in Xiamen and Pingtan. Each of the FTZ has its own policy, focusing on different industry sectors.

Table 7.1 Free-trade zones on national level, approved by the State Council

Province, municipality	Establishment	Towns, districts	Focus industries
Shanghai	2015	Eight areas in Pudong	International trade and finance
Guangdong	2015	Guangzhou, Shenzhen, Zhuhai	Trade, finance, healthcare, education
Tianjin	2015	Three districts of Tianjin City	Aviation, aerospace, shipping, finance
Fujian	2015	Fuzhou, Xiamen, Pingtan	International trade and finance
Liaoning	2017	Shenyang, Dalian, Yingkou	Automotive, aviation, maritime industry
Zhejiang	2017	Hangzhou, Ningbo, Jinyi	AI, fintech, life sciences, oil, gas
Henan	2017	Zhengzhou, Kaifeng, Luoyang	Automobile, biomedicine, robotics, tourism
Hubei	2017	Wuhan, Yichang, Xiangyang	Biomedicine, finance, tourism
Chongqing	2017	Liangjiang, Xiyong, Guoyang	Biotechnology, microelectronics
Sichuan	2017	Chengdu, Luzhou	Diverse
Shanxi	2017	Xi'an, Xianyang	Aviation, finance, tourism, agriculture
Hainan	2018	Hainan Island	International trade and finance
Shandong	2019	Jinan, Qingdao, Yantai	AI, finance, healthcare care, tourism, IT
Jiangsu	2019	Nanjing, Suzhou, Lianyungang	Semiconductors, healthcare, AI, IT
Guangxi	2019	Nanning, Qinzhou, Chongzuo	Finance, logistics, digital services
Hebei	2019	Xiongan, Zhengding, Caofeidian, Daxing Airport	Aviation, life science, biotechnology, IT
Yunnan	2019	Kunming, Honghe, Dehong	Diverse
Heilongjiang	2019	Harbin, Heihe, Suifenhe	IT, new materials, biomedicine, finance, tourism
Beijing	2020	Beijing City	Biomedicine, telecommunication, automotive, fintech, services
Hunan	2020	Changsha, Yueyang, Chenzhou	AI, quantum computing, renewable energies, green tech
Anhui	2020	Hefei, Wuhu, Bengbu	Integrated circuits, AI, fintech

Data sources: Baidu (2022) and FDI China (2022)

In FTZs, imported goods are exempted from customs duties as long as they remain in the zone, corporate tax rates are lower, and additional industries are open to foreign investment (see Sect. 4.2). In addition, the FTZs strive to address special concerns of FIE, for example, restrictions to exchange of foreign currencies and protection of intellectual property rights. The approval and direct supervision of FTZs by the State Council ensures a high degree of legal and political protection.

According to the annual report by the Chinese Academy of International Trade and Economic Cooperation (CAITEC), in 2020, 6472 new FIEs established a presence in the FTZs, 16.8% of all new FIEs in China, investing a total of 1.7638 trillion CNY, 17.6% of the national total foreign investment (YiMagazine, 2021).

A special case of a FTZ is the tropical island of Hainan with a land area of 35,400 km^2 and around ten million inhabitants. Smaller islands in the South China Sea are under the jurisdiction of Hainan Province but are not included in the FTZ. Until April 1988, Hainan was a part of Guangdong Province, before it became the status of a province and a SEZ. In the following decades, Hainan still had only limited economic significance, the main industries being agriculture and tourism. Hainan became a boost as a high-tech location when in 2014 a space launch centre was put into service near Wenchang in the eastern part of the island.

Hainan is now in the preparatory phase to become a large free-trade zone that eventually may reach a freedom of business similar to Hong Kong. Similar to Hong Kong, which is separated by a land border from Guangdong Province, Hainan shall be separated by a 'second line of control', a border within China that separates Hainan from the rest of the country (Hainan Free Trade Port, 2022). By 2025, a system of policies and control points shall be in place, regulating flow of goods and people between Hainan and other provinces. In the following 10 years until 2035, the establishment of the FTZ shall basically be completed. Envisaged measures will be zero customs duties for most imports, strongly reduced corporate and personal tax rates and relaxed visa and working requirements for foreign nationals, supporting free flow of capital, goods, people and data.

Located at the very southern tip of China, Hainan is close to the emerging markets of Southeast Asia. One target of Hainan FTZ is to facilitate China's integration with the ASEAN and RCEP economies.

The details of Hainan FTZ's policies will be formulated in the years to come. However, already now, there are specially policies in place that provide new business opportunities for SMEs. For example, the Lecheng International Medical Tourism Pilot Zone (Lecheng, 2022) has been established in Bo'ao City in the east of Hainan. In that zone, it is possible to apply for a simplified registration (market approval) of drugs and medical devices. Chinese patients that need access to special drugs or medical devices not yet available in other parts of China can go to Lecheng for treatment. Several drug and medical device manufacturers have set up offices in Lecheng to make use of this unique entry point to the Chinese market.

In addition to the 21 FTZs on national level, there is a variety of economic development zones. For example, in 2020, China has established the Integrated National Demonstration Zone for Opening up the Services Sector in Beijing. Together with the Beijing FTZ, they are commonly referred to as the Beijing 'Two Zones' (Government of Beijing Municipality, 2022).

Several free-trade areas have been established to support trade with neighbouring countries, for example, in Kashgar (Xinjiang) close to Pakistan and in Khorgos (Xinjiang) at the border to Kazakhstan. In May 2022, the Lhasa Comprehensive

Bonded Zone in Tibet passed national review; when put into operation, it will facilitate trade with Nepal.

7.3 The Guangdong-Hong Kong-Macao Greater Bay Area (GBA)

The Pearl River (Chinese: Zhujiang, 珠江) in Southern China has a length of more than 2000 kilometres and is the third longest river in China. South of Guangdong's provincial capital Guangzhou, the Pearl River forms a 70-km-long delta and finally flows into the South China Sea. The two SARs Hong Kong and Macao as well as two of the early SEZs Shenzhen and Zhuhai are located on both sides of the delta.

In a transitional period until 1947 and 1949, respectively, Hong Kong and Macao will retain their status as SARs with independent legal systems, currencies and customs authorities. However, to coordinate economic development and avoid overlapping investment, on 01 July 2017, the NDRC and the governments of Guangdong Province, Hong Kong and Macao signed the Framework Agreement on Deepening Guangdong-Hong Kong-Macao Cooperation in the Development of the Greater Bay Area in Hong Kong (Hong Kong SAR Government, 2018).

In addition to Hong Kong and Macao, the GBA includes the nine most developed cities of Guangzhou Province, Guangzhou, Shenzhen, Zhuhai, Foshan, Huizhou, Dongguan, Zhongshan, Jiangmen and Zhaoqing, about 31% of the territory of the province (see Fig. 7.1 Map Greater Bay Area). The total area is of the GBA is around

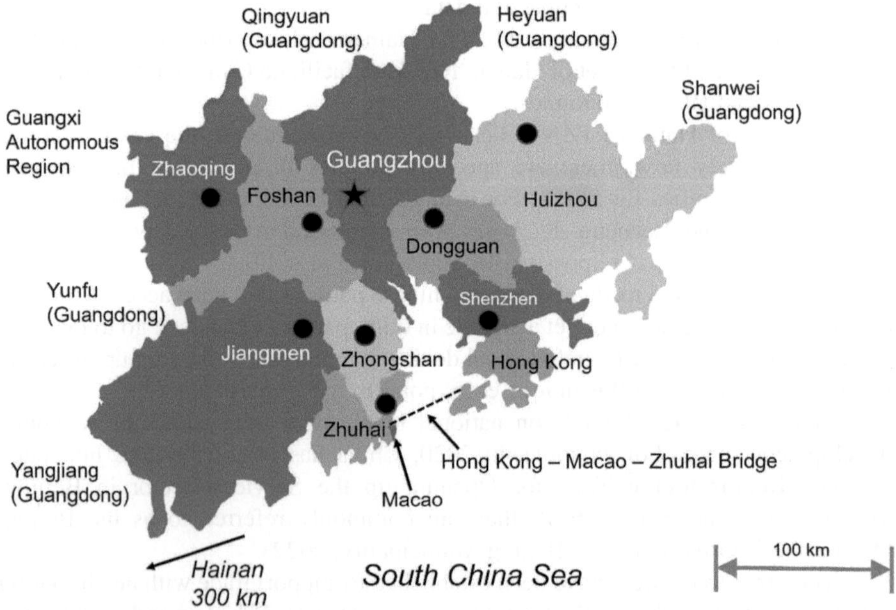

Fig. 7.1 Map of the Greater Bay Area

56,000 km^2, with a population of over 86 million and a GDP of 1668.8 billion US$ in 2020, close to South Korea, the tenth largest economy in the world.

The first stage of the GBA integration focused on improving traffic infrastructure. In October 2018, a Y-shaped sea-crossing bridge was opened, linking Hong Kong with Macao (41.6 km) and Zhuhai (55 km). Travelling time from Hong Kong International Airport to Zhuhai decreased from previously 4 h to about 45 min, incorporating the western side of the Pearl River Delta into an easy reachable commuting radius of Hong Kong. In addition, in 2018, China's high-speed railway network was extended to Hong Kong. In August 2020, the seventh land crossing opened between Hong Kong and Shenzhen. Within Guangzhou Province, additional bridges are built to improve connectivity.

Trans-border cooperation in administration and services has begun with smaller pilot projects. For example, in healthcare, the Shenzhen City Government and Hong Kong University have jointly established a hospital in Shenzhen. Drugs and medical devices that obtained market approval in Hong Kong but not yet in Mainland China are allowed to be administered to patients in this hospital. If successful, it is planned to extend this trial to other cities in the GBA. The Chinese regulator for drugs and medical devices, the National Medical Products Administration (NMPA), has set up a sub-administration in Guangdong to coordinate easier access to new innovative treatment methods (NMPA, 2020). Hong Kong's healthcare service pays for their citizens to seek treatment in Shenzhen's Hong Kong University Hospital. Drug and medical device license holders from Hong Kong and Macao enjoy preferential approval procedures when establishing a manufacture in the GBA.

In the field of education, in September 2022, an external campus of the Hong Kong University of Science and Technology opened in Guangdong's provincial capital Guangzhou. Children of Hong Kong and Macao citizens are given free access to most schools in the GBA area of Guangdong Province. In June 2019, the Hong Kong Education Bureau and the Guangdong Provincial Government signed a letter of intent on cooperation in education, including the exploration of mutual recognition of credits in education and training in the GBA and the promotion of talent exchange.

Additional cross-border cooperations in the GBA started in several other sectors such like financial services, logistics and environmental protection (Hong Kong SAR Government, 2022).

Integration of the GBA is gradual. For the time being, SMEs in the GBA mainly benefit from improved connectivity and easier exchange of personnel. In the future, market access to Mainland China via the free economy Hong Kong will be facilitated, providing new business opportunities for foreign SME.

7.4 Case Study: A Bilateral Cooperation Attracting Foreign SME

In different parts of China, there are several clusters of foreign invested SMEs, where companies headquartered in the same country are concentrated. In most cases, these clusters are supported by bilateral agreements of the Government of China and the respective country.

For an SME, choosing such a cluster as the basis for its business in China has advantages: the sheer number of possible locations in China requires costly and time-consuming marketing studies to find the best location. To 'follow the crowd', investing there, where other companies have already been successful, ensures that such a locality has a business-friendly environment and that basic requirements like a developed infrastructure and ample human resources are fulfilled. A business community connected to their home country is helpful for foreign invested SMEs, especially for newcomers: services like financial reporting and auditing can be outsourced, and information from peers is available to solve typical daily issues. As soon as a certain number of companies from one country have settled down, service providers who specifically address these international clients will follow, for example, financial services, lawyers, entertainment and possibly international schools.

A possible disadvantage to settle down in such a cluster may be a lack of consideration of special requirements of the SME's own industry. For foreign employees, working in an area with many countrymen may slow down integration into the Chinese society and learning Chinese—on a long term negatively influencing business success.

7.4.1 Case Study: German Companies in Taicang

Taicang is a city of 830,000 inhabitants (census 2020), located in the south of Jiangsu Province, bordering Shanghai. The city has an ideal location, only 35 km away from the transport hub Shanghai Hongqiao, which includes an international airport, and has a harbour at the Yangtze River. In 1993, Kern-Liebers was the German company to establish a manufacture in Taicang. In 2000, the German Chamber of Commerce (AHK) Greater China founded a subsidiary in Taicang. In 2007, the number of German companies reached 100 (Taicang Investment, 2022). In 2008, the German Federal Ministry for Economic Affairs and Energy (BMWi) and the MOFCOM recognised Taicang as the first 'Sino-German base for business cooperation', followed by the title 'first Sino-German demonstration zone for SME cooperation' awarded by the Chinese Ministry of Industry and Information Technology (MIIT) (Industrie 4.0 Platform, 2021).

In order to provide German companies with sufficient skilled workers, starting from 2001, Taicang has introduced a professional training system based on German models, with 15 Sino-German dual education training centres. More than 10,000 workers and technicians have graduated from these schools.

In 2016, the world's eighth and China's third German Centre for Industry and Trade opened in Taicang, offering office space and assistance in settlement especially tailored towards German SMEs (German Centre, 2022). In 2022, at least 387 German companies have set up subsidiaries in Taicang (AHK Greater China, 2022) with an annual industrial output of over 50 billion RMB (approx. 6.5 billion €).

In July 2021, the Taicang City Government published the document 'Further deepen the economic and trade cooperation with Germany: 14th Five Year implementation plan on building a Sino-German cooperation demonstration zone for small and medium sized enterprises (SME)' (Government of Taicang, 2021). Taicang plans to create a Sino-German SME cooperation demonstration zone. By the end of the 14th Five-Year Plan period in 2025, Taicang wants to be home to 500 German enterprises, among them over 80 hidden champions and 20 regional headquarters. Within the framework of this cooperation, Taicang will promote carbon reduction to reach China's carbon neutrality goals. German companies will be better integrated into the procurement policies of Chinese companies, opening new market opportunities. General cooperation between China and Germany will be promoted, including investment of local Taicang companies in Germany and cooperation with German cities in the fields of trade and commerce, science and education, culture and city construction (Industrie 4.0 Platform, 2021).

The cluster of German companies in Taicang can be seen as a benevolent cycle: investment by SMEs in China spawns political support, which in turn again attracts more investment. The positive effects of economic and political cooperation spill over to areas like environmental protection and education.

References

AHK Greater China. (2022). Taicang City. Retrieved 30.10.2022, from https://china.ahk.de/market-info/investment-zones/taicang.

Baidu. (2022). Free trade zones. Retrieved 29.10.2022, from https://baike.baidu.com/item/自由贸易试验区/17007974

FDI China. (2022). FDI China Exclusive: The 21 Free Trade Zones Guide 2022. Retrieved 27.10.2022, from https://www.fdichina.com/blog/fdi-china-exclusive-the-21-free-trade-zones-guide-2021/

German Centre. (2022). Die Leistungen für Ihren Erfolg (German). Retrieved 30.10.2022, from https://www.germancentretaicang.com/german-centre/konzept/

Government of Beijing Municipality. (2022). Beijing 'Two Zones'. Retrieved 29.10.2022, from https://open.beijing.gov.cn/

Government of Taicang. (2021). Further deepen the economic and trade cooperation with Germany: 14th Five Year implementation plan on building a Sino-German cooperation demonstration zone for small and medium sized enterprises (SME) (in Chinese). Retrieved 30.10.2022, from http://www.taicang.gov.cn/taicang/zfwj/202107/e30cd3703c094e54a4172816e600dbcf.shtml.

Hainan Free Trade Port. (2022). Overall plan for the construction of Hainan Free Trade Port. http://en.hnftp.gov.cn/policies/Document/202008/t20200818_3288396.html. Retrieved 27.10.2022.

Hong Kong SAR Government. (2018). Greater Bay area overview. By Hong Kong SAR Government Constitutional and Mainland Affairs Bureau: Retrieved 12.11.2022, from https://www.bayarea.gov.hk/en/about/overview.html.

Hong Kong SAR Government. (2022). Policy areas. By Hong Kong SAR Government Constitutional and Mainland Affairs Bureau: Retrieved 12.11.2022, from https://www.bayarea.gov.hk/en/home/index.html.

Industrie 4.0 Platform (2021). Taicang's 14th Five Year Plan for Sino-German SME Cooperation. Retrieved 30.10.2022, from https://www.plattform-i40.de/IP/Redaktion/EN/Downloads/Publikation/China/policy-update-20210910.pdf.

Lecheng (2022). Brief introduction to Hainan Boao Lecheng International Medical Tourism Pilot Zone. By Hainan Boao Lecheng International Medical Tourism Pilot Zone Administration: Retrieved 27.10.2022, from http://en.lecityhn.com/2021-05/31/c_158748.htm.

NMPA. (2020). Policy explanation on the innovative development of the supervision of drugs and medical devices in the GBA (in Chinese). Retrieved 12.11.2022, from https://www.nmpa.gov.cn/xxgk/zhcjd/zhcjdzh/20201111094231196.html

Taicang Investment (2022). Sino-German Cooperation. Retrieved 30.10.2022, from http://invest.taicang.gov.cn/DDHZ.aspx

The Government of Hong Kong. (18. 02 2019). Development Plan Outline for the Guangdong-Hong Kong-Macao Greater Bay Area. Retrieved 12.11.2022, from https://www.bayarea.gov.hk/filemanager/tc/share/pdf/Outline_Development_Plan.pdf

The People's Government of Guangdong Province. (21. 04 2022). Advanced 10 trillion urban agglomeration in the core area of the Pearl River Delta. By Hong Kong and Macao Affairs Office: Retrieved on 12.11.2022, from http://hmo.gd.gov.cn/gdfzcj/content/post_3916304.html.

The State Council of the P.R.C. (21. 12 2010). National main functional area planning: efficient, coordinated and sustainable development pattern of land and space. Retrieved 12.11.2022, from https://web.archive.org/web/20200930184402/http://www.gov.cn/zwgk/2011-06/08/content_1879180.htm

Xinhua (01. 12 2019). Outline of the Yangtze River Delta Regional Integrated Development Plan. By the Central Committee of the Communist Party of China and the State Council: Retrieved 12.11.2022, from http://www.gov.cn/zhengce/2019-12/01/content_5457442.htm.

YiMagazine. (2021). The '2021 Report on Development of the FTZs' has been published: The Degree of Freedom has Created a New Dividend. Retrieved 27.10.2022, from https://baijiahao.baidu.com/s?id=1714776454098815383

Labour Market and Education 8

8.1 Development of Qualified Workforce

The People's Republic of China is after the United States the second largest economy in the world and is expected to exceed the United States in economic output in the next few years. China has achieved rapid economic growth and steadily increased the prosperity of the population in the past 40 years.

The continuously growing population of China exceeded 1.4 billion in 2018. Despite the challenge of an ageing population, there is an enormous available workforce (age group 15–64) at the labour market (see Fig. 8.1). Year after year, the Chinese education system trains a large number of young engineers and technicians as a driving force for sustainable economic development. The education system is currently under reform aiming to shift the focus of academic education from theoretical analysis to more practical solutions in real business world.

However, China still needs to expand the skilled workforce to achieve its ambitious strategic targets of modernisation of the manufacturing sector. According to the 'Manufacturing Talent Development Planning Guide' jointly issued by the Ministry of Education, the Ministry of Human Resources and Social Security and the Ministry of Industry and Information Technology, China is in urgent need of qualified talents in all MIC25 key industry fields (see Fig. 8.2).

Every year, the Chinese government allocates more than 10% of total government expenditure, equivalent to around 4% of the annual gross domestic product (GDP), as national financial education funds to support educational institutions (UNESCO, 2018). In 2020, this figure is as high as 4.4 trillion RMB yuan, equivalent to EUR 519 billion or US$ 621 billion US (National Bureau of Statistics of China, 2022a, b).

In recent years, China has introduced a series of facilitation rules at state and regional levels to make it easier for foreign talents and investors to set foot in China.

T. Dathe et al., *Business Opportunities and Risks in China*, Management for Professionals, https://doi.org/10.1007/978-3-031-31933-4_8

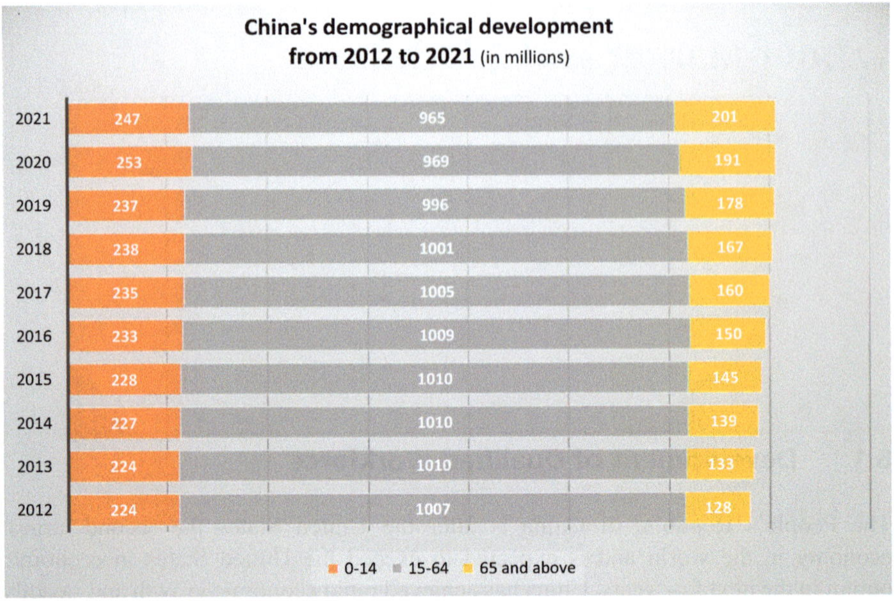

Fig. 8.1 China's demographical development from 2012 to 2021. Data source: (National Bureau of Statistics of China, 2022a, b)

8.2 Education in China

8.2.1 The Education System

The current Chinese education system is divided into primary education, secondary education and higher education (tertiary education). The compulsory education lasts 9 years, consisting of 6 years in primary school and 3 years in junior high school.

Primary education is provided by ordinary primary schools and adult primary schools. Ordinary primary schools enrol children aged 6 to 7, with an education duration of 5–6 years. The primary school for adults is aimed at literacy, in both language and numeracy. Despite the complexity of the language, China has a high literacy rate of 96.8% in the age group 15 years and older. In the age group 15–24 years, the literacy rate is as high as 99.8% (UNESCO, 2018). The total number of adult primary school students is current below 1% of total primary education participants (National Bureau of Statistics of China, 2022a, b).

Secondary education is mainly provided in four different forms: ordinary high school, vocational high school, technical secondary school and technical school. In 2021, the consolidation rate of 9-year compulsory education was 95.4%, and the gross enrolment rate of senior high school was 91.4% (The State Council of China, 2022).

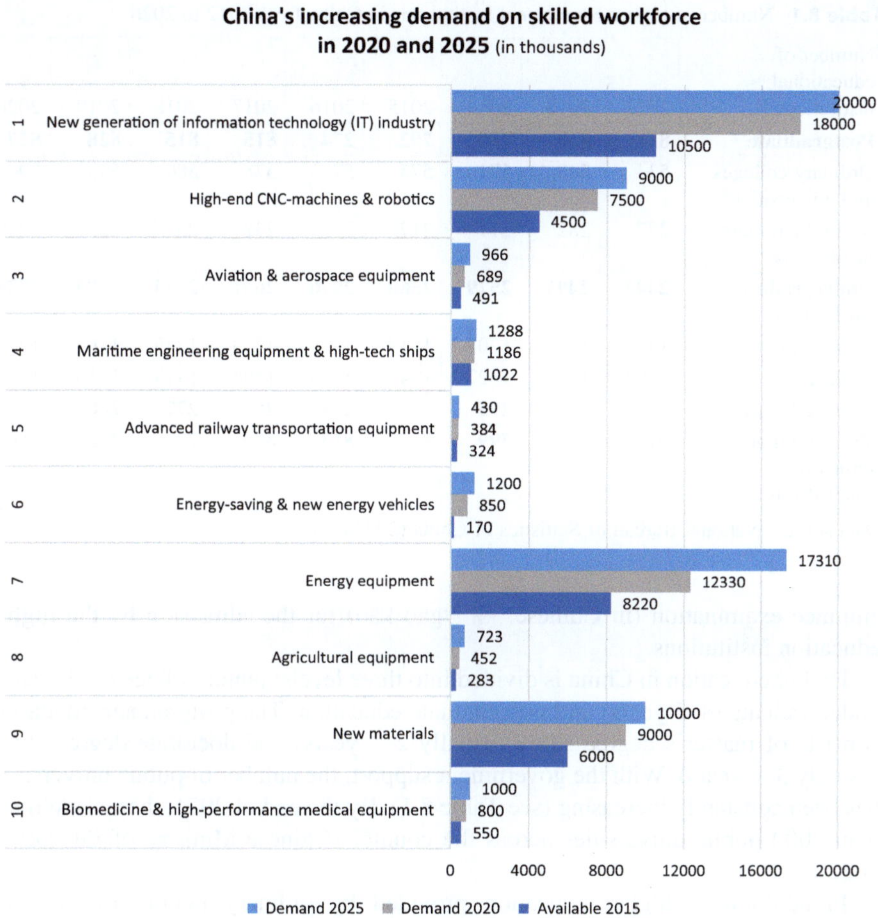

Fig. 8.2 China's demand on skilled workforce in 2020 and 2025. Data source: (Xinhua Network, 2017)

Ordinary high school is divided into two stages: junior high school (3 years) and senior high school (2–3 years; usually 3 years). All students must complete junior high school as a part of the compulsory education. Adults may visit adult junior high school. After graduation from junior high school, students may complete high school education in an ordinary senior high school. As an option, they may also choose one of the vocational secondary education formats, technical school (2–3 years; usually 3 years), secondary vocational school (3–4 years; usually 3 years) or vocational high school (3 years), to complete the secondary education stage. Adult students may visit adult senior high school or adult amateur secondary vocational school (2–3 years).

Ordinary senior high school graduates have restricted access to higher education, while graduates from vocational high schools have only limited access to college study programmes. Both require participation at the national higher education

Table 8.1 Number of higher educational institutions in China from 2012 to 2020

Number of educational institutions	2012	2013	2014	2015	2016	2017	2018	2019	2020
Postgraduate	**811**	**830**	**788**	**792**	**274**	**815**	**815**	**828**	**827**
Ordinary colleges and universities	534	548	571	575	57	578	580	593	594
Scientific research institutions	277	282	217	217	217	237	235	235	233
Undergraduate (ordinary)	**2442**	**2491**	**2529**	**2560**	**2596**	**2631**	**2663**	**2683**	**2738**
Universities	1145	1170	1202	1219	1237	1243	1245	1265	1270
Colleges	1297	1321	1327	1341	1359	1388	1418	1418	1468
Adult education	**348**	**297**	**295**	**292**	**284**	**282**	**277**	**268**	**265**
Private higher education institutions	**823**	**802**	**799**	**813**	**813**	**800**	**784**	**782**	**786**

Data source: National Bureau of Statistics of China (2022a, b)

entrance examination (in Chinese: 高考gao kao) for the admission by the higher education institutions.

Higher education in China is divided into three levels: junior college (2–3 years), undergraduate (4–5 years) and postgraduate education. The postgraduate education consists of master's degree study (usually 2–3 years) and doctorate degree study (usually 3–4 years). With the government support, the number of public universities has been constantly increasing (see Table 8.1). By the end of 2021, there were more than 3000 public universities across the country (Chinese Ministry of Education, 2022).

In addition to higher education provided by ordinary junior colleges and universities, there are a wide variety of distance study programmes, such as the state-run radio and television universities, correspondence studies and evening courses offered by ordinary or independent correspondence junior colleges and universities.

Besides, China also offers a unique low-cost and flexible form of adult higher educational qualifications: self-study examinations. Registered participants receive an exam certificate for each single passed subject examination organised by the national examination agency. Eventually, after passing all examinations and completing the graduation thesis according to the official examination regulations, the participants are awarded the academic degrees. The qualification by self-study is valued on the labour market due to the high challenges on the students in terms of self-motivation and self-organisation.

University graduates have direct access to postgraduate studies, while junior college graduates are subject to further conditions, for example, a waiting period of 2 years after the graduation and additional qualifying examinations.

The education system in China is illustrated in Fig. 8.3.

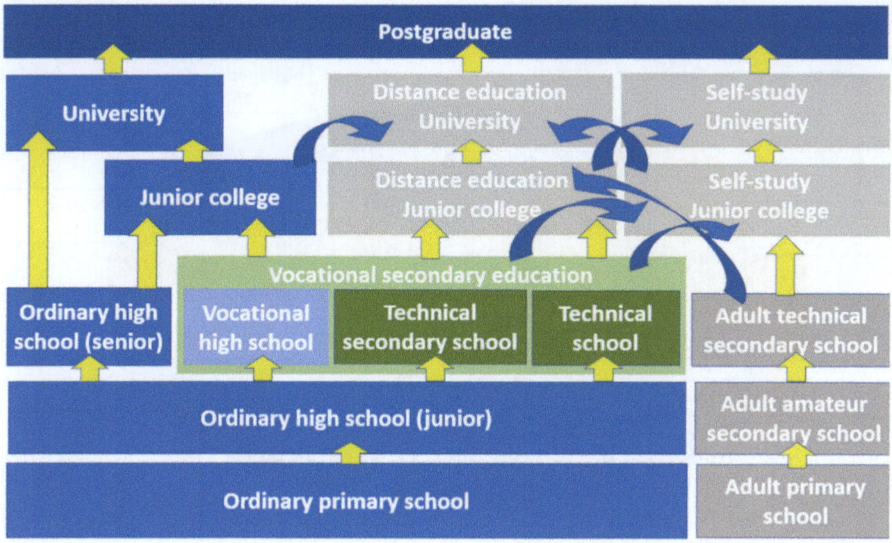

Fig. 8.3 Chinese education system

According to the census results from late 2020, among the total population of over 1.4 billion, over 218 million people have received higher education (college degree or above), 213 million people have senior high school education (including vocational secondary education), 487 million people have junior high school education, and 350 million people have primary school education. In other words, more than 15% of China's population has received higher education (see Fig. 8.4 Educational level of the Chinese population).

8.2.2 Higher Education

China's growing global influence is not confined to its economic power but also demonstrated in the field of education. The top Chinese universities have earned more recognition and become more visible on the world stage over the past decade (see Table 8.2 Top universities of Mainland China on QS World University Ranking List 2023 vs. 2010).

Today, most senior high school students choose to pursue higher education after graduation. From 2012 to 2021, with the continuous expansion of Chinese higher education capacities, the number of undergraduate freshman enrolment increased by 45%, with half in junior college and half in universities (see Fig. 8.5 New enrolments in educational institutions in China from 2012 to 2021). The majors with the highest employment rates for university graduates in 2022 include information security, network engineering, information engineering, microelectronics science and engineering, digital media technology and energy and power engineering and for junior college graduates railway engineering technology, railway power supply

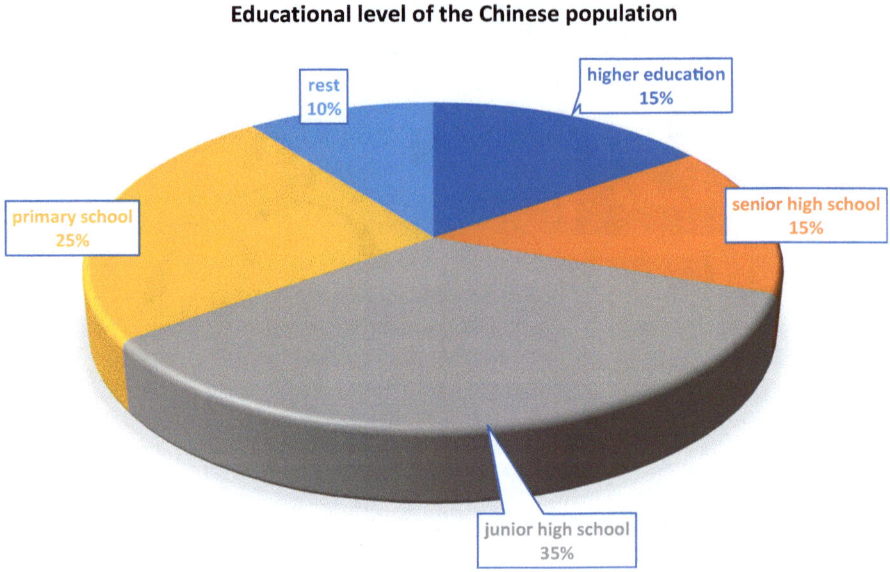

Fig. 8.4 Educational level of the Chinese population. Data source: Ministry of Education of the People's Republic of China (2021)

Table 8.2 Top universities of Mainland China on QS World University Ranking List 2023 vs. 2010

Rank 2023	Rank 2010	University	Location
12	47	Peking University	Beijing
14	54	Tsinghua University	Beijing
34	105	Fudan University	Shanghai
42	218	Zhejiang University	Hangzhou
46	151	Shanghai Jiao Tong University	Shanghai
94	154	University of Science and Technology of China	Hefei
133	177	Nanjing University	Nanjing
194		Wuhan University	Wuhan
212	388	Tongji University	Shanghai

Data source: QS World University Rankings (2022), QS World University Rankings (2009)

technology, social sports, power plants and power systems and road and bridge engineering technology (Sohu, 2022).

In 2021, over 19% of university graduates subsequently attended a master study programme in China or abroad, and there were over one million new enrolments for master studies at Chinese universities (Sohu, 2022) (see Fig. 8.5 New enrolments in educational institutions in China from 2012 to 2021).

As undergraduate degree has become common among young generation in China, more and more Chinese students are choosing adult education courses to accomplish their academic goals (see Fig. 8.5 New enrolments in educational

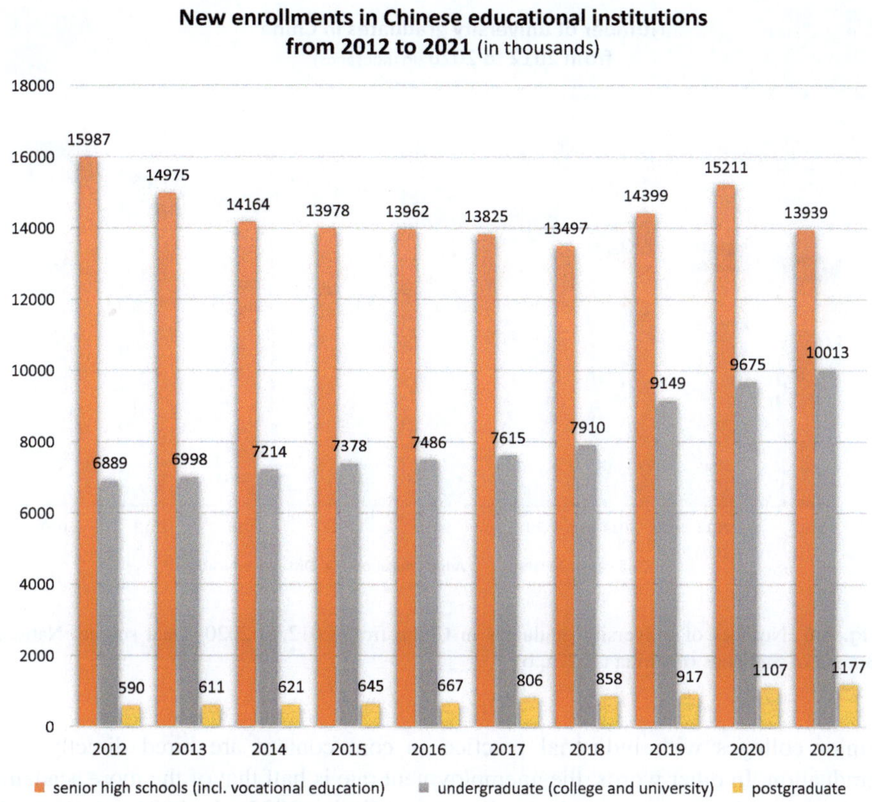

Fig. 8.5 New enrolments in educational institutions in China from 2012 to 2021. Data source: National Bureau of Statistics of China (2022a, b)

institutions in China from 2012 to 2021, Fig. 8.6 Number of university graduates in China from 2012 to 2020 and Fig. 8.7 Number of college graduates in China from 2012 to 2020). One possible explanation for this phenomenon could be the combination of the current employment pressure (job owner being reluctant to give up the employment) and large salary gaps across education levels.

In the recent years, China's economy in transition has been slowing down and in addition affected by negative global economic trends and the Covid-19 crisis. In 2021, over ten million new undergraduate graduates along with over one million postgraduate graduates have further exacerbated the oversupply in the job market. In July 2022, the unemployment rate for the 16–24 age group nationwide has reached nearly 20% (National Bureau of Statistics of China, 2022a, b). The increasing pursuit of postgraduate studies is a way for many to bridge the unemployment after graduation, which only postpones the social problems associated with the overall high unemployment (Agricultural Television Network, 2022).

At the same time, the demand for a more hands-on education is on the rise in the Chinese labour market. According to recent statistics, over 90% graduates from

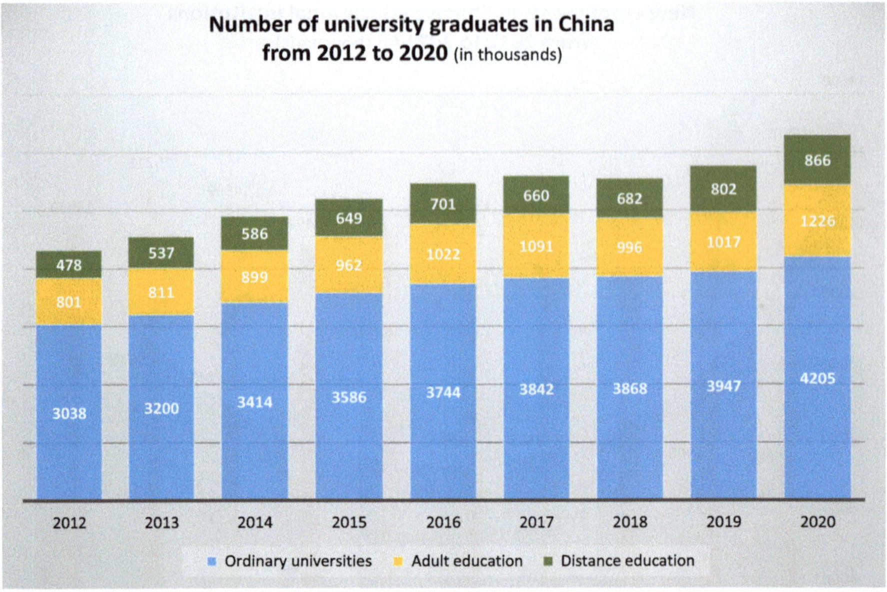

Fig. 8.6 Number of university graduates in China from 2012 to 2020. Data source: National Bureau of Statistics of China (2022a, b)

junior colleges with industrial practice as core content are hired directly after graduation. In other words, the unemployment rate is half that of the more academically focused university students (Economic Daily, 2022). In 2021, significantly fewer majors of energy supply, material and transportation from junior colleges decided to further qualify to a university bachelor's degree, probably because of higher employment rate due to higher market demand (Sohu, 2022).

8.2.3 Vocational Training

Along with the rapid economic growth, China has suffered from a shortage of skilled workforce since many years. As a seemingly paradox, the unemployment is rising among young university graduates at the same time. One of the reasons for the imbalance in the education system is that, despite the high employment rate of the vocational secondary school graduates (currently as high as 95%), the average salaries of the positions that require academic degrees are decisively higher, making the 'return' of academic education appear to be more favourable than vocational education. Moreover, in traditional Confucian understanding, vocational education in China is still commonly perceived as education for unsuccessful students due to its weaker academic focus (Agricultural Television Network, 2022).

In recent years, the Chinese government has launched a series of regulations to promote vocational education. With the Vocational Education Action Plan

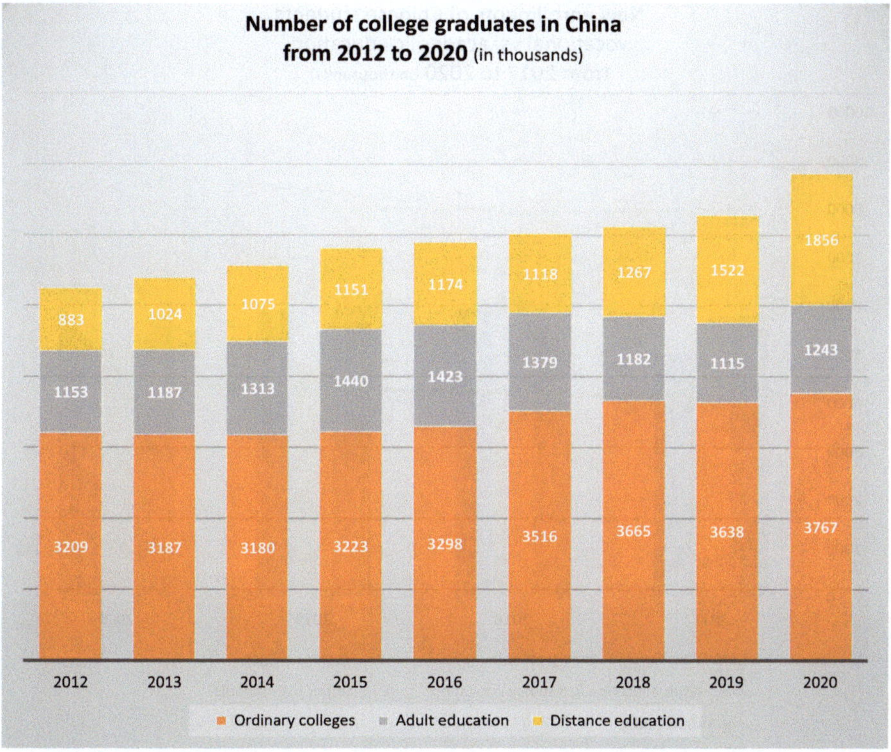

Fig. 8.7 Number of college graduates in China from 2012 to 2020. Data source: National Bureau of Statistics of China (2022a, b)

2020–2023, the state mainly aims to increase the overall capacity of vocational education to a similar scale as the academic education and to improve the social acceptance of vocational education. One of the strategies is to create new vocational higher education institutions by merging independent colleges of universities with vocational secondary schools. The new institutions are usually named vocational universities or vocational technical universities, offering vocational education at undergraduate level (Economic Daily, 2022). As a result of the government policy, the new enrolments at junior colleges with more vocational education content have exceeded the more academic universities (see Fig. 8.8 New enrolments of Chinese students vocational vs. academic education from 2017 to 2020).

Government efforts have significantly improved social acceptance and recognition for vocational education in recent years. Around 55% of junior high school graduates currently complete their secondary education at senior high schools, while 45% of them opt for vocational secondary education (see Fig. 8.8). The government's goal is for 50% of junior high school graduate to attend senior high schools and 50% vocational secondary education in the near future (ifeng.com, 2021).

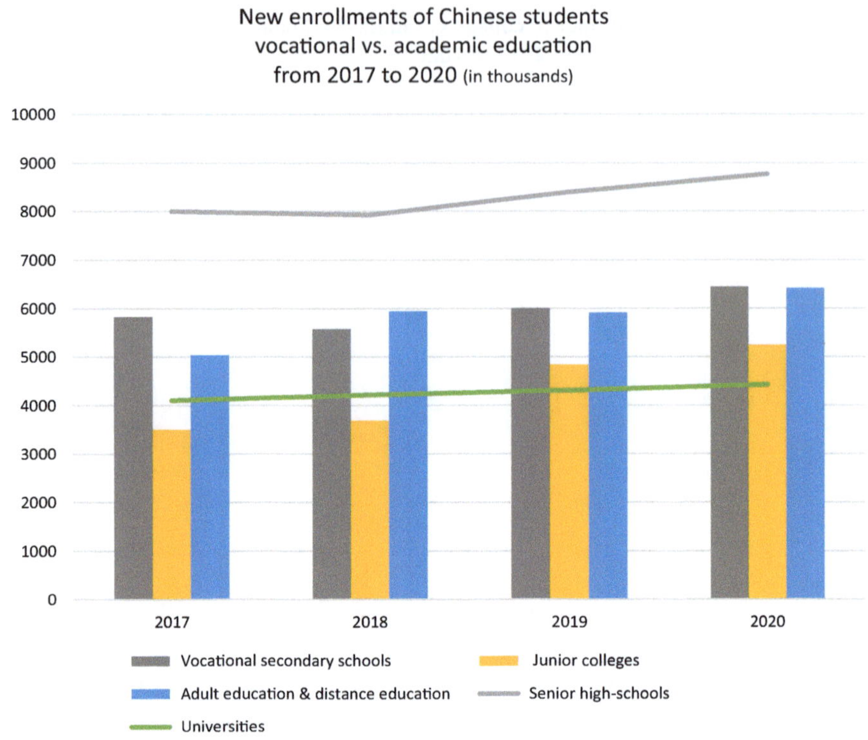

Fig. 8.8 New enrolments of Chinese students vocational vs. academic education from 2017 to 2020. Data source: National Bureau of Statistics of China (2022a, b)

8.2.4 Studying Abroad

For companies dealing with international cooperations, employees with intercultural educational background and/or working experience are special assets.

In 2022, around 170 million people among the Chinese population are between 15 and 24 years old (PopulationPyramid.net, 2022). Through the one-child policy, the Chinese parents have increased their spendings on the education of their cherished offsprings. According to a survey in 2019, most Chinese spend over 20% of their disposable income on education of their children. Moreover, the higher the household income, the higher the share of the children's education expenditure (Chengdu Business Daily, 2021).

To many Chinese parents, studying abroad is a good opportunity to improve the academic skills and intercultural communication skills of their children. From 2010 to 2019, the number of Chinese students studying abroad increased by more than 10% per year on an average. Due to the Covid-19 pandemic and various regional control measures, there was a severe drawback in 2020 (see Fig. 8.9 Number of Chinese students studying abroad from 2010 to 2020). Most of Chinese students abroad choose to study the so-called STEM subjects. STEM stands for Science,

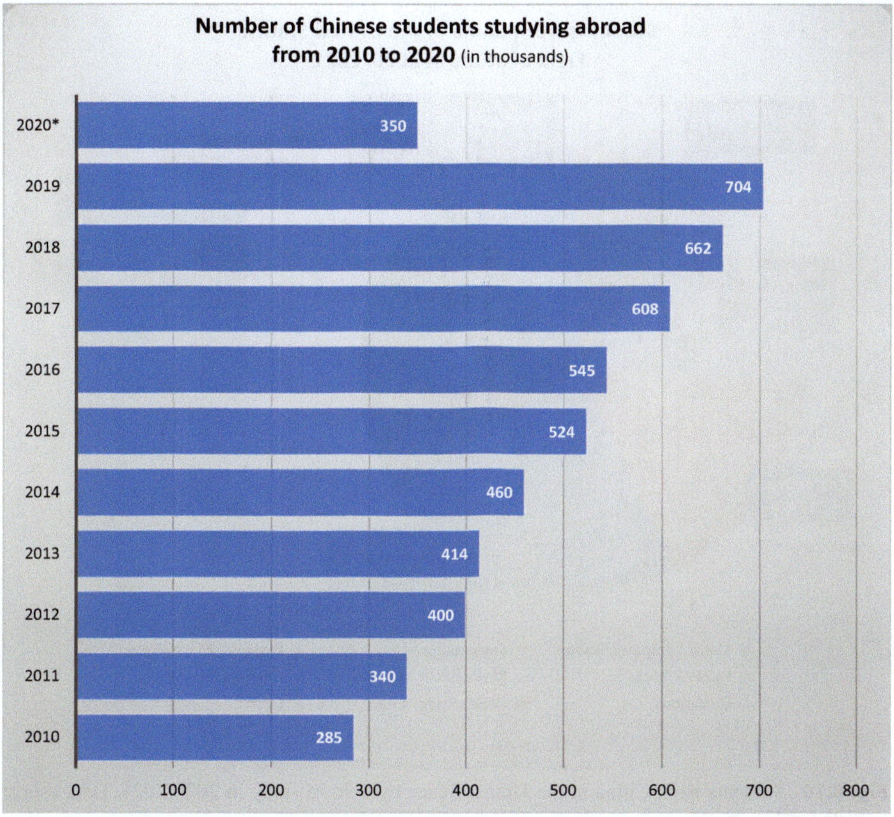

Fig. 8.9 Number of Chinese students studying abroad from 2010 to 2020. Data source: (Statista, 2022a, b, c). * Prognosis

Technology, Engineering and Mathematics (see Fig. 8.10 Students from China in the United States by field of study in 2020/2021).

In consideration of the global influence of the American universities, the United States has been the most favoured destination for Chinese students for many years. In 2019 and 2020 before the pandemic outbreak, Chinese students made up around one third of foreign students in the US universities, creating $60 billion income for the US economy. The higher out-of-state tuition fees paid by Chinese students were important funding sources for education of domestic students (The Wall Street Journal, 2022).

However, the deteriorating geopolitical conflicts between the two nations have also affected the academic field. As of 24 August 2022, the US government has included 13 Chinese universities and research institutions on the entity list for

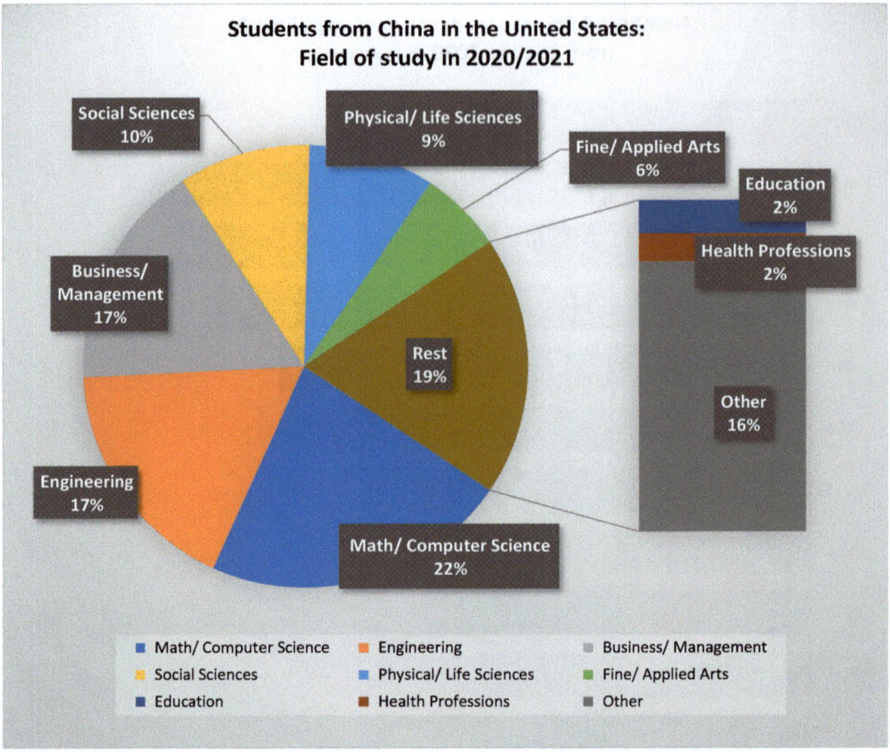

Fig. 8.10 Students from China in the United States by field of study in 2020/2021. Data source: Statista (2022a, b, c)

sanction (U.S. Department of Commerce, 2022), all of those being pioneers in the fields of cutting-edge technologies such as national defence, aviation and quantum computing. Compared to the previous year, the number of US student visas issued to Chinese nationals in the first half year 2022 dropped by 50%. Restrictions were imposed especially on STEM students (The Wall Street Journal, 2022).

A plethora of reasons have softened the enthusiasm of Chinese students and their parents for the United States, for example, the descending hospitality towards Asians, increasing political uncertainty and discrimination as well as travel restrictions (The Wall Street Journal, 2022). Meanwhile, the United Kingdom and some Asian regions, for example, Japan, Singapore and Hong Kong, have become alternative destinations for overseas studies (see Fig. 8.11 Preferred destinations for Chinese students studying abroad (2015 vs. 2022)) (Forbes, 2022).

Meanwhile, China is not only a source of international students, but has become the destination country for overseas students. In 2016, China's Ministry of

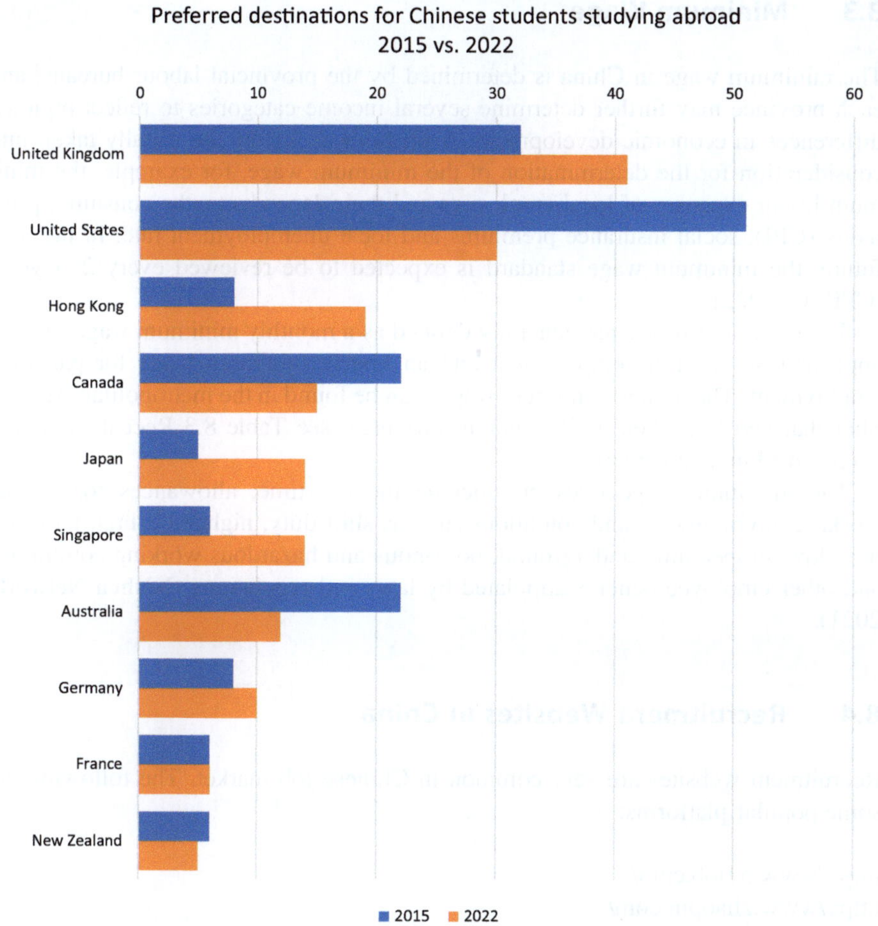

Fig. 8.11 Preferred destinations for Chinese students studying abroad (2015 vs. 2022). Data source: Statista (2022a, b, c)

Education introduced the Belt and Road Initiative (BRI) Education Action Plan to strengthen educational cooperations between China and the BRI countries in Central Asia, the Middle East, Africa and Europe. The Chinese universities have launched 'going out' projects to promote their internationalisation, for example, Peking University HSBC Business School has set up a campus in Oxford, UK, and Tsinghua University established a partnership with the University of Washington with the first overseas presence of Global Innovation Exchange Institute (GIX) at campus Seattle, USA. In addition, China has also introduced massive open online courses in English for global learners on the platforms XuetangX and iCourse (University World News, 2021).

8.3 Minimum Wage

The minimum wage in China is determined by the provincial labour bureaus, and each province may further determine several income categories to reflect regional differences in economic development. A plethora of factors are usually taken into consideration for the determination of the minimum wage, for example, the minimum living expenses of local employees and their dependents, the consumer price index (CPI), social insurance premiums and local unemployment rate. In the near future, the minimum wage standard is expected to be reviewed every 2–3 years (CPPCC, 2022).

The minimum wages are generally defined as a monthly minimum wage that are applicable to full-time employment and an hourly minimum wage for part-time employment. The highest minimum wages can be found in the metropolitan Beijing, Shanghai and Shenzhen in Guangdong Province (see Table 8.3 Recent minimum wages in Mainland China).

The minimum wage does not include the overtime; allowances for special working environments and conditions such as shift duty, nightshift, high temperature, low temperature, underground, poisonous and hazardous working conditions; and other employee benefits stipulated by laws and regulations (Xinhua Network, 2021).

8.4 Recruitment Websites in China

Recruitment websites are very common in Chinese job market. The following are some popular platforms:

http://www.51job.com/
http://www.zhaopin.com/
http://www.chinahr.com/
http://www.lagou.com/
http://www.rrlt.com/
http://www.liepin.com/

For international companies:

https://www.ahk.de/,
https://www.europeanchamber.com.cn/en/home.

Table 8.3 Recent minimum wages in Mainland China

Province/region	Minimum wage (in CNY)								
	Monthly				Hourly				Effective date
Class	I	II	III	IV	I	II	III	IV	
Beijing	2320				25.3				01.08.2021
Tianjin	2180				22.6				01.07.2021
Hebei	1900	1790	1680	1580	19.0	18.0	17.0	16.0	01.11.2019
Shanxi	1880	1760	1630		10.8	10.1	9.4		01.10.2021
Inner Mongolia	1980	1910	1850		20.8	20.1	19.5		01.12.2021
Liaoning	1910	1710	1580	1420	19.2	17.2	15.9	14.3	01.11.2021
Jilin	1880	1760	1640	1540	19.0	18.0	17.0	16.0	01.12.2021
Heilongjiang	1860	1610	1450		18.0	14.0	13.0		01.04.2021
Shanghai	2590				23.0				01.07.2021
Jiangsu	2280	2070	1840		22.0	20.0	18.0		01.08.2021
Zhejiang	2280	2070	1840		22.0	20.0	18.0		01.08.2021
Anhui	1650	1500	1430	1340	20.0	18.0	17.0	16.0	03.12.2021
Fujian	2030	1960	1810	1660	21.0	20.5	19.0	17.5	01.04.2022
Jiangxi	1850	1730	1610		18.5	17.3	16.1		01.04.2021
Shandong	2100	1900	1700		21.0	19.0	17.0		01.10.2021
Henan	2000	1800	1600		19.6	17.6	15.6		01.01.2022
Hubei	2010	1800	1650	1520	19.5	18.0	16.5	15.0	01.09.2021
Hunan	1930	1740	1550		19.0	17.0	15.0		01.04.2022
Guangdong	2300 (Guangzhou)/2360 (Shenzhen)	1900	1720	1620	22.2	18.1	17.0	16.1	01.12.2021
Guangxi	1810	1580	1430		17.5	15.3	14.0		01.03.2020
Hainan	1830	1730	1680		16.3	15.4	14.9		01.12.2021
Chongqing	2100	2000			21.0	20.0			01.04.2022
Sichuan	2100	1970	1870		22.0	21.0	20.0		01.04.2022
Guizhou	1790	1670	1570		18.6	17.5	16.5		01.12.2019

(continued)

Table 8.3 (continued)

	Minimum wage (in CNY)								
Province/region	Monthly				Hourly				Effective date
Class	I	II	III	IV	I	II	III	IV	
Yunnan	1900	1750	1600		18.0	17.0	16.0		01.10.2022
Tibet	1850				18.0				01.07.2021
Shaanxi	1950	1850	1750		19.0	18.0	17.0		01.05.2021
Gansu	1820	1770	1720	1670	19.0	18.4	17.9	17.4	01.09.2021
Qinghai	1700				15.2				01.01.2020
Ningxia	1950	1840	1750		18.0	17.0	16.0		01.09.2021
Xinjiang	1900	1700	1620	1540	19.0	17.0	16.2	15.4	01.04.2021

Data source: Renshetong (2022) as of August 2022

References

Agricultural Television Network. (30. 07 2022). High employment rate, promising prospects: Would you choose vocational education? Retrieved 10.10.2022, from https://www.163.com/dy/article/HDI3J4JK0511DJHA.html

Chengdu Business Daily. (2021). How much does a Chinese family spend on education for their children every year, have you calculated? Retrieved 06.05.2021, from https://www.163.com/dy/article/G9ABD2P20512GMQ3.html

Chinese Ministry of Education. (01. 03 2022). The main results of the national education statistics in 2021. By Ministry of Education Website: Retrieved on 12.10.2022, from http://www.gov.cn/shuju/2022-03/01/content_5676225.htm

CPPCC. (01. 04 2022). Many places usher in an increase of wages. By Chinese People's Political Consultative Conference: Retrieved 10.10.2022, from http://cppcc.china.com.cn/2022-04/01/content_78142668.htm

Economic Daily. (22. 08 2022). "China Vocational Education Development White Paper" released: the employment rate of graduates of secondary and higher vocational education exceeds 90%. Retrieved 10.10.2022, from https://china.huanqiu.com/article/49LDkR3Olv3

Forbes. (11. 08 2022). American Universities Are Losing Chinese Students To Rivals: U.S.-China Business Forum. By Russell Flannery: Retrieved 16.10.2022, from https://www.forbes.com/sites/russellflannery/2022/08/11/american-universities-are-losing-chinese-students-to-rivals-us-china-business-forum/?sh=194aa37e2cec

ifeng.com. (08. 06 2021). In many places, the merger and transfer of independent colleges and vocational colleges has been suspended. By The Observer Network: Retrieved 10.10.2022, from https://news.ifeng.com/c/86tu9JLvpKb

Ministry of Education of the People's Republic of China. (12. 05 2021). The results of the seventh national census show that China's educational level among population has improved significantly in the past ten years. Retrieved 16.10.2022, from http://www.moe.gov.cn/jyb_xwfb/s5147/202105/t20210512_530993.html

National Bureau of Statistics of China. (2022a). Annual data. Retrieved 10.10.2022, from https://data.stats.gov.cn/easyquery.htm?cn=C01

National Bureau of Statistics of China. (July 2022b). urban unemployment rate survey. Retrieved 10.10.2022, from https://data.stats.gov.cn/easyquery.htm?cn=A01

PopulationPyramid.net. (2022). China 2022. Von Retrieved 10.10.2022, from https://www.populationpyramid.net/china/2022/

QS World University Rankings. (2009). QS World University Rankings 2010. Retrieved 10.10.2022, from https://www.universityrankings.ch/results/QS/2010

QS World University Rankings. (08. 06 2022). QS World University Rankings 2023: Top global universities. Retrieved 10.10.2022, from https://www.topuniversities.com/university-rankings/world-university-rankings/2023

Renshetong. (August 2022). Minimum wage standards for each province and city (released before August 2022). Retrieved on 14.10.2022, from https://m12333.cn/policy/wrib.html.

Sohu. (20. 06 2022). 2022 Employment Blue Book: IT industry continues to lead the industry salary list, but the increase is low. Retrieved 14.10.2022, from https://www.sohu.com/a/559179741_120129517.

Statista. (2022a). Chinese students' preferred destinations for studying overseas in 2015 and 2022. Retrieved 10.10.2022, from https://www.sohu.com/a/559395259_362042: https://www.statista.com/statistics/1108708/china-students-preferred-destinations-for-study-abroad/

Statista. (August 2022b). Number of students from China going abroad for study from 2010 to 2020. Retrieved 10.10.2022, from https://www.statista.com/statistics/227240/number-of-chinese-students-that-study-abroad/

Statista. (2022c). Students from China in the United States in the academic year 2020/21, by field of study. Retrieved 10.10.2022, from https://www.statista.com/statistics/295988/students-from-china-in-the-us-by-field-of-study/

The State Council of China. (01. 03 2022). The main results of the national education statistics in 2021. By Ministry of Education (Website): Retrieved on 10.10.2022, from http://www.gov.cn/shuju/2022-03/01/content_5676225.htm

The Wall Street Journal. (12. 08 2022). Chinese Student Visas to the U.S. Tumble. Retrieved on 10.10.2022, from https://www.wsj.com/podcasts/google-news-update/chinese-student-visas-to-the-us-tumble/6571551e-0536-4108-a36d-a0c0dd1022b3

U.S. Department of Commerce. (24. 08 2022). Supplement No. 4 to Part 744—ENTITY LIST. Von Bureau of Industry and Security: Retrieved 16.10.2022, from https://www.bis.doc.gov/index.php/documents/regulations-docs/2326-supplement-no-4-to-part-744-entity-list-4/file

UNESCO. (2018). China: Education and literacy. By Unesco Institute for Statistics: Retrieved 10.10.2022, from http://uis.unesco.org/en/country/cn

University World News. (02. 10 2021). How China is bidding for global intellectual dominance. By Romi Jain: Retrieved 16.10.2022, from https://www.universityworldnews.com/post.php?story=20210929100204424

Xinhua Network. (2017). Made in China 2025 is coming, how should the education system train manufacturing talents? http://www.xinhuanet.com. Retrieved 27.02.2017, from http://www.xinhuanet.com//politics/2017-02/27/c_129496516.htm

Xinhua Network. (12. 10 2021). The minimum wage has been raised in many places! By China Daily: Retrieved 10.10.2022, from http://www.news.cn/fortune/2021-10/12/c_1127947194.htm

Understanding the Chinese Culture 9

9.1 Culture Models in Cultural Research

The prominent cultural researcher Geert Hofstede describes culture as 'the collective programming of the mind' that divides people into individual cultural groups and considers cultural values as the core elements of cultures (Hofstede, 1980; Hofstede, 2007). Fundamentally, the interpersonal relationships are influenced by cultural values (Hofstede, 2007). In a business context, the management aiming at the coordination of people's efforts for common goals expressed by corporate strategies should be designed under consideration of cultural appropriateness (Hofstede, 2007)—'Being Rome, do what Romans do'.

Cultural understanding is a definite advantage when doing business in a foreign country. In cultural research, cultural models are commonly used for comparative studies on versatile cultures. The following presents two cultural models that exemplify important aspects of the Chinese culture. Due to its distinctive and lengthy history, Chinese culture differs remarkably from the Western cultures in many ways.

9.2 VSM Model by Hofstede

During a long-term research project, the Dutch cultural scientist Geert Hofstede collected survey data at international branches of the company IBM in 74 countries between 1967 and 1976. Based on the statistical analysis of empirical data, he later developed the Values Survey Model (VSM) which remains till this day among the most commonly used cultural models for academic research and business practice in the field of intercultural communication (Hofstede, 1980; Hofstede, 2007).

In the VSM model, cultures are described and measured in the following dimensions (Hofstede, 1980; Hofstede, 2007; Hofstede et al., 2010):

- Power distance.
- Individualism vs. collectivism.

T. Dathe et al., *Business Opportunities and Risks in China*, Management for Professionals, https://doi.org/10.1007/978-3-031-31933-4_9

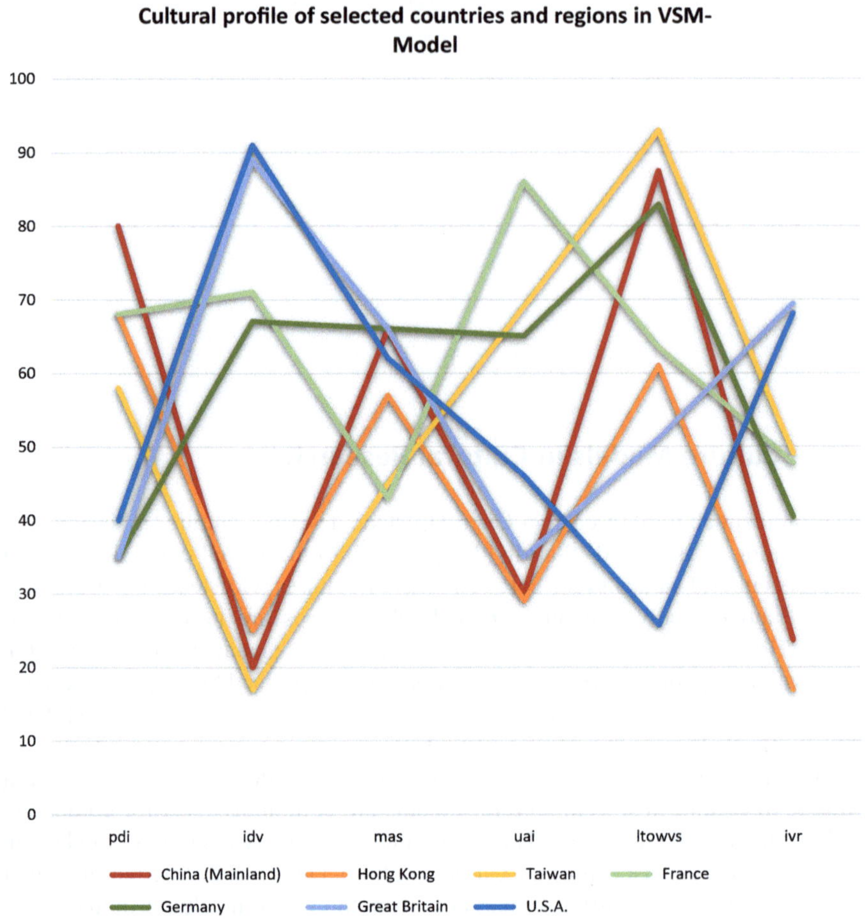

Fig. 9.1 Cultural profile of selected countries and regions in VSM model by Geert Hofstede. Data source: (Geerthofstede.com, 2015)

- Masculinity vs. femininity.
- Uncertainty avoidance.
- Long-term orientation.
- Indulgence vs. restraint.

Figure 9.1 illustrates the Chinese culture in the VSM model in comparison with some Western cultures. In addition, the regional profiles of Mainland China, Hong Kong and Taiwan demonstrate clear similarities and nuances among the subcultural groups.

The following sections explain the content of these cultural dimensions in more detail.

9.2.1 Power Distance (pdi)

Power is distributed unequally in every society. The term power distance stands for the readiness of those with little influence in the society to accept the difference in individuals' power of influence. This measure implies the extent to which a society is prepared to accept the general inequality (Hofstede, 2007). In a culture with little power distance, the mainstream aims to minimise the inequality of individual people. In cultures with great power distance, on the contrary, inequality is considered normal, and behaviours against the hierarchical rules are seen as violations of social rules scored that ought to be penalised (Dathe & Helmold, 2018). Compared to most Western cultures, the Chinese culture is characterised by high power distance (see Fig. 9.2).

In the Confucian tradition, a hierarchical structure can be observed in every aspect of life in the Chinese society. A classic Chinese company is run like a family, whereas the management takes parental care of the employees. The managers are expected to make business decisions in general interest of all employees, however without formal involvement of the workforce. The authority of the superiors should be respected and never challenged openly, which means, for example, their formal decisions and statements at meetings are not to be questioned in the public, and

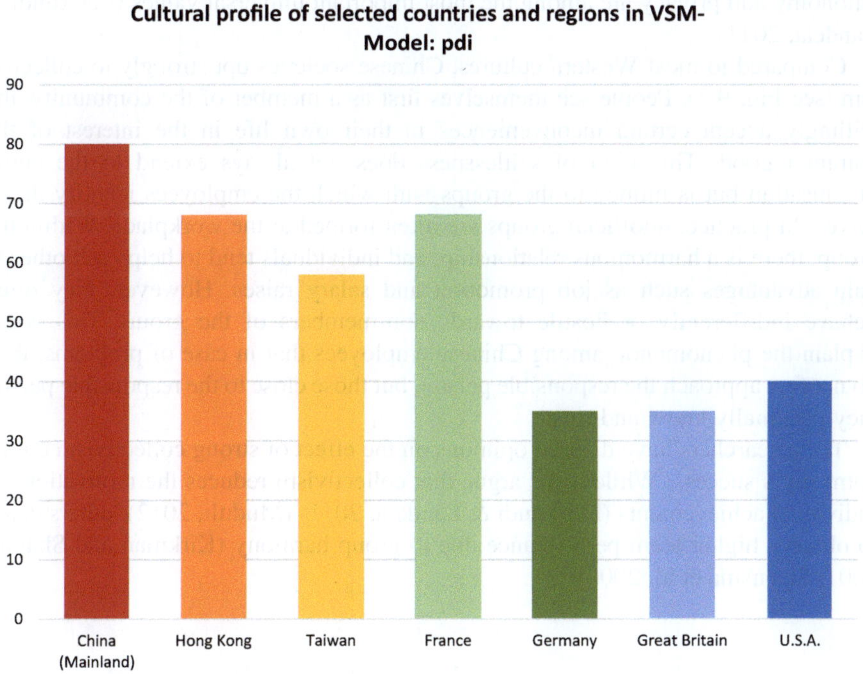

Fig. 9.2 Cultural profile of selected countries and regions in VSM model: pdi. Data source: (Geerthofstede.com, 2015)

company rules such as overtime requirements according to business operational circumstances are widely accepted.

High power distance enables managers to effectively make quick decisions with their authority; however, on the other hand, there is higher risk of wrong business decisions. In addition, previous studies indicate that uncontrolled power could lead to abuse of office or corruption (Chia et al., 2007; Lee & Oh, 2007).

The fair opportunity of social advancement is a very important element in the Chinese Confucian culture. Regardless of origin, everyone should be able to improve his social status and earn additional power with excellent performance and hard work. Such self-earned achievements bring honour to the Chinese families.

9.2.2 Individualism Vs. Collectivism (idv)

Individualism in a society implies that the individuals in the group only provide for themselves and their immediate families. Collectivism is the opposite of individualism and stands for mutual caring among the individuals in the society. This cultural dimension describes the extent to which individuals in a society depend on each other (De Mooij & Hofstede, 2010). In a community dominated by collectivism, compliance with social norms and participation in collective activities are important social values. When individualism dominates, however, independence, individual autonomy and privacy are among the most important universal values (Lertxundi & Landeta, 2011).

Compared to most Western cultures, Chinese societies opt strongly to collectivism (see Fig. 9.3). People see themselves first as a member of the community and willingly accept certain inconveniences in their own life in the interest of the common good. This kind of selflessness does not always extend to the entire organisation but is limited to the groups with which the employees identify themselves. In practice, unofficial groups are often formed at the workplace. Within the group, there is a harmonious relationship, and individuals tend to help each other to gain advantages such as job promotion and salary raises. However, they often behave indifferently or hostile towards non-members of the group. This could explain the phenomenon among Chinese employees that in case of problems, they do not first approach the responsible person, but those close to the responsible person they personally know and trust.

The researchers have divided opinions on the effect of strong collectivism on the company's success. While some argue that collectivism reduces the motivation for individual achievements (Lertxundi & Landeta, 2011) (Muduli, 2012), others claim to observe higher team performance due to group harmony (Kirkman and Shapiro 2001; Steensma et al. 2000).

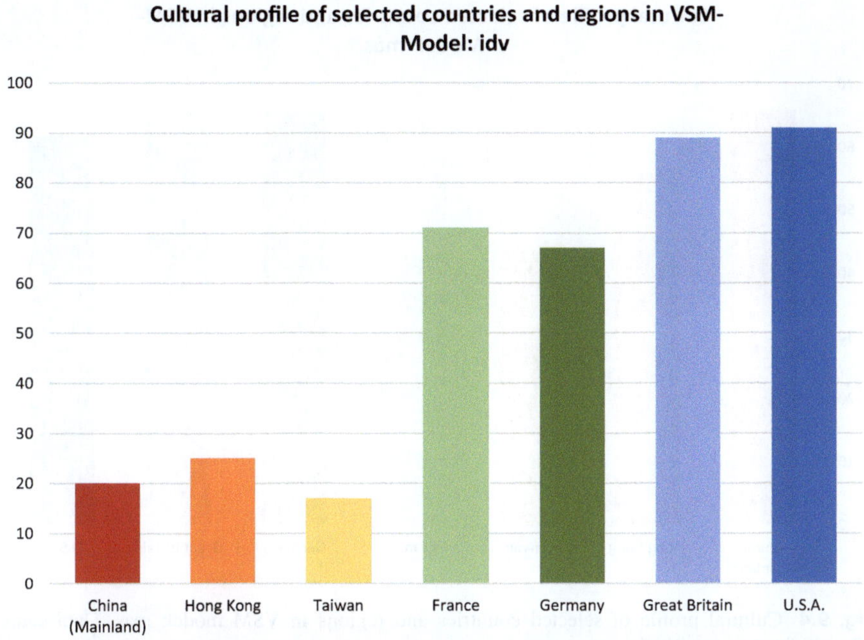

Fig. 9.3 Cultural profile of selected countries and regions in VSM model: idv. Data source: (Geerthofstede.com, 2015)

9.2.3 Masculinity Vs. Femininity (mas)

This cultural dimension measures the dominant values that motivate the individuals in a society. The masculine values are those associated with personal achievements and success. The feminine values are fondness for one another and quality of life (De Mooij & Hofstede, 2010). In a masculine culture, the majority strives for professional success and readily accepts the therefore caused disturbance in their private lives. In a culture dominated by feminine values, a stress-free private life is valued more, and interference from work in private life is not tolerated (Hofstede & Hofstede, 2011).

Like in most industrial countries, China is dominated by masculine values (see Fig. 9.4). However, the public stimulation of competitiveness could be shocking to those who are not familiar with the social life in the Chinese culture. Chinese children are motivated by the ranking of their individual performance as early as in preschool age. A transcript of grades with the names is made public after almost every exam in school. This tradition continues later in professional life, and sometimes even salary information is 'leaked' as a stimulus for individual performance of all employees (Dathe & Helmold, 2018).

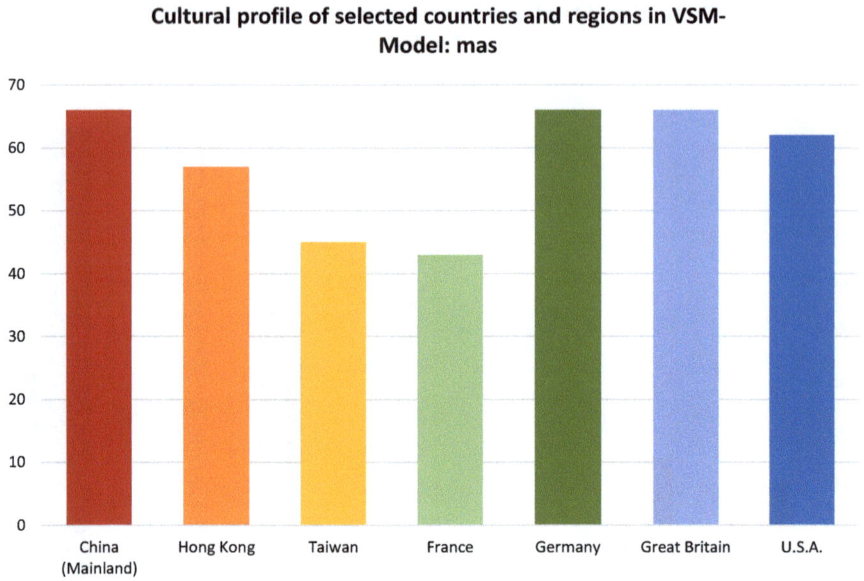

Fig. 9.4 Cultural profile of selected countries and regions in VSM model: mas. Data source: (Geerthofstede.com, 2015)

9.2.4 Uncertainty Avoidance (uai)

Uncertainty avoidance describes the extent to which one avoids ambiguities or feels threatened in unfamiliar situations. A culture with high uncertainty avoidance is characterised by a strong need for regulations and formalities; individuals tend to trust experts and reject changes (Hofstede & Hofstede, 2011).

The Chinese culture demonstrates a rather low level of uncertainty avoidance. Most Chinese people share a pragmatic attitude towards changes in their living environment and are open to technological innovations (see Fig. 9.5). Ambiguity of information does not cause mental stress to most Chinese people. Job descriptions in China often contain less details than, say, in Germany. To many Chinese employees, the absence of excessive information provides them room to adapt quickly to the changing environment.

9.2.5 Long-Term Orientation (ltowvs)

The long-term orientation describes the willingness of individuals to give up pleasure in the present, in expectation of benefits in the future—in other words, the willingness to invest in one's own future (Hofstede & Hofstede, 2011).

The Chinese culture is characterised with strong long-term orientation (see Fig. 9.6). As a result, the overall job satisfaction heavily depends on job security or career prospects in the company (Bryson et al., 2011; Batt, 2002). Chinese

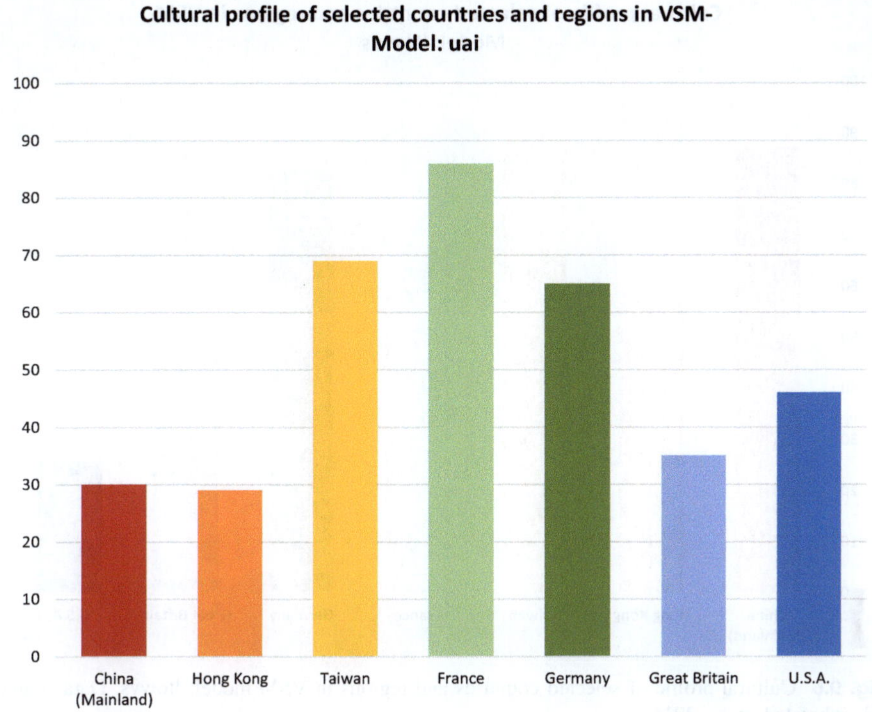

Fig. 9.5 Cultural profile of selected countries and regions in VSM model: uai. Data source: (Geerthofstede.com, 2015)

employees work hard to secure their professional future. In general, Chinese entrepreneurs prefer long-term business partnerships to riskier business opportunities that promise higher profit.

9.2.6 Indulgence Vs. Restraint (ivr)

This cultural dimension describes the extent to which people express their desires and impulses. *Indulgence* means succumbing to human needs, whereas the opposite *restraint* stands for self-control (Hofstede et al., 2010). Cultures with high indulgence values are characterised by properties such as an optimistic mood, many extroverted personalities and less moral discipline, while free time and leisure are considered important for the quality of life. Cultures with tendency to restraint, on the other hand, are characterised by the opposite features, such as a pessimistic or cynical mood, many introverted personalities, a high priority of work ethics, high moral discipline, etc. In a culture dominated by restraint, the individual behaviours are primarily controlled by social norms, and succumbing to one's own desires and impulses counts as a misconduct (Hofstede et al., 2010).

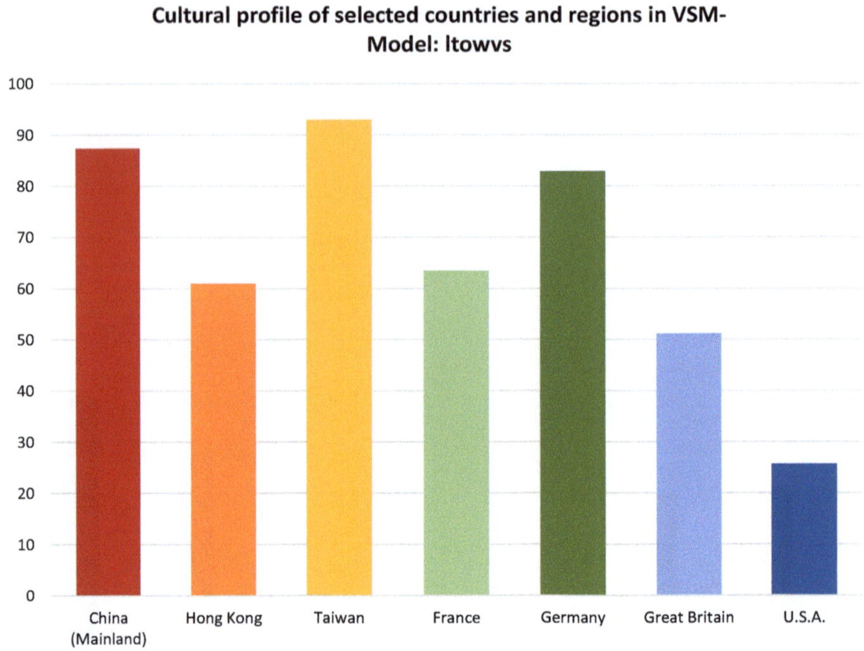

Fig. 9.6 Cultural profile of selected countries and regions in VSM model: ltowvs. Data source: (Geerthofstede.com, 2015)

Compared to most Westerners, the Chinese apt clearly to restraint in this cultural dimension (see Fig. 9.7). To most Chinese people, professional obligations have a much higher priority than private life. To improve the family income and their social status, millions of Chinese migrant workers leave home to work in a factory in a distant city. The neglect of children and loneliness of the elderly among the left behind family members have led to a social problem than has drawn the attention of the policymakers.

The Chinese rule of conduct requires that one should downplay the importance of his own success in public. Addressing one's own accomplishments openly is often perceived as an act of indulgence and is seen as pushy and boastful. However, a lack of due recognition from superiors and colleagues could lead to great dismay, although the disappointment might remain hidden to the untrained eye.

9.3 Cultural Dimensions According to E.T. Hall

The American anthropologist and ethnologist Edward Twitchell Hall Jr. is considered the founder of intercultural communication. He describes cultures in several facets including:

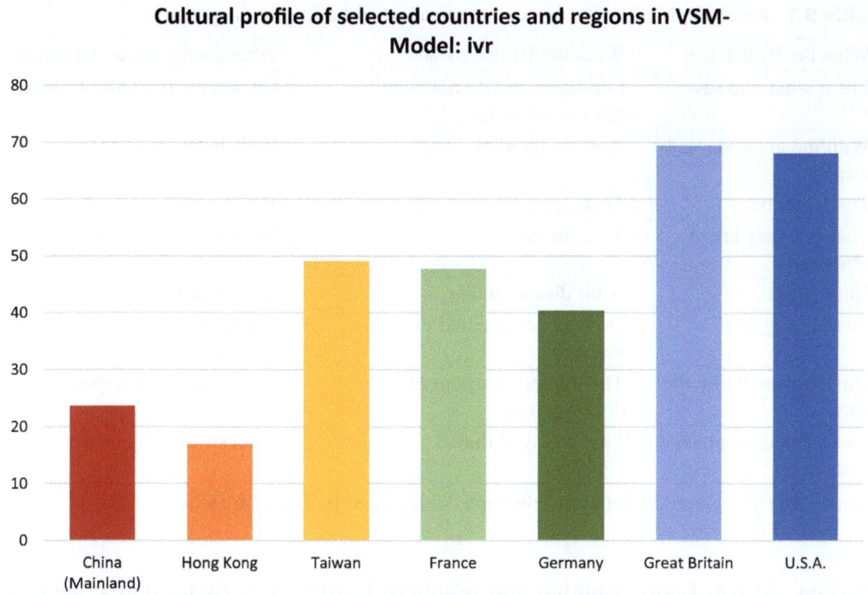

Fig. 9.7 Cultural profile of selected countries and regions in VSM model: ivr. Data source: (Geerthofstede.com, 2015)

- Contextual orientation.
- Monochronic vs. polychronic understanding of time.
- Understanding of space.

The cultural dimensions according Hall's theories will be briefly explained in the following sections.

9.3.1 Context Orientation

Hall uses context orientation to describe the importance of networking in communication, especially in processing information during the communication.

In low-context cultures, the communication partners act directly on each other and try to provide precise and explicit information. The personal relationships play no significant role during the communication process. In high-context cultures, however, much information is not explicitly encoded in the verbal messages but assumed to be known based on the relations of the communication partners and their common understanding of contextual communication influence factors, for example, facial expressions, or the circumstances of their encounters. The personal relationships are of great importance for contextual communication. The United States, Canada, the Scandinavian countries, the Benelux countries and Great Britain are usually considered cultures with weak context orientation, while many countries

Table 9.1 An example of contextual communication in the English language

What the British say	What the British mean	What foreigners understand
I hear what you say	I disagree and do not want to discuss it further	He accepts my point of view
With the greatest respect	You are an idiot	He is listening to me
That's not bad	That's good	That's poor
That is a very brave proposal	You are insane	He thinks I have courage
Quite good	A bit disappointing	Quite good
I would suggest ...	Do it or be prepared to justify yourself	Think about the idea, but do what you like
Oh, incidentally/by the way, ...	The primary purpose of our discussion is ...	That is not very important
I was a bit disappointed that ...	I am annoyed that ...	It doesn't really matter

Source: The Telegraph 2017 (www.telegraph.co.uk), cited by Dathe & Helmold (2018)

in Asia, Africa, Latin America and Southern Europe (e.g. Spain and France) are considered cultures with strong context orientation (Hall, 1976).

As an example for context reference in verbal communication, Table 9.1 An example of contextual communication in the English language illustrates how the communication in Great Britain could mislead strangers in the culture.

Chinese culture is characterised by a high degree of context orientation. Unspoken rules or information and knowledge are often involved during the communication process. Chinese business partners usually attempt to build up personal trust and mutual understanding in communication at the beginning of important business relationships. The sensitivity to the prevailing type of communication in the cultural circle could largely improve the chance of long-term business success in China.

9.3.2 Monochronic Vs. Polychronic Understanding of Time

The understanding of time is often very different in various cultures. In his work *The Dance of Life: The Other Dimension of Time*, Hall compares the monochronic with the polychronic cultures.

According to Hall's definition, it is common practice in a monochronic culture to do one thing at a time and to stay focused on one task at a time. Individuals in a monochronic culture usually make great efforts to keep to the schedules. A monochronic culture is often also a culture with weak context orientation, because precise information is required for precise planning to achieve the set goals. Privacy is generally respected, and interpersonal relationships are often of relatively short duration (Hall, 1983).

In a polychronic culture, multiple activities are often performed simultaneously. While prone to distractions, one is quick to respond to changes and find new solutions. The schedule is only a reference and of less importance than in a monochronic culture. Long-term interpersonal relationships contribute largely to the flexibility of individual reactions under continuously changing circumstances, and a strong context orientation is common in polychronic societies (Hall, 1983).

While many industrial countries are characterised by a monochronic culture, the polychrome setting is widespread in the Chinese society. For example, someone with changing professional fields in the CV probably raises browse of a German HR manager, who is likely to see this circumstance as an indication of disorientation. The same applicant, however, is likely to be considered by a Chinese manager as a multi-talent and valued for his professional flexibility. Understanding this cultural difference could improve intercultural cooperations and avoid potential conflicts or frustrations.

9.3.3 Understanding of Space

According to Hall, every human being requires a certain space around himself as his own. Depending on the familiarity between the persons, such distant zones can be further distinguished as intimate, personal, social and public distance zone. Intruders in the invisible distance zones without permission can cause discomfort. In particular, entering the intimate zone is perceived as an act of aggression. On the other hand, keeping too large a distance can also be interpreted negatively, for example, as a lack trust or even hostility (Hall, 1976). The extent of such sensible distance zones varies from culture to culture (Hall, 1966).

In general, the Chinese require a rather large intimate distance compared to Europeans. Physical contact in business life is rare and often confined to a handshake. In private life, a friendly hug from less familiar people could cause discomfort. On the other hand, due to permanent lack of space in the large cities, the Chinese are used to a smaller public distance, allowing strangers to be physically close to them in most public places, such as in the overcrowded subway or in the restaurant, where people could easily follow the conversation at the neighbouring tables. Compared to European cultures, more physical contact without an intimate background is maintained among the same sex; two adult friends walking in the park might hold hands (Dathe & Helmold, 2018).

9.4 Cultural Diversity within China

Within international companies, awareness of cultural diversity has increased with progressing globalisation; intercultural trainings are now widely available to prepare foreign employees for work and life and China. However, what is often overlooked is the immense diversity of Chinese culture.

In addition to the Han Chinese majority, the Chinese population includes 55 officially recognised ethnic minorities. China's land area is 2.23 times larger than that of the EU, stretching from sub-arctic Heilongjiang Province to the mainly tropical

Hainan Province. Until roughly 30 years ago, most Chinese rarely ever left the town or county where they were born; as a consequence, different local cultures rarely mixed.

For example, working attitude varies in different parts of China. While not in line with Chinese labour law, working on Saturdays and extreme overtime are quite common and widely accepted among employees in the 'factory of the world' Guangdong Province, while working style is more relaxed in Northern and especially Western China.

Within China, there are even different concepts of time. In most parts of China, public transport is super-punctual. In contrary, on the Qinghai-Tibetan highland, many long-distance busses don't leave according to a fixed schedule, but when they are full. Lunch breaks don't have a dedicated length; the driver will continue the journey when all passengers have finished their meal—a human-orientated concept of time completely different from other parts of China.

Stereotypes—positive and negative—abound in China: business-savvy people in Guangdong, a laid-back living style in Sichuan and patriotism and political consciousness in Beijing. Each employee's and business partner's individual's character and their professional abilities are shaped by many factors, the place of birth only being one of them. However, local cultural factors do have an influence, and foreign managers should be aware of them.

In addition, culture is permanently changing, but different parts of the country do so at different speeds. The early SEZs Shenzhen and Zhuhai—and to a lower degree also Beijing, Shanghai and Guangzhou—have become cultural melting pots, the majority of the workforce are migrant workers from all parts of China, and these cities are very open to absorb international cultural influence. On the other hand, in smaller towns, especially in Western China, there are few people from other provinces, and lifestyle and culture are much more traditional.

For international companies, it has become common practice to care for the mental well-being of foreign employees. However, often overlooked is the fact that employees from ethnic minorities or simply other parts of the country may have the same or even greater difficulties to adjust to their new location. Chinese culture emphasises a deep connection with one's roots. Cultural concepts of homesickness (思乡病) and non-adaptation (水土不服) are deeply engrained in Chinese thinking. While in most cases, foreign employees will consider a lack of ability to adapt as their own shortcoming, for Chinese, this is quite acceptable.

Chinese migrants often form—formal or informal—hometown or home-province groups, in which they can speak in their native dialect and cook home-style food together. This is a way of relieving cultural stress. However, this kind of associations may become a challenge when many employees from one area are working together, which is often the case in large factories. Natives from one home-province may isolate themselves from their colleagues, forming factions and undermining team spirit.

The generally acknowledged advantage of multicultural teams is the diversity of abilities. The management needs to put the right employee in the right position; according to common stereotypes, an employee from southern China's coastal provinces is probably a good sales representative, while a native Beijinger is probably more suitable for government relations.

Because of the fast overall development of China, cultural competency—just like general China know-how—needs to be maintained regularly. For example, just 20 years ago, it was very common in China to share private information like salary details with strangers. This has changed completely. As another example, in the past, an 'exotic' European face on an advertisement would give the product an international appeal and draw a lot of attention. While this may still be an advantage in Western China, in the developed coastal cities, the presence of foreigners is nothing special anymore.

One astonishing effect of China's modernisation is the popularisation of standard Chinese (Putonghua or 'mandarin'). Nowadays, meetings with business partners or government officials are generally held in standard Chinese. However, outside of melting pots mentioned above, foreign employees still should consider learning the local dialect. In informal settings, in most cases, locals will switch to their dialect. Anyone who just speaks Putonghua will remain an outsider.

Much literature has been written about Chinese versus 'Western' management styles (King & Zhang, 2014). In reality, there is hardly any uniform Chinese management style. Many of the early private entrepreneurs came from the countryside, strongly influenced by Confucian traditions. As a result, they often manage their companies like a patriarch, caring for their employees like a father and demanding strict obedience. On the other hand, since the late 1990s, a whole generation of Chinese top managers went through international degrees in business, becoming heavily influenced by Western management theories. Management in SOEs is influenced by administrative practices in government departments; however, nowadays, management in Chinese SOEs is also very target oriented.

In the past, economic underdevelopment and a society favouring collectivism did not leave much room for subcultures. Nowadays in China, all conceivable types of living style exist in parallel. This opens new niche markets for European companies. For example, not long ago, many well-educated urban Chinese felt superior to peasants and were reluctant to do manual labour. Nowadays, there is a new trend that young urban professionals move to the countryside to grow green food, creating a completely new market for do-it-yourself tools that local companies have hardly addressed so far.

Finally, product marketing also needs to consider local cultural factors. There are two examples: although China is the world's largest consumer of pork, products—not just food—containing raw materials from pigs should at least be clearly labelled, as they will not be acceptable to the minority Muslim population. Han Chinese, like most East Asians, prefer a pale 'white' complexion; cosmetics are specially designed for this customer group. However, this preference is not shared by some of China's ethnic minorities.

9.5 Case Study: Finding the Right Sales Representative in Western China

In Western China, international companies may find it difficult to find good staff members, and local job candidates have less international experience and seem to be less business-orientated than their peers in coastal regions. When establishing a new office in Western China, an international company mostly selected graduates from universities in coastal areas, where they had acquired the 'mindset' that made them fit for work in an international company.

Finally, there was one position for a sales representative left. Two candidates were shortlisted: Candidate A had already worked for foreign companies, with sophisticated manners and good English. The female candidate B grew up in the countryside, somewhat coarse in her appearance and the only one in her village who had worked her way up to university. Despite a lot of resistance from the team, the chief representative insisted on employing candidate B. First, he knew people from that area are particularly honest and loyal, which are important qualities for sales representatives, whose often have their own agenda. Second, the well-being of candidate B's whole family would depend on her salary, which meant she would work extremely hard to fulfil her filial duties. Third, and perhaps most important, she would match the cultural habits of the company's customers, who almost all grew up in that province and felt a culture gap when they encountered Westernised behaviour.

Needless to say, candidate B delivered excellent sales results. In this case, a right mix of employees was the key to success: managers educated in coastal areas with good organisational skills and the ability to interact with the company's China headquarters and sales representatives who could relate well to local customers.

References

Batt, R. (2002). Managing customer services: Human resource practices, quit rates, and sales growth. *Academy of Management Journal, 45*(3), 587–597.

Bryson, A., Buraimo, B., & Simmons, R. (2011). Do salaries improve worker performance? *Labour Economics, 18*(4), 424–433.

Chia, H.-B., Egri, C., Ralston, D., Fu, P. P., Kuo, M. C., & Lee, C. (2007). Four tigers and a dragon: Values differences, similarities, and consensus. *Asia Pacific Journal of Management, 24*.

Dathe, T., & Helmold, M. (2018). *Erfolgreich im Chinageschäft: Strategien und Handlungsempfehlungen für kleinere und mittlere Unternehmen (KMU)*. Springer Gabler Verlag.

De Mooij, M., & Hofstede, G. (2010). The Hofstede model. *International Journal of Advertising, S, 29*(1), 85–110.

Geerthofstede.com. (08. 12 2015). Dimension data matrix. Von 6 dimensions for website.xls: https://geerthofstede.com/research-and-vsm/dimension-data-matrix/abgerufen

Hall, E. (1966). *The hidden dimension*. Garden City.

Hall, E. (1976). *Beyond culture*. Garden City.

Hall, E. (1983). *The dance of life: The other dimension of time*. Anchor Books.

Hofstede, G. (1980). *Culture's consequences: International differences in worked-related values*. Sage Publication.

Hofstede, G. (2007). Asian management in the 21st century. *Asia Pacific Journal of Management, 24*(4) S., 411–420.

Hofstede, G., & Hofstede, G. J. (2011). *Lokales Denken, globales Handeln: Interkulturelle Zusammenarbeit und globales Management* (5th ed.). Munich DTV.

Hofstede, G., Hofstede, G. J., & Minkov, M. (2010). *Cultures and organizations: Software for the mind, 3. Auflage*. McGraw-Hill Books.

King, P., & Zhang, W. (2014). Chinese and western leadership models: A literature review. *Journal of Management Research, 6*(2):1

Kirkman, B., & Shapiro, D. (2001). The impact of cultural values on job satisfaction and organizational commitment in self-managing work teams: The mediating role of employee resistance. *Academy of Management Journal, 44*(3), 557–569.

Lee, S.-H., & Oh, K. (2007). Corruption in Asia: Pervasiveness and arbitrariness. *Asia Pacific Journal of Management, 24*(1), 97–114.

Lertxundi, A., & Landeta, J. (2011). The moderating effect of cultural context in the relation between HPWS and performance: An exploratory study in Spanish multinational companies. *International Journal of Human Resource Management, 22*(18), 3949–3396.

Muduli, A. (2012). Business strategy, SHRM, HR outcome and organizational performance: Evidence from an Indian industry. *Global Management Journal, 4*(1/2), 111–125.

Steensma, H., Marino, L., Weaver, K., & Dickson, P. (2000). The influence of natinal culture on the formation of technology alliances by entrepreneurial firms. *Academy of Management Journal, 43*(5), 951–973.

10 General Business Environment

10.1 Legal System of China

In order to be successful in doing business in China, it is essential to be familiarised with the relevant local laws and government regulations. The Chinese civil law system is similar to that of continental European model. Interpretations of the People's Supreme Court are, however, in contrast to the supreme court in Germany, treated almost as laws, which reminds of the Anglo-American legal system further developed by judicial laws (Dathe & Helmold, 2018).

The highest source of law in China is the Constitution. The court system adjudicates with constitution-related laws, civil law, commercial law, economic law, social law, criminal law, administrative and non-procedural law, etc. In conformity with the Constitution and laws, the State Council may formulate administrative statutes, and the people's congresses and their standing committees of provinces, autonomous regions and municipalities directly under the central government, cities and autonomous prefectures may formulate local statutes and regulations. The ministries and committees of the State Council, the People's Bank of China, the National Audit Office and the directly affiliated institutions with administrative functions may formulate regulations within the scope of their own competence in accordance with laws and administrative regulations, decisions and orders of the State Council. Although China is not a country of case law, previous judicial interpretations by the Supreme People's Court could provide guidance in judicial practice (Ministry of Commerce of the People's Republic of China, 2022).

Since the introduction of opening-up policy in 1978, there has been an upheaval in China's economic and legal system. In the early days, the utilisation of foreign capital was ruled by the 'Three Foreign Investment Laws' including 'Sino-Foreign Equity Joint Venture Enterprise Law of the People's Republic of China', 'Law of the People's Republic of China on Wholly Foreign-Owned Enterprises' and 'Sino-Foreign Cooperative Joint Venture Enterprise Law of the People's Republic of China'. In March 2019, the 'Three Foreign Investment Laws' were replaced by the 'Foreign Investment Law of the People's Republic of China' which serves as the

T. Dathe et al., *Business Opportunities and Risks in China*, Management for Professionals, https://doi.org/10.1007/978-3-031-31933-4_10

basic legal framework for foreign investment in China ever since (Ministry of Commerce of the People's Republic of China, 2022).

In accordance with the Foreign Investment Law, the entry of foreign investment at the Chinese market is ruled by special administrative measures based on the principle of 'Pre-Establishment National Treatment and Negative List'. That means, at the stages of establishment, acquisition and expansion of enterprises in fields outside the negative list, foreign investors and their investments are entitled to no less favourable treatments than domestic investors and their investments ('Pre-Establishment National Treatment'). The 'negative list' refers to industrial fields prohibited for foreign investment (Ministry of Commerce of the People's Republic of China, 2022).

Although the Hong Kong and Macao SARs as well Taiwan are officially considered a part of China, international treaties that apply in the People's Republic of China do not per se apply in those three regions each with an individual legal system.

10.2 FIE Business Registration

Foreign investors may establish their business organisations (foreign invested enterprises, FIEs) in China mainly in two forms: corporations and partnerships. According to the chosen legal organisation, all FIEs established after 1 January 2020 are governed by the Company Law of the People's Republic of China and the Partnership Enterprise Law of the People's Republic of China. In other words, FIEs will no longer be divided into Sino-foreign joint ventures, Sino-foreign cooperative enterprises and wholly foreign-owned enterprises as in the past (Ministry of Commerce of the People's Republic of China, 2022).

In accordance with the Foreign Investment Law, foreign investors in China enjoy the same opportunities and rights in fields beyond industry sectors on the negative list as domestic investors ('Pre-Establishment National Treatment and Negative List'). The procedure for FIE registration is illustrated in Fig. 10.1 Business registration procedures for FIEs in China.

As an alternative to the establishment of a foreign invested enterprise (FIE), foreign companies may also choose to establish resident representative offices ('representative offices') in China. However, the business operations of a representative office are limited to non-profit activities, such as market research, exhibitions, publicity activities and liaison activities related to sales of products and services, domestic procurement and domestic investment of foreign enterprises (Ministry of Commerce of the People's Republic of China, 2022).

10.3 Foreign Exchange Control

China pledged to gradually liberate its capital market when acceding to the World Trade Organization (WTO). Over time, state control measures have been successively lifted to facilitate cross-border capital flows under the 'closed' capital account

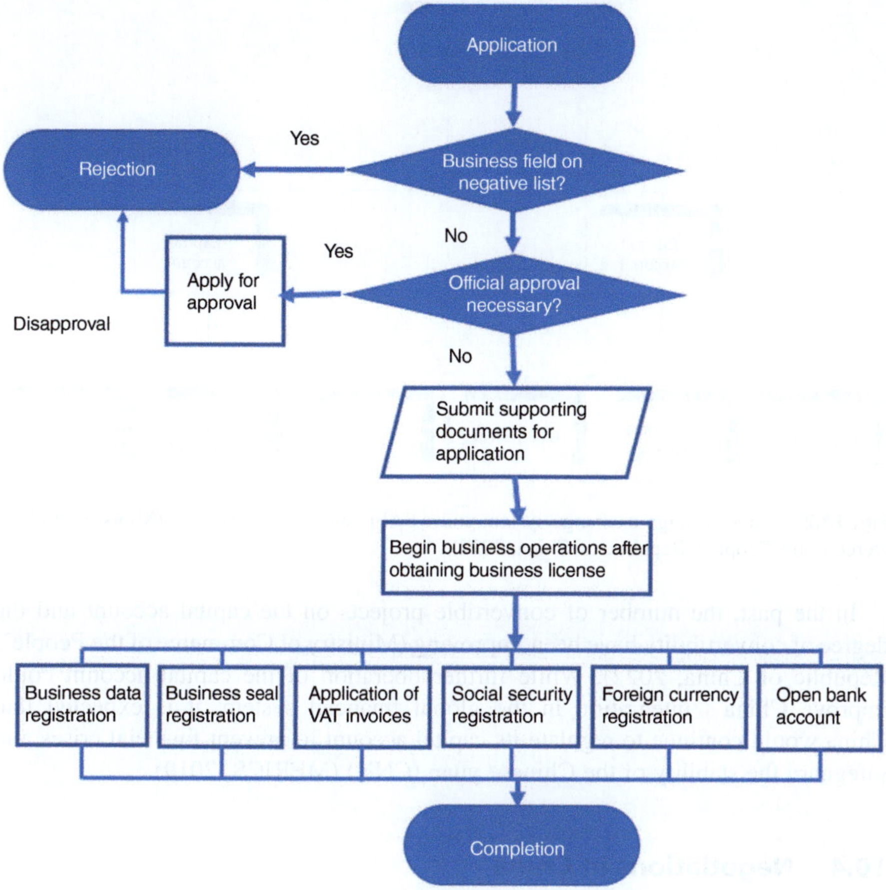

Fig. 10.1 Business registration procedures for FIEs in China. Information source: (Ministry of Commerce of the People's Republic of China, 2022)

policy. The national regulatory agency that oversees the foreign exchange market in China is the State Administration of Foreign Exchange (SAFE).

In general, the flow of foreign exchange in China is divided into two accounts: the current account and the capital account. While cross-border payments for business transactions on the current account are free convertible, transactions on the capital account are subject to control measures by the State Administration of Foreign Exchange (SAFE). The current account refers to ordinary recurring business transactions, including payments for foreign trade receipts, non-trade exchange (e.g. interest payments on foreign debts and repatriation of after-tax profits/dividends) and free transfers. The capital account refers to capital import and export, including foreign direct investment (FDI), cross-border security investment and cross-border lending (see Fig. 10.2 China's foreign exchange system under SAFE supervision).

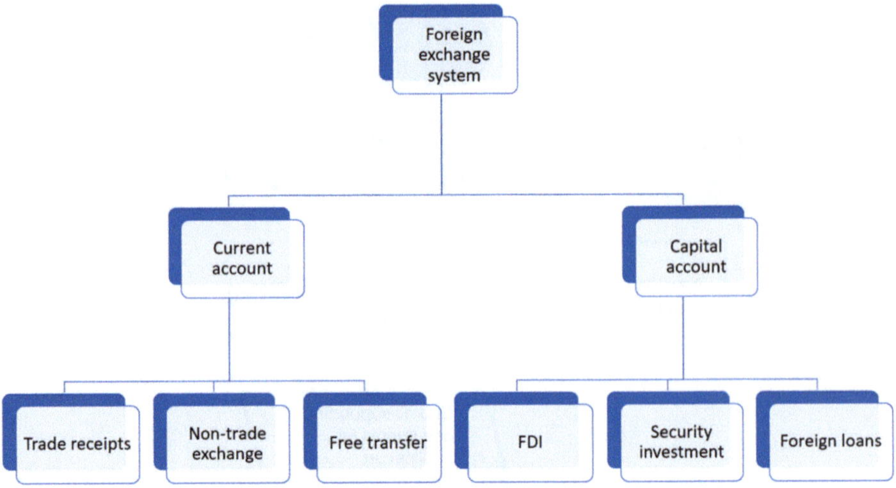

Fig. 10.2 China's foreign exchange system under SAFE supervision. Source: (Ministry of Commerce of the People's Republic of China, 2022)

In the past, the number of convertible projects on the capital account and the degree of convertibility have been improving (Ministry of Commerce of the People's Republic of China, 2022). While further liberation of the capital account could improve China's integration in the global financial system, it is expected that China would continue to regulate its capital account to prevent financial crises and safeguard the stability of the Chinese yuan (CNY) (MERICS, 2019).

10.4 Negotiations in China

The following checklist based on suggestions of the American negotiation specialist Jeswald Salacuse could be helpful for the preparation for negotiations in any cultural settings (Salacuse, 1991):

I. Negotiation Partner

1. Are we dealing with the producers of the desired deliveries directly? (Sometimes, the Chinese intermediaries pretend to be the manufacturers.)
2. Are we negotiating with the right persons or departments in the organisation? (Decision power of negotiation partner)
3. Should other parties (e.g. higher instance in the organisation, authorities, etc.) be present at the negotiating table?
4. Are we well informed of the status of all participants of the counterparty?

II. The Goals

5. What are our goals and interests in this negotiation? Our maximum targets? Our minimum targets?
6. At what point is it better to give up the business and end the negotiation?
7. What are the goals and interests of the counterparty? At what point would they probably give up the negotiation?
8. What is the history or our relationship with the counterparty? How will this relationship affect the discussions?
9. Who are our competitors in this business?
10. What advantages do we have over our competitors?
11. What advantages do our competitors have over us?
12. What specific decision-making authority does our team have to act in the negotiation, in order to make binding commitments?
13. Who will bear the exchange rate risk in this deal? How should we protect ourselves if we will?

III. Organisational Questions

14. Where will the negotiation take place?
15. When will the negotiation take place? Did we consider the local holidays of our negotiation partners which may cause schedule conflicts for the negotiation process?
16. How much time should we allow for the negotiation? (Abundant time should be planned, especially if we don't know the negotiation partners well.)
17. When should our team arrive at the venue? Will we have enough time to acclimatise and get prepared for the discussions before the negotiation starts?
18. When will we leave the venue? Have we informed the counterparty about our arrival and departure schedules?
19. Have we arranged a specific time during the day with our contact person in the 'headquarters'?
20. Which language will be spoken at the negotiation table? In which language should the contract be drafted?
21. Will an interpreter be required? Who will provide the interpreter?
22. If we will provide the interpreter, have we informed the interpreter of the type of project, the terminology, etc.?
23. Have the specific tasks such as logistics, communication, record-keeping, etc. been assigned to individual team members?
24. Are there further tasks? Who will be responsible for those tasks?

IV. Tactical Planning

25. Who are the members of our negotiation team? Does our team have the right mix in terms of expertise, language skills, knowledge of the country and negotiation experience?

26. Who will be the spokesperson for our team?
27. Did we agree on an agenda with the counterparty?
28. Which other topics should be brought up for discussion?
29. What are the key issues in the negotiation? (Topics should be evaluated with the scale of 1–10.)
30. What is our strategy for each topic? In which order should we deliver the arguments? (Compare with the strategy described at the beginning of this section. Tip: Better to save the 'bonus' for the negotiation partner for the end of discussion.)
31. Are there any issues we should avoid? If yes, do we have a response should those topics be addressed?
32. Did our team sit down to discuss and simulate specific negotiation situations and to formulate necessary draft contracts?
33. Does our team plan to get together at the end of each day to discuss the progress and the plan for the next few days?
34. Will any social occasions arise during the negotiations that bring us together with the negotiation partners? Do we know how to respond to the local culture properly? (The Chinese do not expect a foreigner to know everything about the Chinese culture. The host is pleased to the interested to explain his culture to the guest from afar. A decent guest should show respect and interest.)
35. Are there ideological factors that might cause conflicts with our counterparty? (Tip: Never criticise the local culture and politics before you get to know the host well!)

V. Information and Documentation

36. What information do we need about the other country, the partner organisation, the transaction, etc. before the negotiation starts? How can we get hold of the information?
37. What information do we need about the counterparty's team members? How can we get this information? Till when do we need the information?
38. Which draft contracts, presentation materials, reports and publications need to be prepared for the negotiation?
39. Which books, magazines, reports, documents and equipment should our team bring to the negotiation location?
40. Do we need to hire local consultants and professionals? Should they participate in all negotiations?
41. Are we well informed of the formal terms of the transaction or cooperation? How would those affect us?

VI. Opening of Negotiation

42. Did we introduce all members of our team adequately?
43. Did the counterparty team introduce all members of their team adequately?

44. Do we know who the leader of counterparty team is, and do we know the role of the members of the counterparty team?
45. What is the seating arrangement at the negotiating table, and how is the environment of the meetings?
46. Did we dedicate enough time to each member of the counterparty team to get to know them?
47. Will we make a detailed opening statement? What content should be included in it?
48. Did we go through the agenda with the counterparty?
49. Do we know the exact negotiating power of the counterparty? Does the counterparty team know our negotiating power exactly?

VII. Negotiation dynamics

50. Have we received sufficient information from the counterparty? Are we listening to them carefully? Do they know that we are listening to them carefully? Shall we ask questions?
51. How should we react if the counterparty doesn't seem to be listening to us? (For example, the negotiation partners attend to their business e-mails or cell phones while we are speaking: Friendly reminder or repetition of important points?)
52. Are we paying attention to both non-verbal and verbal communication of the counterparty?
53. At what point should we present our draft contract as a basis for the negotiation?
54. How should we react if the counterparty presents their draft contract?
55. Are we keeping minutes of the negotiation sessions? Is approval for the minutes by the counterparty necessary?
56. What options does the counterparty have to meet their goals and interests?
57. What options do we have to pursue our goals and interests? Can we justify our various options according to objective criteria?
58. Are we sure that we really understand and respect the goals and interests of the counterparty?
59. Are we sure that the counterparty really understands our goals and interests?
60. Have we sufficiently clarified what type of transaction we are proposing? Is the counterparty fully aware of the deal and aware of its consequences?

VIII. Completion

61. If an agreement is concluded, can we be sure that it will be permanent?
62. What future events and trends might affect this deal? How do we protect ourselves against these events?

63. How should we structure the agreement to limit future uncertainties to a minimum?
64. Is the deal good for both sides? The negotiation process in China may differ significantly from the traditional negotiation training concepts in Europe. Especially for large state-owned enterprises (SOEs), the official conclusion of a specific deal (e.g. a large purchase order) or a project (e.g. founding a joint venture) is celebrated in abundance, with the invited representatives of the business partners and sometimes the government agencies as guests of honour. However, this is only a declaration of intent. Important details still have to be determined in subsequent tough negotiations, usually starting with the technical questions, followed by financial conditions. The price is set at the very end of the process. The decision-makers are regularly informed about the progress, but do not personally take part in the negotiations. It may take weeks or months to resolve all pending issues, and a festive banquet is then organised for the delegation members of the contract partners to celebrate the signing of the contract (Dathe & Helmold, 2018).

Traditional negotiation tactics are also applicable for interactions with Chinese business partners, for example (Dathe & Helmold, 2018):

- Know yourself and your opponent better than he himself.
- Always be well prepared.
- Strike when your opponent doesn't expect it.
- Always set the pace.
- Give in on trivial matters, to give in on essential points to assert your interests.

The Chinese are mostly well-prepared tough negotiators who resolutely pursue their interests. Thus, a negotiation strategy is extremely important when negotiating with the Chinese business partners. In addition, the cultural differences can pose a major challenge for European partners. The seemingly ambiguous information due to contextual communication may look like an unnerving beating about the bush. Maybe it helps to know that the European 'stubbornness and obsession with details' or 'disregard for the give-and-take principle' can also be annoying for the Chinese partners, although their feelings often remain hidden from untrained eyes. To achieve mutual success, it is important to show a lot of patience, to try to understand the meaning behind the spoken words and to always show respect and interest while emphasising the mutual benefits.

10.5 关系Guānxì (Connection), 面子Miànzi (Face) and Business Dinner

There are some major reasons why personal networks in the China business world are of great importance such as (Dathe & Helmold, 2018):

- It is much easier to implement intended business plans with the support of a higher-ranking ally. Because of his status, the general acceptance of his opinion is greater.
- To many employees, only the networked members in the organisation are reliable associates. Less cooperation is expected for the non-allies because they might pose a potential threat.
- The jurisprudence in China still leaves a relatively large scope for interpretation by the competent officials. Under circumstances, a personal favour could therefore be decisive for the business success.

To achieve success in China, it is important to manage the interpersonal relationships based on the understanding of the critical cultural concepts such as '关系 (guānxì)' and '面子(miànzi)'.

关系guānxì means useful personal connections which are considered among the most powerful resources in Chinese companies. Good connections are always helpful: Familiar business partners offer each other favourable conditions; good relations with the authorities may provide the decisive advantage at the critical moment. Sharing influential 关系guānxì is perceived as an act of true friendship. In contrast to the European way of life, the Chinese often mix their contacts from different areas of life to maximise the personal networks, e.g. the college friends and the friends from elementary schools are introduced to each other.

The word 面子miànzi means literally the face or surface. In context of interpersonal relationships, it may be roughly understood as the concept of 'status' in social science, i.e. someone's reputation and the associated rights thereof in an organisation or a social group (Thomas, 2011). One receives 面子miànzi from others due to his organisational position or professional qualifications. On the other hand, giving others 面子miànzi or doing favours helps to develop 关系guānxì (connections). Moreover, it is important not to make others lose face (面子miànzi) as that would be a public disgrace.

Business dinners are especially important in China. There is a famous Chinese saying: 民以食为天mín yǐ shí wéi tiān (food is heaven for the people). There is also a very popular one Chinese TV series titled 舌尖上的中国shé jiān shàng de Zhōngguó (China on the tip of the tongue), which presents numerous culinary specialties in China. But the primary purpose of a business meal goes far beyond the culinary delights. Business dinners are also the best occasions to demonstrate one's knowledge and skills in managing 关系guānxì and 面子miànzi.

The organisation of the business dinner already provides a first impression of the host's appreciation of the business partner, for example, the event location, the number of dishes and quality of the food, the choice of participants, the seating arrangement and possibly even the dressing code of the stakeholders. Such information indicates the status of the guests from the host's perspective. Before the most senior person at the table or the most important guest has started eating, no one touches the food.

Today, quiet partitioned areas in high-end restaurants are usually reserved for discreet business meetings. Traditionally, however, Chinese restaurants are known for their noisy atmosphere because the Chinese regard eating together as a happy event and the joy must be expressed out loud. Especially in Northern Chinese tradition, challenging each other with drinking alcoholic beverages is considered a way of giving 面子miànzi. The mood at the dinner grows more positive with increasing alcohol consumption. Drinking alcohol may be declined with personal health issues or simply because one has to sit behind the wheel afterwards. With the current anti-corruption campaigns in China, however, alcohol consumption at official or business meetings has become quite limited.

Although many contracts are made around the dinner table, the conversation usually begins with small talks. The conclusion of contract may depend on how the mood develops during the conversation, so that the choice of topics for small talks could just matter.

The Chinese really appreciate it when a foreigner learns about their culture or the history of the country. In case of absence of such knowledge, there are many 'safe' subjects such as the food culture in general, interesting stories from family life or superficial discussions on feng shui, kung fu, etc. 'Unsafe' topics should be avoided before a personal trust relationship is developed, for example, politics, religion or any issues that could put the country in unfavourable light. Especially negative comments based on misinformation might trigger strong hostility.

At the end of the business dinner, people stand up to shake hands and bid farewell. Valued guests are given special attention and escorted out of the dining room or up to the elevator. The highest form of 面子miànzi can be given by the host by waving at the departing guest until he/his vehicle disappears from view. (Dathe & Helmold, 2018).

References

Dathe, T., & Helmold, M. (2018). *Erfolgreich im Chinageschäft: Strategien und Handlungsempfehlungen für kleinere und mittlere Unternehmen (KMU)*. Springer Gabler Verlag.

MERICS. (2019, June 19). *China's caution about loosening cross-border capital flows*. By Mercator Institute for China Studies. Retrieved October 26, 2022, from https://merics.org/en/report/chinas-caution-about-loosening-cross-border-capital-flows

Ministry of Commerce of the People's Republic of China. (2022, September). *Invest in China: Legal system in China*. By Ministry of Commerce People's Republic of China. Retrieved October 26, 2022, from https://fdi.mofcom.gov.cn/come-newzonghe.html?parentId=124&name=%E4%B8%AD%E5%9B%BD%E6%B3%95%E5%BE%8B%E4%BD%93%E7%B3%BB%E4%BB%8B%E7%BB%8D&comeID=3

Salacuse, J. (1991). *Making global deal—Negotiating in the international market place*. Houghton Mifflin.

Thomas, A. (2011). Interkulturelle Handlungskompetenz-Versiert, angemessen und erfolgreich im internationalen Geschäft. In A. Thomas, Interkulturelle Handlungskompetenz-Versiert, angemessen und erfolgreich im internationalen Geschäft (S. 80). Gabler Verlag.

11 Positioning in a Complex Market

11.1 Prosperity Gap Within China

To evaluate China's level of development is far from easy. China's cities have a world-class infrastructure; many urban citizens own large, very expensive apartments and modern cars. On the other hand, in 2021, China had a per capita GDP of S$12,556, slightly above Bulgaria (US$11,635) and considerably behind Romania (US$14,862), the EU poorest and second poorest country (The World Bank, 2022).

One obvious factor is the unbalanced level of development. Already in imperial China, parts of South China had become prosperous by international trade, while Central and Western China, especially mountainous remote areas, were incredibly poor. Today, Beijing Municipality (at the same administrative status as a province) has a per capita GDP of US$25,847, higher than Portugal (US$24,262) or Saudi Arabia (US$23,586). Gansu, a province in north-western China, is at the bottom of the provincial ranking with a per capita GDP of just US$5748, 10% lower than Albania (US$6494) (Baidu, 2022; Caiti, 2022) (see Fig. 11.1 Per-capita GDP by Province, 2000 vs. 2021).

Even within a province or municipality, prosperity levels differ considerably. For example, Beijing has a population of 21.8 million people and an area of 16,410 km^2, more than ten times as large as Greater London. 2.72 million of Beijing's inhabitants are classified as rural population. Lifestyle and consumption patterns in villages at the outskirts of Beijing are more similar to neighbouring Hebei Province than to central Beijing.

In addition, like in most emerging economies, there is a huge gap of income and assets within the Chinese cities. In 2020, the average income of the Chinese population was around 30,000 yuan, while 600 million people had a monthly income of 1000 RMB or below (Huanqiu Net, 2020).

Despite these facts, per capita GDP underestimates the level of Chinese economic development. A better index is the purchasing power parity (PPP), figuring in the

T. Dathe et al., *Business Opportunities and Risks in China*, Management for Professionals, https://doi.org/10.1007/978-3-031-31933-4_11

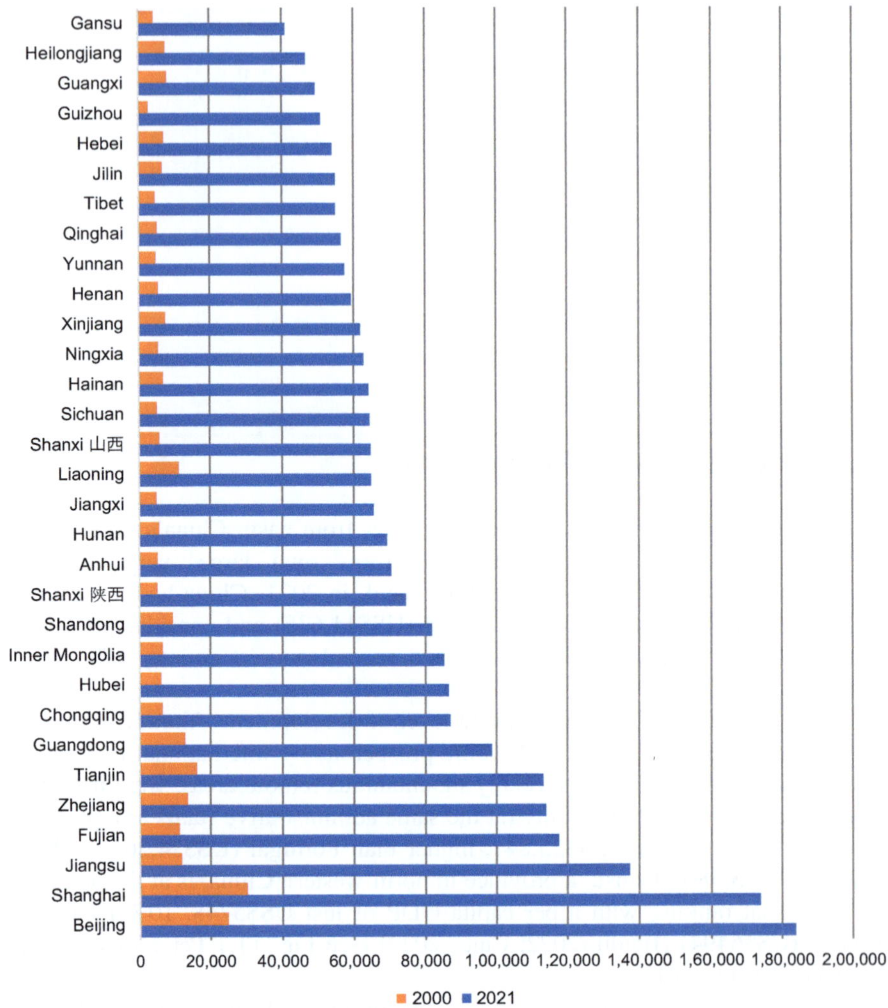

Fig. 11.1 Per capita GDP by province, 2000 vs. 2021. Data sources: Caiti (2022) and Baidu (2022)

cost of living. In terms of PPP, already in 2016, China has exceeded the United States as the world's largest economy (Compare Economy, 2021).

What makes things more complicated, calculation of PPP does not mean an equal factor for all goods and services. Within Chinese cities, different population groups have different patterns of consumption. For example, while some international consultants rate Shanghai as one of the most expensive cities in the world for expatriates, well-integrated foreign employees find costs of living in Shanghai still rather low.

Currently, the Chinese middle class is estimated at 400 million people with a household income between 25,000 and 250,000 yuan (China Briefing, 2019). Most foreign companies focus on this market segment. Local Chinese companies serve the low-income population very well; hence, it is difficult for foreign companies to compete in the low-end market. Some FIEs have adopted a special China market positioning, for example, the German supermarket chain Aldi is serving the low-cost market in Central Europe, while in China it is targeting the premium market segment (Aldi Reviewer, 2019). However, in addition to providing high-end products, an additional market opportunity is to provide the same level of quality and functionality at lower costs. For example, innovative treatment methods that reduce the number of days patients stay in hospital and reduce overall treatment costs have very good chances on the hospital market in China.

China is changing rapidly; this is also true for the prosperity gap. In the past, due to its mountainous terrain, southwestern Guizhou was by far the poorest province. After building transportation and power supply infrastructure, in recent years, Guizhou managed to attract Chinese high-tech companies, raising Guizhou to place 28 of 31 within Mainland China's provincial GDP ranking. For many years, Tibet was China's second poorest region; now, it's per capita GDP exceeds the old industrial bases Heilongjiang and Jilin in the northeast. Key for Tibet's development was also construction of the infrastructure, making Tibet one of China's favourite tourist destinations, allowing sales of its rich agricultural products to other provinces and also attracting companies to set up subsidiaries in Lhasa (Müller, 2022b).

After declaring that it has eradicated absolute poverty in 2020, one of China's next most important tasks is to promote 'common prosperity' with the target of narrowing the prosperity gap (CGTN, 2021). While this is a giant task in a country of 1.4 billion people, it is safe to predict that the Chinese middle class will continue to grow and a larger fraction of the population will be able to buy products from international brands.

11.2 Chinese and International Competitors

In Chinese, the term competition (竞争, jìngzhēng) has a very positive connotation. The Chinese culture promotes a sense of competition as early as in kindergarten and elementary school; teachers and parents encourage children to perform better than their peers. For international companies active in China, it is important to understand that competition and friendship are not a contradiction. Two companies may be fierce competitors in one project and cooperate well in another one. Competition exists in all business areas: competition for best personnel, the best location for a sales outlet, for government-sponsored research projects and for fastest delivery from a supplier. In this chapter, we will focus on competition on the sales market.

With the beginning of China's market reforms, there were two distinct market segments:

- Cheap, low-cost products manufactured in China by local companies
- Expensive, high-end imported products

Starting in the 1980s and accelerating quickly after China's accession to the WTO in December 2001, foreign companies established factories in China to benefit from lower costs and closer distances to customers and suppliers. This created a third market segment: 'foreign brands' manufactured in China. International companies typically started to relocate manufacture of relatively simple and cheap products to China; therefore, this third market segment addressed the gap between cheap local and expensive imported products.

Over time, boundaries of the three market segments have blurred. In the important government procurement market, there is no longer any distinction between products made in China by indigenous Chinese companies and by FIEs (China Government, 2021). Quality and also costs of manufacture of top Chinese brands have increased; in many industries, Chinese companies are now directly competing with international brands. In a survey in early 2022, 19% of European companies listed competition by Chinese companies—12% by Chinese private companies and 7% by SOEs—as one of the three main business challenges in China (EU Chamber of Commerce in China, 2022a).

In China, not only competition with local Chinese brands but also competition with other international companies may be much fiercer than in the home market. The size and growth rate of China's market attract companies from all over the world; in China, foreign brands may face non-Chinese manufacturers they have not competed against in other markets. Because of the geographic proximity and cultural similarity, in many industries, Japanese and South Korean companies are stronger in China than in Europe or North America. In 2022, the main three exporting countries to China were (Trading Economies, 2022):

• South Korea	US$199.67 billion	8.1% share of China's imports
• Japan	US$184.50 billion	7.5% share
• United States	US$178.96 billion	7.2% share

Companies from emerging markets are also undertaking increased efforts to gain a market share in China. In 2022, the 4 BRICS countries Brazil, Russia, South Africa and India had a combined share of 11.0% of the world's total exports to China:

• Brazil	US$109.52 billion	4.4% share	Rank 9
• Russia	US$114.15 billion	4.6% share	Rank 6
• South Africa	US$32.54 billion	1.3% share	Rank 22
• India	US$17.48 billion	0.7% share	Rank 31

Taking the automobile market in Germany and China as an example: German car manufacturers are doing very well in China; in 2018, almost one quarter of all cars sold in China were German brands, and Volkswagen sold more than 40% of its global car sales in China and BMW and Daimler more than one third. However, despite this strong performance of German brands, the market share of manufacturers in the German and Chinese market is completely different [data sources: Statista (2022) and Carsalesbase (2021)]:

- Among the 20 top-selling brands in China, there are 11 Chinese brands; in Germany, there is not a single Chinese one.
- Not a single European, non-German brand is among the top-selling brands in China.
- In China, 3 Japanese brands are among the top 20, but only 1 of them (Toyota) is among the top 20 in Europe.
- In China, 2 US brands are among the top 20, but again, only 1 of them (Tesla) is among the top 20 in Europe.

This means, in China, German car manufacturers have to compete with 16 strong brands that are de facto not present on the German market.

As a consequence, for international companies, when developing a market strategy and positioning in China, it is necessary to compare one's products not only with competitors known in the home market but also with local Chinese companies and a much wider range of international competitors.

11.3 Niche Markets and Chances for International SMEs

According to a definition, 'a niche market is a market segment identified by a unique set of needs or preferences. These needs may follow from the purchaser's budget, location, interests, attitude toward the product, or other factors' (Diggity Marketing, 2022). Newcomers in the Chinese market may be misguided by the sheer size of the market with 1.4 billion people consumers, a fast-growing B2B market and strong government investment. However, like in other economies, there are already sufficient suppliers serving the mainstream needs of the Chinese market. For newcomers, to carve out a market share is not an easy task. Another misconception is to consider China as a homogeneous market. A considerable prosperity gap exists within China (see Sect. 11.1), and China is culturally very diversified (Müller, 2022a); very different living styles exist in parallel.

Because of the size of the Chinese population, in absolute figures, even a relatively small niche market may be large. Many international SMEs and foreign individuals have managed to establish successful businesses in China, often related to special professional skills or products related to their home country. A few examples are as follows:

- A German baker founding a bakery, first starting to serve the German community in China, but his bread quickly found customers among local Chinese.
- An Indian yoga teacher, opening a yoga school.
- A German bodybuilder, founding a fitness centre and working as fitness trainer.
- International architects are employed to meet China's demand for futuristic buildings and city architecture.
- A German trick cyclist, establishing a bicycle manufacture in China.

The last example is a specially enlightening one in terms of finding a niche market. For decades, China has been the 'kingdom of bicycles'. There are about 1800 bicycle manufacturers in China, including some of the world's most successful brands. Therefore, it is certainly not feasible for a SME to compete with these strong players in the mainstream market. The German SME focused on a very special niche market: individual design of bicycles according to special wishes of affluent customers. Big companies are strong in mass production; to care for such a small niche market would distract them from their core business.

There is no easy way to identify a niche market; expensive market studies are mainly designed for mainstream markets. One possible approach is to analyse international markets and trends. With China's growing internationalisation, it is likely that international lifestyles and fashion trends will also be adapted in China; typical examples are mountaineering, sailing or horseback riding. Riding has been a traditional form of transportation and sports in Inner Mongolia and on other grass lands, but only recently has become a leisure activity for a very small number of Chinese and expatriates in economically developed regions of China.

For SMEs with a limited budged, marketing and sales need to be very targeted. For example, China doesn't have a culture of sport clubs like in Europe. Chinese often find together on the internet and social media to form groups for leisure activities. Advertisement on social media is essential to reach these customer segments. In most cases, sales and delivery of products are most efficiently organised via the big Chinese internet platforms. Customers looking for niche market products will very likely use these platforms to search for suppliers.

Niche markets are not limited to the consumer market. One example from the medical field are drugs and medical devices for the cure of rare diseases. In the EU, an illness is defined as a rare disease, if it affects less than 0.05% of the population; there are more than 6000 (Chinese scientists say more than 7000) known rare diseases (German Federal Ministry of Health, 2022), and only 5% of them currently have an available treatment option. The first challenge for manufacturers is to find a sufficient large number of patients for clinical trials to prove the efficacy and safety of their products. In China, an incidence rate of 0.05% still means more than 700,000 patients. More than 10 million people suffer from rare diseases, so that clinical trials can be finished in a reasonable time. In addition, in China, there is a sufficient large market that justifies the investment. In recent years, the Chinese drug and medical device regulator NMPA has considerably lowered the market approval threshold for drugs and medical device against rare diseases. A remaining challenge is the—compared with Western European standards—limited reimbursement by the public health insurance (EU Chamber of Commerce in China, 2022b).

Chinese companies are active in all industries, including agriculture, manufacture and service, and many of them need very specialised suppliers. Focusing on a niche market is a very promising strategy for international SME.

11.4 Case Study: A German SME in the Chinese Medical Device Market

To illustrate the importance of positioning in the Chinese market, we summarise the example of a German medical device manufacturer.

Background: a small German medical device manufacturer (here called: The SME) produces high-risk, life-sustaining medical equipment. Within its home country Germany, the market for these products is dominated by one multinational company; most of The SME's products are exported to emerging markets. The SME wants to expand its manufacturing capacity, reduce costs of manufacture and increase sales; therefore, it decides to set up its first subsidiary, and the obvious country to do so is China. The tasks of the subsidiary shall include manufacture, sales, after-sales service and regulatory affairs (product registration and post-market surveillance).

Before establishing the subsidiary in China, The SME had been represented by a distributor, who acted independently. The SME itself had hardly any information about the medical device market in China and no general China know-how. The SME founds the subsidiary with the help of a China consultancy; in the next step, it employs a German citizen as general manager (GM) with long-time experience in China and good knowledge of the medical device market.

The GM employed a good sales team; however, in the first year, sales remained far behind expectations. A market analysis gives the following results: The high-end and medium-quality/functionality market is dominated by two multinational companies. These two companies have sales representatives and service engineers based in each major province. They have built up customer relations with main hospitals for about 20 years and provide a well-balanced product range of top-end imported equipment and locally manufactured standard devices. Malfunction of this type of devices may put the life of patients at risk; availability of service engineers close to the hospital is essential. To build up a nationwide service network in China, a country 27 times larger than Germany, was out of reach for The SME. Other medical device manufacturers from other European countries and emerging economies, who were quite successful in their home markets, were also not able to compete with the two dominant players.

On the other hand, the low-end market was served by domestic Chinese manufacturers, who produced equipment at much lower prices than The SME.

The SME decided to target a niche market: hospitals in medium-sized town (in China called 'tier three' and 'tier four' towns). Some of these hospitals wanted to upgrade their equipment and buy medical devices from foreign, especially German brands, but had no financial resources to buy from the big international companies. So the niche was a market segment between well-known international brands and cheap Chinese products.

To solve the challenge of after-sales service, The SME trained engineers of provincial distributors to provide service to final customers. Applying a rigid quality management system, The SME could prove that the failure rate of its equipment was close to German standards, a competitive advantage compared with Chinese manufacturers.

The SME's market share was still very low compared with the big international brands, but within The SME, in the second year after the founding of the subsidiary, China became the number one in global sales.

Though competitors on the market, The SME established a very positive professional relationship with one of China's local manufacturers. To expand its product portfolio, The SME in cooperation with this Chinese manufacturer jointly developed a new medical device, specifically targeting emerging markets. Within 1 year after product launch, this device became The SME's best-selling equipment.

The conclusions for SMEs:

- The Chinese market is huge and very diverse. For a SME, even a niche market may offer sufficient opportunities to justify establishment of a subsidiary in China.
- Investment in China should not be a one-way business. The subsidiary in China may contribute its expertise and creativity to drive the worldwide development of The SME (Müller, 2022c)

References

Aldi Reviewer. (2019). *Aldi opening 2 stores in China*. Retrieved November 19, 2022, from https://www.aldireviewer.com/aldi-opening-2-stores-in-china/

Baidu. (2022). *Per-capita GDP Beijing* (in Chinese). Retrieved November 25, 2022, from https://www.baidu.com/s?wd=北京人均GDP

Caiti. (2022). *Newest ranking of the per-capita GDP of all Chinese provinces* (in Chinese). Retrieved November 25, 2022, from https://www.cadforex.com/gdp/94700.html

Carsalesbase. (2021). *China car sales analysis October 2021*. Retrieved November 20, 2022, from https://carsalesbase.com/china-car-sales-analysis-october-2021/

CGTN. (2021). *Xi's "Common Prosperity": The deep message*. By China Global Television Network (CGTN). Retrieved November 19, 2022, from https://news.cgtn.com/news/2021-10-15/Xi-s-Common-Prosperity-The-deep-message-14nx5Q0jn8c/index.html

China Briefing. (2019). *China's middle class in 5 simple questions*. Retrieved November 19, 2022, from https://www.china-briefing.com/news/chinas-middle-class-5-questions-answered/

China Government. (2021). *Notification on the equal treatment of domestic and foreign invested companies in government procurement* (in Chinese). Retrieved November 19, 2022, from http://www.gov.cn/zhengce/zhengceku/2021-10/26/content_5644953.htm

Compare Economy. (2021). *Gross domestic product (PPP)*. Retrieved November 19, 2022, from https://compareeconomy.com/gdp/gdp_ppp#:~:text=Top

Diggity Marketing. (2022). *What is a niche market?* Retrieved November 25, 2022, from https://diggitymarketing.com/niche-market/

EU Chamber of Commerce in China. (2022a). *Business confidence survey 2022*. Retrieved November 19, 2022, from https://www.europeanchamber.com.cn/en/publications-business-confidence-survey

EU Chamber of Commerce in China. (2022b). *Pharmaceutical working group position paper 2022/23*. Retrieved November 25, 2022, from https://europeanchamber.oss-cn-beijing.aliyuncs.com/upload/documents/documents/Pharmaceutical_EN2022[1027].pdf

German Federal Ministry of Health. (2022). *Rare diseases* (in German). By German Federal Ministry of Health (BMG). Retrieved November 24, 2022, from https://www.bundesgesundheitsministerium.de/themen/praevention/gesundheitsgefahren/seltene-erkrankungen.html

Huanqiu Net. (2020). *Li Keqiang: 600 Million People in China have an Income of 1000 Yuan, the Aver-age Income is 30,000 Yuan* (in Chinese). Retrieved November 19, 2022, from https://baijiahao.baidu.com/s?id=1667980339187579197

Müller, V. (2022a). *One country, many cultures chances and challenges of China's incredible diversity*. Retrieved May 13, 2023, from https://www.eurobiz.com.cn/one-country-many-cultures/

Müller, V. (2022b). *Tibet—Buddhismus und Wirtschaft zwischen Tradition und Moderne*. Retrieved November 19, 2022, from https://china-wiki.de/tibet-buddhismus-wirtschaft-tradition-moderne/

Müller, V. (2022c). *We Must Talk – How to increase China expertise in European headquarters to improve communication with Chinese subsidiaries*. Retrieved May 13, 2023, from https://www.eurobiz.com.cn/we-must-talk/

Statista. (2022). *Market shares of the leading car brands in Germany in 2022, by number of new car registrations*. Retrieved November 19, 2022, from https://www.statista.com/statistics/1005575/leading-car-brands-market-share-new-registrations-germany/

The World Bank. (2022). *GDP per capita (current US$)*. Retrieved November 19, 2022, from, https://data.worldbank.org/indicator/NY.GDP.PCAP.CD

Trading Economies. (2022). *China imports by country*. Retrieved November 18, 2022, from https://tradingeconomics.com/china/imports-by-country

12 Marketing Strategy in China

12.1 Direct Approaches to Sales in China

In 2021, China's goods import trade value exceeded US$2.6 trillion, making China the second largest importing nation worldwide (Statista, 2022). China's share of global merchandise imports stands at 11.9%. In addition, many international brands manufacture in China; locally manufactured goods don't count as imports. For example, in 2021, the German and Japanese passenger cars manufactured in China reached a sales volume of around US$1.1 billion each. Though in recent years quality and brand building of local Chinese firms have greatly improved, international brands still have a very good image among consumers and decision-makers in procurement departments. Almost all foreign brand consumer goods sold in Chinese supermarkets are manufactured in China.

For international SMEs, China is an extremely attractive market, in terms of both sales and procurement; a challenge is to find the optimum way how to tap China's market potential. As China has adopted all trade rules of the WHO, in principle, all marketing approaches used in user countries are also feasible in China. However, like in other countries, there is no 'one-fits-all' approach to gain a market share in China; the best way depends on each company's product portfolio and available resources.

SMEs with a limited budget may want to start with a low-level engagement. To start export to China, it is not necessary to establish a presence in the country and not even to have a local distributor. Chinese final customers can directly order from an international company, the Chinese customer becoming responsible for customs clearance and compliance with Chinese laws and regulations. However, a good quality management system (QMS) of the international manufacturer should ensure knowledge of and compliance with Chinese relevant laws and regulations, for example, whether the products delivered need a Chinese label and Instructions for use.

An increasingly attractive way for SME to sell products to China is cross-border e-commerce. Online shopping is a favourite way of Chinese urban consumers, a

T. Dathe et al., *Business Opportunities and Risks in China*, Management for Professionals, https://doi.org/10.1007/978-3-031-31933-4_12

trend that accelerated during the Covid-19 pandemic. In December 2021, about 842 million people in China had purchased goods online at least once. In 2020, China's cross-border e-commerce import reached a value of US$88.2 billion, an increase of 16.5% over 2019 (US International Trade Administration, 2022). The large Chinese online shopping platforms have their international departments, providing Chinese consumers easy access to imported products. For example, Jingdong, a platform with its own very sophisticated nationwide delivery system, has its own international department Jingdong Worldwide.

In total, China has more than 30,000 companies related to cross-border e-commerce. The government has established 132 so-called cross-border e-commerce pilot zones in all parts of the country, which provide a variety of trade services including logistics, payment, law, taxation and customs clearance to support cross-border e-commerce (State Council, 2022a).

To establish a presence in China has obvious advantages: a physical office in China proofs a higher degree of commitment to the Chinese market. This helps to build trust among customers; this is especially important if selling complicated, long-lasting products that may need maintenance and repair. An office in China shortens the distance to customers and regulators, and changes in the Chinese market can be sensed early and the business strategy be adjusted accordingly.

12.2 Sales via Chinese Distributors

Before China's economic reforms, most SMEs sold their products through large international trading companies. Typically, these trading companies had a presence in Hong Kong, from there selling to partner companies in Mainland China. This kind of trading companies still exists, but their significance greatly diminished. As direct trade with China has become very easy, most manufacturers prefer to cooperate directly with specialised local distributors.

Contacts to distributors can be established, for example, on trade fairs or via the internet. Some industry organisations and investment promotion agencies offer matchmaking events.

The number of distributors and traders in China is enormous. For example, in late 2020, 788,000 companies had obtained a valid medical device trading license (CN-Healthcare, 2021). This figure does not include distributors of low-risk class I medical devices, who don't need a special trading license. The scope of business of most of these medical device trading companies is very small, covering only a few hospitals and a small range of products. The challenge for SMEs is to find a distributor that is well established in the target market and fulfils the sales targets. The typical arrangement is to entrust one general distributor who in turn will cooperate with local traders. This carries the risk that the complete China business depends on the business relationship with just one company. Cooperating with several distributors in different parts of China is possible, but management of complex sales channels is difficult without presence in China. If distributors are limited to sell in a certain region, mostly one province, it is necessary to prevent out-of-area sales, so that distributors don't compete with each other.

The most important criteria to select a promising distributor is its proven sales record at the manufacturer's potential key customers with similar but not competing products. Market research in China identifying the decision-makers at key customers is recommended before selecting a distributor.

For example, the decision to buy mid-size medical equipment in a hospital is typically made by a clinical department, not by the hospital procurement department, which is only responsible for ordering and payment. If the distributor is successful to sell consumable medical devices to a hospital, it will still be difficult for him to sell medical equipment, because these two types of devices are chosen by different decision-makers.

If market approvals (e.g. for food) are necessary for import into China, it is advisable that the foreign manufacturer applies for the licences through a specialised registration agent, not through the distributor; otherwise, the manufacturer will become too dependent on the distributor. A webinar on best practices to cooperate with Chinese distributors is recorded at EUSME (2021).

Customers and Chinese regulators will turn to the importer, if products are defective or don't comply with Chinese standards and regulations. Nevertheless, the manufacturer is responsible for product quality and compliance with Chinese legal requirements. Distributors must be given sufficient training, including necessary maintenance and safe disposal of the product. The distributor must keep the manufacturer informed on changing legal requirements, for example, new versions of standards. Manufacturer and distributor need to agree on procedures how to handle customer complaints, repair and possible recalls.

Sales to China via distributors will not receive the best possible sales results, but for SMEs, it is an easy way to test the market with limited risk.

12.3 Control by a Representative Office

Until the 1990s, at a time when commercial activities of foreign invested companies in China were still rather restricted, establishment of a representative office (rep office) was the favourite investment form of many foreign companies, especially SMEs. As the name says, a rep office is not a company; it cannot directly engage in profit-generating activities. The main advantage of rep offices is its easy establishment and little administrative overhead in managing the entity. After China joined the WTO in 2001, the procedure of founding a foreign invested company in China has been simplified, and restriction for foreign companies has been lifted; therefore, rep offices have become a less attractive option. Nowadays, only about 10% of foreign invested entities in China are rep offices (Globalizationpedia, 2022).

A rep office cannot sell products or services to a customer. The rep office may prepare a deal, but the final contract and payment transaction have to be concluded between the Chinese customer and the rep office's headquarters. This may delay the time of delivery of goods. If the Chinese customer has no foreign trading license, it may require additional efforts and increase expenses, to transfer the payment in foreign currencies. Especially procurement of services from abroad by Chinese companies still faces restrictions.

In general, the main task of rep offices is to select and supervise distributors and participate in marketing activities like trade fairs. The rep office may provide training to business partners and final customers, but the rep office cannot invoice this training. For companies sourcing in China, a rep office may be feasible to select and supervise suppliers.

The head of a rep office is called chief representative. Up to four foreign nationals can be employed in a rep office; they need to sign a working contract with the headquarters abroad. Possible labour disputes should be settled under the laws of that country. A rep office cannot directly employ Chinese staff members; this must be done through a human resources agency. This is not a disadvantage; the rep office is free to select suitable candidates; all legal obligations of the employer like payment of income tax and social security contributions are outsourced to the agency.

Though rep offices don't have income in China, they are subject to business tax in China. Tax is calculated based on the expenses of the office, in general by a flat rate of 15% (China Briefing, 2018). The logic behind the taxation rule: a rep office creates profit for its mother company. As this profit is not visible in the books of the rep office, it is roughly assumed that the profit is linked to the level of activities of the rep office; the more the expenses, the more the profit.

Within an international company, targets and success criteria need to be well communicated. A rep office is a cost centre, not a profit centre. When business in China develops well, this is not reflected in the books of the rep office.

There is no procedure in place to upgrade a rep office to a company. If a foreign company plans to extend its activities, the subsidiary needs to be newly established and the rep office closed. Working contracts of expatriates and local employees need to be newly signed by the new company.

Despite the restrictions listed above, establishment of a rep office in China is a fast, cheap way to get a first foothold in China; this is especially attractive for SMEs.

12.4 Subsidiaries

The next higher level of commitment to China is the founding of a trading company as a foreign invested enterprise (FIE). Many international companies start their engagement in China with a representative office and, if successful, establish a company a few years later. Like any other company, a subsidiary in China is responsible for profit and loss, so the subsidiary has a clear commercial responsibility.

Chinese cities and industrial parks compete for investment. Local investment promotion agencies as well as international organisations provide comprehensive support (see Sect. 17.2).

A typical business scenario: the Chinese subsidiary buys products from the company's headquarters and sells them with a mark-up to customers in China. If necessary, the Chinese subsidiary applies for market licences (e.g. medical device registration certificates) and provides training and after-sales service to final customers.

The main advantage of establishing a trading company in China: the FIE can control the whole sales channel in China and directly engage in business activities like sales to final customers. Local distributors often require high mark-ups, making the final price less competitive. In a fast-growing economy like China, local distributors and dealers often focus on short-term profit, their ownership may change, or they adjust their business focus. Controlling the sales channel by the FIE makes operation independent from business partners.

To reduce necessary investment and limit the headcount, many functions of a company like customs clearance, accounting and human resources can be outsourced. High-quality service providers are available at all larger Chinese cities; many of them focus on FIEs and are, for example, familiar with international accounting standards.

The structure of an adequate sales network depends on the industry. In the consumer market, many international foreign invested enterprises (FIEs) sell via Chinese online sales platforms and local supermarket chains only. In the B2B and business-to-government market, direct sales to final customers is more common. In this case, the size of China with a land area 27 times larger than Germany must be considered. A subsidiary in China can employ sales representatives in different parts of the country, but it is unrealistic for most FIE to cover whole China by its own sales staff. In many cases, FIEs choose a mixed approach, selling directly to final customers in the province where the subsidiary is registered plus a few key cities and cooperating with distributors in other parts of the country.

Compared with a representative office, a company has far-reaching legal responsibilities. The company bringing imported products into the market must ensure that they comply with Chinese standards, which may deviate from international ones, for example, electric plugs. Products must work under extreme environmental conditions (temperature, high altitude) and must be delivered with Chinese labels and instructions for use. A company is the direct employer of Chinese employees and responsible for compliance with Chinese labour laws. Nowadays, Chinese customers and employees are well aware of their legal rights. The complexity of China's market regulation is comparable with Central European standards. Many regulations have been harmonised with international practices, but differences exist. For FIEs with limited headcount in China, it is a challenge to become and stay familiar with all applying laws and regulations. A wide range of consultants and law firms are present to provide the necessary expertise.

Nearly all restrictions to founding a FIE have been lifted since China's accession to the WTO. Nowadays, most foreign invested trading companies are wholly foreign-owned enterprises (WFOE); there is hardly any reason to founding a trading company together with a local partner (joint venture).

As China wants to attract foreign investment, establishment of a company in China has become quite straightforward. The required time to register a business depends on the location and the industry; the typical time frame is between 2 and 6 months (EUSME, 2019).

After registration with the local Bureau of Commerce, the FIE will receive a business licence, describing the scope of business. Sales by a subsidiary in China is not limited to products manufactured by its headquarters; the subsidiary may also source and sell products from third parties. However, the products must fit into the scope of business in the business licence. For example, a pharmaceutical company is not allowed to sell food supplements, if this type of products is not listed in the business licence. When applying for a business licence, it is advisable to define a broader scope of business. When the scope of business shall be extended, it is possible to apply for a modification of the business license (Generis, 2021).

When applying for the business licence, two points are important:

- The applicant needs to stipulate the registered capital. The registered capital basically covers all fixed assets and daily expenses before the subsidiary reaches a break-even.
- A feasibility study or business plan must be submitted to the Bureau of Commerce. Chinese approval authorities want to avoid that FIEs fail in China. The business plan needn't be very detailed, and it is not required to disclose any business secrets.

In addition to the Bureau of Commerce, the newly established company must be registered with several other authorities, for example, customs, tax authorities and statistics bureau. The registration procedures can be done by the company itself or by a local consultancy. The last step is to register a bank account; when this is finished, the FIE can start to do business transactions.

For some industries with high-risk products, for example, pharmaceuticals, medical devices and food, in addition to normal business registration, it is necessary to apply for an industry-specific trading licence with the responsible authority, in case of pharmaceuticals and medical devices with the NMPA.

Around 83% of businesses establishing a presence in China create a WFOE (Globalizationpedia, 2022); this is the most common option for both multinational companies and SMEs.

12.5 Servicing Goods and Trade in Service

When providing service to customers, two cases need to be distinguished:

- Service as integrated part of trade in goods
- Genuine trade in services, not connected to trade in goods

A wide range of goods, especially long-lasting fixed assets, need accompanying service, including user training, maintenance and repair. The price for service may be included in the contract price of goods or charged separately. Many international companies are promoting service contracts in China; however, until now, the number of Chinese customers willing to sign service contracts is lower than in most developed economies.

If an international manufacturer has no subsidiary in China, it is possible to provide service from the headquarters, either by sending service engineers to China or by shipping a defective machine to the headquarters for repair. This process is obviously very slow and expensive. In most cases, it is advisable to provide service from a base within China. For some medium- and high-risk products, for example, medical devices, having a responsible company providing after-sales service within China is a mandatory condition of market approval.

After-sales service can be provided by the Chinese subsidiary of an international company or be outsourced to a third party, including in-house serving by a final customer. Quality of after-sales service must be ensured, independent of who provides the service. Contractual agreements between the manufacturer and its local service agents in China should lay down the share of responsibility.

Representative offices in China can only provide a very limited scope of services. Rep offices cannot invoice customers for services provided, and they cannot overtake legal responsibility.

A new trend in servicing is remote maintenance: the manufacturer can access a machine via the internet and remotely run analysis routines to find the reason of a malfunction. If remote maintenance involves access to sensitive data, for example, in hospitals, the manufacturer needs to check whether international data transfer complies with China's data protection and cyberspace security regulations.

In a broader sense, trade in services include all non-physical, intangible parts of the economy. A definition of the OECD lists the following economic activities as service: 'transport (both freight and passengers), travel, communications services (postal, telephone, satellite, etc.), construction services, insurance and financial services, computer and information services, royalties and license fees, other business services (merchanting, operational leasing, technical and professional services, etc.), cultural and recreational services, and government services not included in the list above' (OECD, 2020).

The provision of certain types of services, for example, homecare and senior citizen care, requires a physical proximity of customer and supplier, making it difficult to serve the Chinese market from Europe or Northern America. In addition, China was (and is) labelled the 'factory of the world'; in the last several decades, trading with China has focused on goods. However, trading of services plays an increasingly important role. In 2021, China was the third largest partner for EU exports of goods (223.3 billion euros, 10.2%) and the largest partner for EU imports of goods (472.2 billion euros, 22.4%) (Eurostat, 2022a). In comparison, in 2020, Mainland China was the fourth largest partner for EU exports of services (47 billion euros, 5%) and the sixth largest partner for EU imports of services (31 billion euros,

4%) (Eurostat, 2021). In trading of services, the EU has a strong trade surplus with China.

For China, promotion of trading in services is one key tool to transform its economy from resource-intensive industrial manufacture to a modern, highly efficient and ecological economy.

As it is often the case in China, reform policies are first implemented in a small part of the country and, if successful, may be rolled out nationwide later. A pilot programme for opening up the service sector started 2015 in Beijing; Tianjin, Shanghai, Hainan and Chongqing began separate pilot programmes in 2021, and another six cities, Shenyang, Nanjing, Hangzhou, Wuhan, Guangzhou and Chengdu, in late 2022 received approval by the State Council for 3-year trial programmes (State Council, 2022b).

Beijing's Plan for Building an Integrated National Demonstration Zone for Opening up the Services Sector is the most ambitious pilot programme. By 2030, 'Beijing's services sector will be among the world's best in terms of economic scale and international competitiveness' (Beijing Government, 2020). Key components of Beijing's development include smoothening of cross-border capital flow, attracting more international talent and facilitating cross-border dataflow.

China specifically promotes trading of knowledge-intensive services (KIS). A definition of KIS is given in Eurostat (2022b). From January to November 2021, KIS reached 44.2% of China's total trade in services, in absolute terms a growth of 8% compared with the same period of 2020 (State Council, 2021).

Since 2012, the MOFCOM and the Beijing Municipal Government co-host the annual China International Fair for Trade in Services (CIFTIS), the only large-scale trade fair specially dedicated to trade in services. Together with the longstanding China Import and Export Fair (Canton Fair) in Guangzhou and the China International Import Expo (CIIE) in Shanghai, CIFTIS has developed to one of the three leading cross-industry trade fairs. For international SMEs, CIFTIS is a main entry points to sell and source services in China (CIFTIS, 2022).

12.6 Manufacture in China

Most multinational companies have established their own manufacture in China or entrust Chinese companies to contract manufacture, for sales both in China and on the international market.

From the sales point of view, also for SME, manufacture in China for the local Chinese market is an attractive option, and main advantages include:

- Lower costs of manufacture compared with developed economies
- No customs clearance required
- Lower costs of transportation and logistics
- Proximity to suppliers of components and raw materials
- Fast delivery to customers
- Use of site of manufacture for repair and maintenance

- Smooth market access, even if procurement of imported products is restricted (government procurement)

There are basically two options to manufacture in China: establishment of a factory or contract manufacture.

There is no unambiguous definition of contract manufacture. The basic concept: the international company has the complete ownership of and legal responsibility for the product. The international company sells the product under its own brand and with its own product name; however, manufacture is entrusted to a third party in China.

Roughly two different cases are distinguished when outsourcing production to a contract manufacturer: original equipment manufacturing (OEM) and original design manufacturing (ODM).

In the case of OEM, the international product owner has developed and designed the product. The product may be identical with that manufactured at the headquarters, slightly modified to match Chinese requirements (e.g. modified electric plugs) or specifically developed for the Chinese market and potentially other emerging markets.

ODM means the international product owner provides a rough specification only and the cooperation partner overtakes development and design and sometimes even whole product life cycle services.

The optimum details of contract manufacturing depend on each individual case. In general, the advantages of contract manufacture are low investment and quick time to market, as existing licences and infrastructure can be used. The main disadvantage is a transfer of value creation to the contract manufacturer, resulting in a lower margin for the international company. In addition, contract manufacture causes a commercial and technical dependence from the manufacturer.

Compared with contract manufacture, building up one's own factory in China requires a much higher degree of commitment to the Chinese market. However, also for SMEs with limited financial resources, building its own factory in China is an attractive option to become independent from contract manufacturers and control the complete value creation chain.

In the 1980s when China opened up to foreign investors, in most cases, establishing a factory in China was only possible together with a Chinese partner company in the form of a joint venture. In many cases, the Chinese partner contributed land and factory buildings. Joint ventures were formed because of legal requirements, not because the Chinese and foreign partner wanted to combine their strengths. When China joined the WTO and restrictions to foreign investment were lifted, most international companies opted to form wholly foreign-owned enterprises (WFOE), and the proportion of investment in WFOE increased from 27% in 1995 to 77.4% in 2010 (China Briefing, 2011). However, quite a large number of 'legacy joint ventures' still exist, for example, in the automotive industry, where the last restrictions to foreign ownership were only lifted in 2022.

For some SMEs serving multinational companies in China, it may be mandatory to manufacture in the country. Multinational companies may require that their suppliers manufacture close to their own plants to ensure exact time of delivery as well as simplify communication and quality control.

Establishment of a factory in China is not very different from the process in other countries. Application for founding factory is part of the registration of a foreign invested company. In addition to the documents required to founding a non-manufacturing company, the applicant needs to submit (Dezan Shira, 2022):

- A feasibility study, considering whether the factory will have special requirements, for example, to energy and water supply or transportation infrastructure
- An environmental impact assessment, including an on-site environmental impact assessment, and report approval from authorities in charge

Before the factory can start operation, it must be audited by the local fire brigade, a rather strict procedure comparable to most developed economies. In some industries, factories need additional approval by the relevant authorities, for example, an auditing according to Good Manufacturing Practice (GMP) by the National Medical Products Administration (NMPA) for pharmaceutical plants.

Founding a factory in China needs an especially careful selection of the location. Many industrial parks have incentive policies, for example, favourable rent of standardised factory buildings, often tailored for specific industries. One important point to consider: To save expenses, it may be attractive to have its office within the factory building. However, Chinese cities are large; industrial parks are usually located in the outskirts far away from the city centre. Convenient commuting for office workers to the factory is a precondition to employ and retain qualified personnel.

References

Beijing Government. (2020). *Plan for building an integrated national demonstration zone for opening up the services sector through the integrated pilot program for further opening up Beijing's services sector*. Retrieved December 25, 2022, from http://english.beijing.gov.cn/investinginbeijing/WhyBeijing/lawpolicy/policies/202009/t20200918_2065917.html

China Briefing. (2011). *China joint ventures: The basics*. Retrieved December 27, 2022, from https://www.china-briefing.com/news/china-joint-ventures-the-basics/

China Briefing. (2018). *Setting up a representative office in China*. Retrieved November 27, 2022, from https://www.china-briefing.com/news/setting-up-a-representative-office-in-china/

CIFTIS. (2022). *Background*. Retrieved December 19, 2022, from https://www.ciftis.org/article/9126321912672256.html

CN-Healthcare. (2021). *How many medical device companies exist in China? Figures have been published* (in Chinese). Retrieved December 4, 2022, from https://www.cn-healthcare.com/articlewm/20210318/content-1200262.html

Dezan Shira. (2022). *An introduction to doing business in China 2023*. Retrieved December 28, 2022, from https://www.asiabriefing.com/store/book/introduction-doing-business-china-2023.html

Eurostat. (2021). *International trade in services*. Retrieved December 19, 2022, from https://ec.europa.eu/eurostat/statistics-explained/index.php?title=International_trade_in_services#General_overview

Eurostat. (2022a). *China-EU—international trade in goods statistics*. Retrieved December 19, 2022, from https://ec.europa.eu/eurostat/statistics-explained/index.php?title=China-EU_-_international_trade_in_goods_statistics

Eurostat. (2022b). *Glossary: Knowledge-intensive services (KIS)*. Retrieved December 19, 2022, from https://ec.europa.eu/eurostat/statistics-explained/index.php?title=Glossary:Knowledge-intensive_services_(KIS)

EUSME Centre. (2019). *How to establish a foreign-Invested enterprise in China*. Retrieved December 3, 2022, from https://www.eusmecentre.org.cn/publications/how-to-establish-a-foreign-invested-enterprise-fie-in-china-2019-update/

EUSME Centre. (2021). *Indirect sales & business partners in China: How to identify, approach, select and secure them*. Retrieved December 3, 2022, from https://www.eusmecentre.org.cn/events/indirect-sales-business-partners-in-china-how-to-identify-approach-select-and-secure-them/

Generis Global. (2021). *Complete guide to starting a subsidiary in China*. Retrieved December 3, 2022, from https://generisonline.com/complete-guide-to-starting-a-subsidiary-in-china/

GlobalizationPedia. (2022). *Setting up a representative office in China*. Retrieved November 27, 2022, from https://globalizationpedia.com/the-representative-office-in-china-explained/

OECD. (2020). *Trade in services*. Retrieved December 19, 2022, from https://data.oecd.org/trade/trade-in-services.htm

State Council. (2021). *China's trade in services a new vista to watch*. Retrieved December 19, 2022, from http://english.www.gov.cn/news/topnews/202101/16/content_WS60025002c6d0f72576943eb4.html

State Council. (2022a). *Cross-border e-commerce pilot zones forge a promising future for China's foreign trade*. Retrieved December 14, 2022, from https://english.www.gov.cn/policies/policywatch/202202/15/content_WS620b7167c6d09c94e48a511a.html

State Council. (2022b). *China launches pilot programs to further open up service sector*. Retrieved December 23, 2022, from https://english.www.gov.cn/policies/latestreleases/202212/20/content_WS63a131eec6d0a757729e497c.html

Statista. (2022). *Imports to China—Statistics & facts*. Retrieved December 14, 2022, from https://www.statista.com/topics/1471/imports-to-china/

US International Trade Administration. (2022). *China cross-border ecommerce channels*. Retrieved December 14, 2022, from https://www.trade.gov/market-intelligence/china-cross-border-ecommerce-channels

13 Managing Global Supply Chain

13.1 Objectives of Supply Chain Management (SCM)

All business organisations need to coordinate sourcing of raw materials and services from suppliers and the distribution of their own products and services to customers. The process of planning, implementing and managing the flow of materials and services is the subject of supply chain management (SCM). While the flow of material of services suppliers is referred to as upstream supply chain, the term downstream supply chain is for the distribution to customers (see Fig. 13.1).

The main objectives of supply chain management (SCM) are optimal quality of products and services, cost efficiency, quick and reliable delivery time and risk management especially in terms of avoidance of disruptions. In the past decades, modern business organisations increasingly shifted peripheral activities to suppliers, in order to make the best use of limited resources at hand by focusing on the value-adding core competencies. This circumstance encourages interorganisational collaborations and, subsequently, results in interdependency of firms within the global supply chain network (Helmold et al., 2022).

In supply chain management, all activities related to integrated planning, coordination, implementation and control of the flow of goods including the goods-related information from the sources of origin (suppliers) to the end consumers (customers) are described as logistic processes. Logistics costs can account for more than 40% of the total costs for bulky components. In case of special transport and air freight, the proportion of logistic costs can be even higher. With regular transport and innovative logistics chains, logistics costs can sometimes be optimised to a value of 2% to 5% of the total costs (Helmold et al., 2022).

The assessment of logistic processes is frequently discussed based on the principle of '7 Rs of logistics' (Dathe & Helmold, 2018):

- Getting the *Right* products.
- in the *Right* quantity,
- in the *Right* condition,

T. Dathe et al., *Business Opportunities and Risks in China*, Management for Professionals, https://doi.org/10.1007/978-3-031-31933-4_13

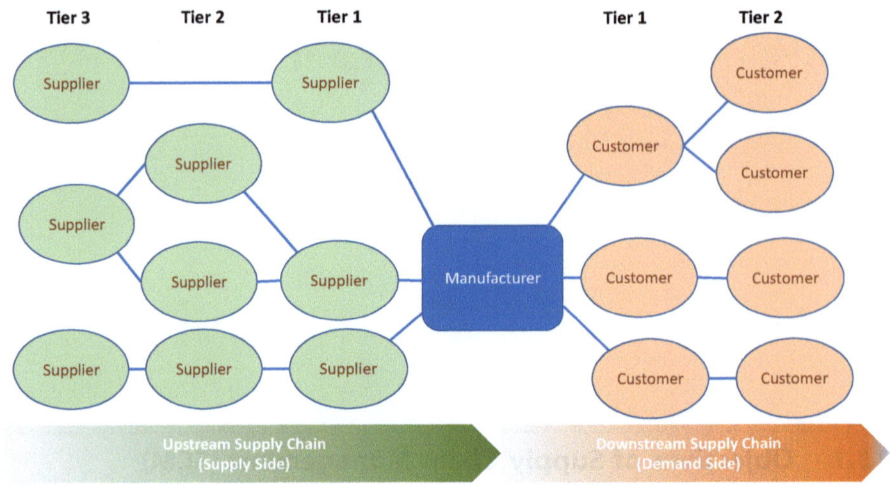

Fig. 13.1 An illustration of supply chain. Source: According to (Laudon & Laudon, 2021)

- at the *Right* place,
- at the *Right* time,
- to the *Right* customer, and,
- at the *Right* costs.

In consideration of the increasing importance of the sustainability aspect, the 7 Rs principle can be extended to the 8 Rs framework by the adding the aspect of 'with the *Right* resources' (Helmold et al., 2022).

To stay competitive at the increasingly transparent global market, it is important especially for manufacturers to minimise waste along the supply chain, in order to obtain cost leadership and other delivery advantages. Waste is any activity that consumes limited resources (e.g. money, time, etc.) without creating value (in fulfilling the 7 Rs of logistics) for the customers. The continuous effort in minimising waste along the supply chain is described as lean supply chain or lean production in academic studies (Helmold et al., 2022).

A popular instrument for lean supply chain management is the 5S worksite management concept originated by the Japanese carmaker Toyota in Nagoya, Aichi, including the following aspects (Helmold et al., 2022):

1. Sort (Seiri 整理). Sorting contents at the workplace and removing all unnecessary items. This helps to reduce waste of time for locating the needed items and may improve the use of space and safety by eliminating avoidable obstacles. The shadow board is an example for the implementation of the Seiri principle.
2. Straighten (Seiton 整頓). Putting all necessary items at workplace in optimal places to best fulfil their functions according to the production process.
3. Shine (Seisō 清掃). Cleaning and inspecting tools and machinery at workplace on a regular basis. The cleanliness prevents distractions and disruptions to

employees. By keeping the workplace clean, the production processes can be carried out swiftly, and potential disturbance can be detected easily.

4. Standardise (Seiketsu 清潔). Standardising the processes of the first three 'S' activities. This helps to improve the efficiency of those repetitive procedures. Additional mechanism could be implemented in the standardised processes to be mistake-proofing (jap.: poka-yoke).
5. Sustain (Shitsuke 躾). Training the workers to be self-disciplined and do the right things without being told. This could ensure the fulfilment of the 5S principles in a complex, changing environment.

In the past, China has successfully adapted many advanced techniques for the management of global supply chains and developed an overall comprehensive industrial infrastructure for most business sectors in the world.

13.2 Global Supply Networks

In the recent decades, the main focus of supply chain management (SCM) is no longer confined to the manufacturer's improvement of internal processes. To a large extent, today's supply chain managers primarily act on exchange of information and exploitation of collaborations with (potential) business partners in a complex global network. Especially supplier management plays a critical role in the continuous improvement of processes along the global supply chain. Due to the complexity of the modern global supply chain, the supply chain can no longer be handled by the manufacturers alone, but must rely especially on a worldwide innovative, efficient and flexible supplier network (Helmold et al., 2022). The traditional push-based supply chain—that is, the manufacturer organises the supply chain based on his anticipation of the market demand—has largely been replaced by the market-driven pull-based strategy (see Fig. 13.2) (Laudon & Laudon, 2021).

During the globalisation process, enterprises tend to maximise their economic benefits by concentrating on their core competence and outsourcing non-critical production steps. As a result, a mutual specialisation has taken place, that is, external providers have developed their own business models to achieve cost leadership or qualitative advantages by focusing on certain types of components for a large number of customers worldwide. Special processes which are designed for the continuous smooth flow of goods and services within and across various organisations, such as through just-in-time (JIT) or just-in-sequence (JIS) or Kanban systems, become widespread to achieve optimal logistic performance and cost advantages (Helmold et al., 2022).

Furthermore, global megatrends such as increasing digitisation, urbanisation as well as globalisation and deglobalisation play a major role in China's future as a sourcing country. Global digitisation has triggered innovations in terms of both new products and radical changes of traditional business models. The internet-driven digital technologies have long become foundations for digitalised manufacturing (e.g. 'smart factory') and the global networking of manufacturers with their

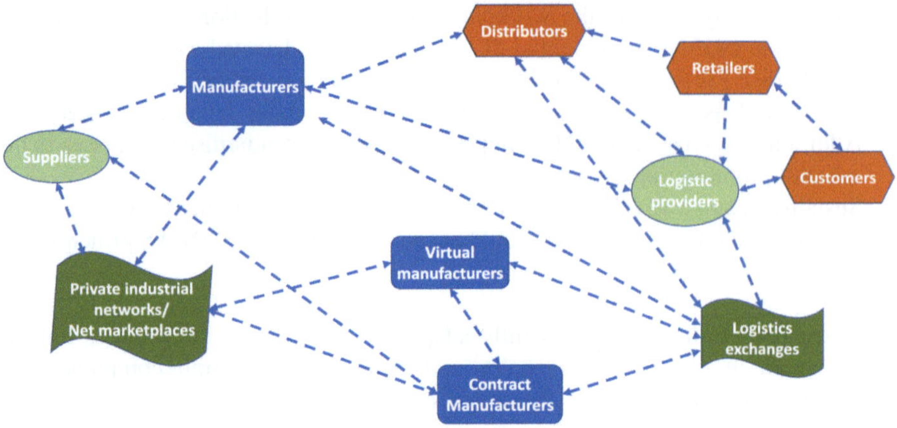

Fig. 13.2 Push-based vs. pull-based supply chains. Source: Adapted from (Laudon & Laudon, 2021)

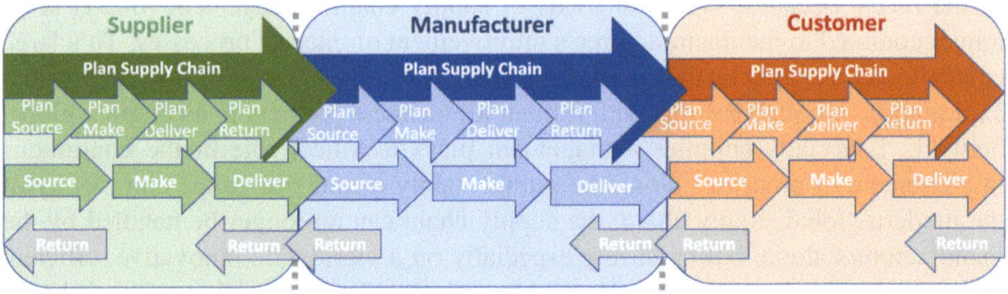

Fig. 13.3 An internet-driven digital logistics nervous system. Source: Adapted from (Laudon & Laudon, 2021)

customers and suppliers. The almost unlimited exchange of information among (potential) business partners immensely increases the market transparency over a large part of the value-added activities along the global supply chains, for the supply of both goods and services (Dathe & Helmold, 2018). As a result of intensified competition at the global market, further specialisation in the global supply chain has taken place. The modern digital logistics systems based on internet technology resemble a complex nervous system. The container transport is traced by GPS-based real-time data monitoring covering the location, temperature, humidity, pressure, etc. of the cargo (Laudon & Laudon, 2021). Moreover, new roles in the global logistic networks such as virtual manufacturers, virtual marketplaces for professional material sourcing and logistic exchange hubs have emerged to bundle tasks independently from geographical proximity and create value for customers (see Fig. 13.3).

The coordination of cross-border flows of goods and services and collaborative information exchange in today's comprehensive logistic networks poses an enormous challenge for modern supply chain management. To facilitate the

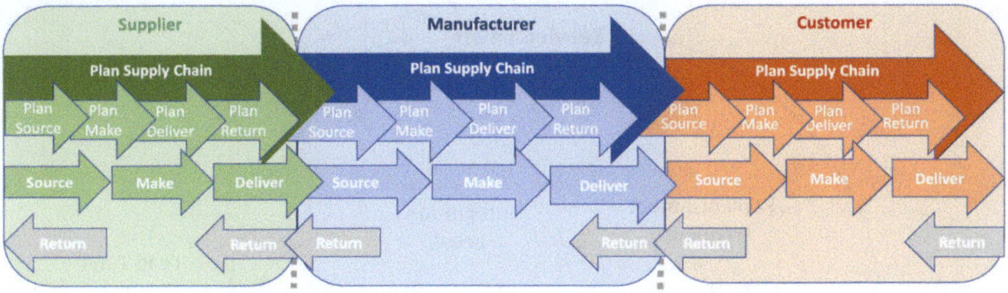

Fig. 13.4 SCOR: key supply chain management processes. Information source: (CIO, 2021)

cross-organisational communication on complex logistic transactions, the Supply Chain Council (SCC) has designed the Supply Chain Operations Reference (SCOR) model based on expertise from different industry sectors. In practice, this reference model is often utilised as a standard diagnostic tool for the design and troubleshooting in a global supply chain based on five key management processes (see Fig. 13.4) (CIO, 2021):

1. *Plan*: Defining resources, requirements and chain of communication and allocating resources in line with the overall business plan.
2. *Source*: Identifying suppliers, scheduling deliveries and managing inventory, in order to obtain adequate goods and services to meet the market demand.
3. *Make*: Scheduling and implementing production to meet the market demand (made to order, made to stock or engineered to order).
4. *Deliver*: Selecting carriers and planning delivery routes for distribution of finished products and services to customers.
5. *Return*: Dealing with post-delivery customer claims.

In addition, there are the enable processes aiming to ensure other supply chain management processes by providing business rules, data resources, necessary contracts and risk management guidelines.

For the design of a global supply chain, multiple critical aspects must be considered, especially (see Fig. 13.6):

- Service level: The likelihood that customer demand can be fulfilled within the expected delivery time (the past performance is measured by fill rate—the fulfilment of customer orders).
- Cost.

The supply chain performance can be effectively controlled by operating management decisions to influence the performance indicators such as replenishment frequency, integration level, inventory level, frequency of information exchange and lead time (time needed to make the goods and services available after the customers

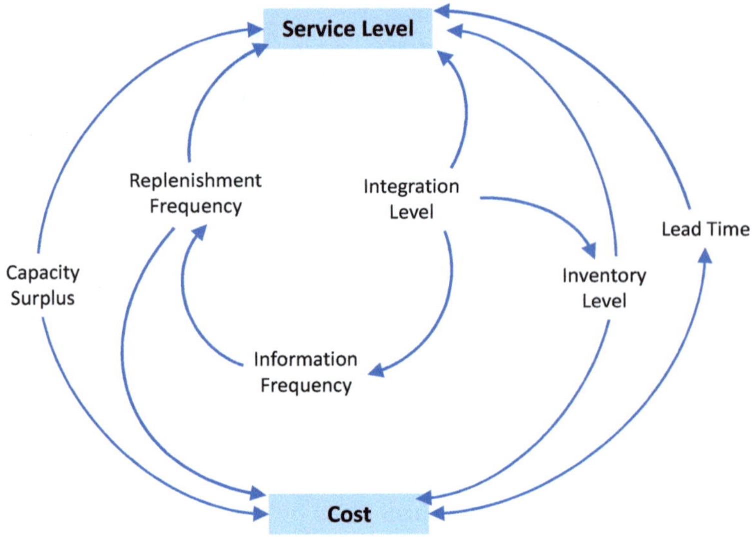

Fig. 13.5 Assessment criteria for supply chain performance and influence factors. Source: Adapted from (Sinha et al., 2020) with modifications

have placed orders). Essentially, supply chain management aims to balance the competing goals service level and cost. For example, reducing inventory level could save storage costs; however, it could decrease service level (see Fig. 13.5).

Resilience is a further requirement for supply chains. That is, supply chains must be stable and robust to be able to overcome disruptions. A disruption can be described as an unplanned event that significantly impacts a firm's normal operations in a negative manner (Sinha et al., 2020).

In the recent years, there have been several major events that have caused disruptions in global supply chains and drawn public attention to supply chain resilience issues (see Sect. 13.3).

13.3 Covid-19 Pandemic and Supply Chain Resilience

Through decades of globalisation process, a specialisation mainly based on local resources and infrastructure has taken place along the global supply chains, resulting in cost benefits for consumers around the world. Goods and services are constantly moved in global supply chain networks, mostly with a combination of different transport means (intermodal logistics transport) in both domestic regions and overseas (Helmold et al., 2022). The intertwining supply chain increases the risk of disruptions. That is, local disruptions in the supply chain can easily affect significantly larger regions in other countries (Sinha et al., 2020).

The long-lasting Covid-19 pandemic slowed the world economy and caused global recessions (IMF, 2022). To reduce mortality caused by the lethal virus,

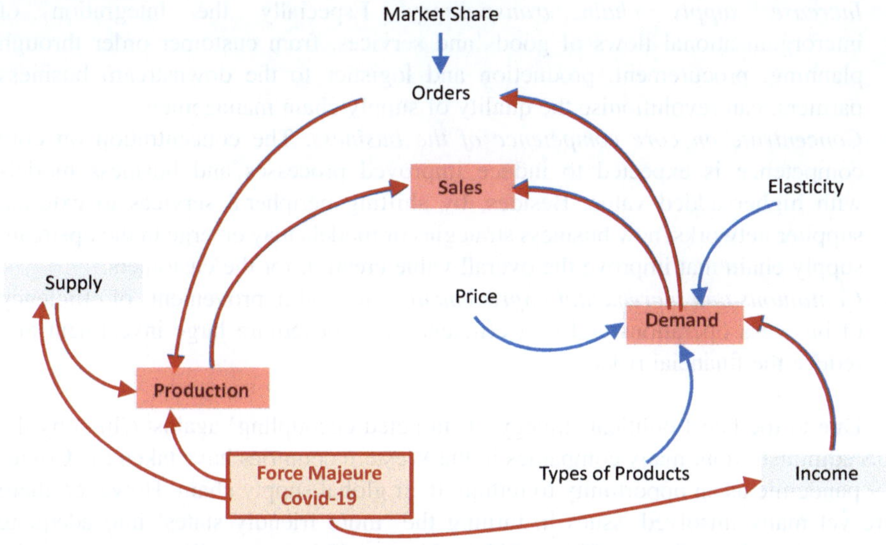

Fig. 13.6 Supply chain disruptions caused by Covid-19 pandemic (initial impacts). Source: Adapted from (Sinha et al., 2020) with modifications

governments implemented quarantine and lockdown measures to enforce social distancing. Such measures, however, caused disastrous results on the global supply chain in multiple aspects, especially (Sinha et al., 2020) (see Fig. 13.6):

- Delays in upstream delivery.
- Extended production lead time causing shortage of market supply and increasing prices.
- Reduced household income leading to falling demand on the consumer market.
- Liquidity pressure on companies associated with declining market demand and increasing inventory, leading to bankruptcies and falling demand in the investment market.

Due to the above development, supply chain resilience has become a major requirement in the latest development of supply chain management. The adaptability of the supply chain to respond to disruptions cannot be simply achieved by building up the inventory. On the contrary, growing inventory potentially leads to increasing obsolescence. The subsequent liquidation pressure often forces companies to scale down the business operations or even bankruptcy (Sinha et al., 2020).

There are no one-size-fits-all solutions to overcome dramatic supply chain disruptions such as collapsing in incoming orders and sales or upstream delivery disruptions. However, experts propose several approaches to stabilise the operating income and short-term liquidity, including (Helmold & Tracy, 2022):

- *Increase supply chain transparency.* Especially the integration of interorganisational flows of goods and services, from customer order through planning, procurement, production and logistics to the downstream business partners, can revolutionise the quality of supply chain management.
- *Concentrate on core competence of the business.* The concentration on core competence is expected to induce improved processes and business models with higher added value. Besides, by shifting peripheral services to external supplier networks, new business strategies or models may emerge in the upstream supply chain that improve the overall value creation for the customers.
- *Continuous and incremental improvements.* Gradual improvements of efficiency of business operations and cost efficiency do not require large investment and reduce the financial risks.

Due to the latest political strategy of 'targeted decoupling' against China by the US administration, many companies in the Western countries have taken the Covid-19 pandemic as an opportunity to rethink their global supply chain. However, there are yet many unsolved issues in turning the 'more friendly states' into adequate outsourcing alternatives to China. Although many Chinese suppliers are serving the European sales markets or European manufacturers ('extended workbench'), the sales market is of growing importance due to the increasing middle class in China. At present, China still offers significant advantages as a production location, thanks to its comprehensive infrastructure, skilled labour market, price advantages as well as political consistency (China-CEE Institute, 2022).

In spite of the political conflicts between China and the industrial countries under the leadership of the United States, the Chinese market is too attractive for many European companies to give up. To counteract on the potential pressure for decouple from the Chinese economy, foreign companies in China have commonly adopted the 'in China for China' strategy. For example, the German cleansing equipment manufacturer Kärcher, one of the global Fortune 500 companies, recently announced the plan to invest RMB 1 billion yuan (approximately 140 million EUR) in the coming years to expand their production capacity in China to develop more products for the local market (Financial Times, 2022).

More discussions on risk management strategies for business in China are presented in Chap. 16.

13.4 International Commercial Terms (Incoterms) 2020

When trading with international business partners, a series of questions of commercial importance must be considered, such as:

- Who is responsible for the arrangement of transport, the import and export clearance, etc.?
- Who should pay for which interval of transport of the ordered products?
- Who is liable for the loss and damage of goods during the transportation?

In order to help traders around the world, especially those with different business conventions and legal standards, to set up a common set of rules and guidelines to define their individual responsibilities and codify the contract terms in international trade, the International Chamber of Commerce (ICC) composed a series of pre-defined contract terms called the International Commercial Terms or Incoterms for the first time in 1936. Since then, the Incoterms rules have gone through several amendments. In practice, the Incoterms should be quoted with reference to the year of publication. The latest version is Incoterm 2020 (ICC, 2020).

The Incoterms use a series of abbreviations to describe specific rules for the sale of goods. Due to the wide acceptance of the Incoterms rules, they are frequently adopted voluntarily by business partners to specify the desired trade contract terms. The adoption of Incoterms is not confined to cross-border trading but can also be applied to domestic transactions. Understanding the Incoterms is rather helpful for the negotiation of commercial contracts with trading partners and service providers.

Incoterm 2020 which contains 11 rules is subdivided into 2 categories: I. rules for any transport mode and II. rules for transport by sea and inland waterway only (ICC, 2020).

Among rules for any transport mode, there are the following terms (IncotermsExplained, 2020):

- EXW = Ex Works. This term places the minimum obligation on the seller and the maximum obligation on the buyer. The seller is responsible for making the goods available with appropriate packaging at the seller's factory or warehouse. In contrast, the buyer is responsible for the collection of goods (including loading at the place of origin), all export procedures and the transport to the destination. The risk is transferred to the buyer when the products are handed over at the place of manufacture.
- FCA = Free Carrier. The seller is responsible for the delivery of goods to a carrier nominated by the buyer. In case the named place of delivery is under control of the seller, the seller is responsible for loading the goods to the carrier—this is a major difference to EXW. In other named places of delivery, for example, a transport hub or the forwarder's warehouse, the risk of loss and damage of goods passes to the buyer upon arrival at the agreed place of delivery. FCA is often chosen for containerised goods.
- CPT = Carriage Paid To. The seller bears the freight costs to the named place of destination, however not for the insurance of the goods in transit. The risk is transferred to the buyer upon hand-over to the first carrier in the country of export.
- CIP = Carriage and Insurance Paid To (named place of destination). In addition to the conditions of CPT, the seller is obliged to insure the goods in transit.
- DPU = Delivered at Place Unloaded. In the previous Incoterms 2010, this rule was referred to as Delivered At Terminal (DAT). The seller bears all transport costs including unloading from the carrier at the place of destination. The named place can be, for example, a transport hub or the buyer's warehouse. The risk passes to the buyer when the goods are unloaded at the destination port or terminal. The buyer is responsible for import clearance.

- DAP = Delivered At Place. The seller is responsible for making the goods available to the buyer at the place of destination (including appropriate packing for safe transport to the final destination) and clearance of export. The buyer is responsible for unloading at the named place—this is the main difference from DPU.
- DDP = Delivered Duty Paid. The seller arranges and pays for the delivery of goods at the named place of destination, import clearance and all relevant taxes and duties. The buyer is responsible for unloading of goods from the arriving carriage. The risk passes from the seller to the buyer when the goods are delivered to the name place of destination and ready for unloading.

The rules for transport by sea and inland waterway only are applied to bulk cargos such as oil, coal and non-containerised goods, whereas the exporter can load the goods directly onto the vessel for transport. Incoterms 2020 contains the following rules of this category:

- FAS = Free Alongside Ship. This rule only applies to goods transport by sea or inland waterway, usually for bulk cargos or non-containerised goods (e.g. oil and coal). The Incoterm FCA is usually used for containerised goods. Under the FAS rules, the seller is responsible for the delivery of goods to the vessel at the named port of shipment. The buyer takes over the risk and costs for loading the goods and the transport thereafter.
- FOB = Free On Board. The seller arranges and pays for the delivery to the named port of shipment including loading onto the vessel, as well as export clearance.
- CFR = Cost and Freight. The seller is responsible for the delivery to the named port of destination. However, the risk passes to the buy after the loading of goods on board the vessel in the country of export.
- CIF = Cost, Insurance and Freight. The seller is responsible for the delivery and insurance of the goods in transit to the named port of destination. The risk passes to the buy after the loading of goods on board the vessel in the country of export.

The Incoterms rules are primarily intended to describe the delivery of goods, but not the payment terms or place of jurisdiction. The obligation to take out transport insurance is not regulated by the majority of Incoterms rules, except for the terms CIF and CIP upon which the seller is required to obtain transport insurance for goods in transit.

Based on the logic of the rules, the above Incoterms may be put into four groups (see Fig. 13.7) (IncotermsExplained, 2020):

1. Buyer assumes responsibility for all carriage: EXW.
2. Buyer assumes responsibility for main carriage: FAS, FOB and FCA.
3. Seller assumes responsibility for main carriage; risk passes after main carriage: DPU, DAP and DDP.
4. Seller assumes responsibility for main carriage; risk passes before main carriage: CFR, CIF, CPT and CIP.

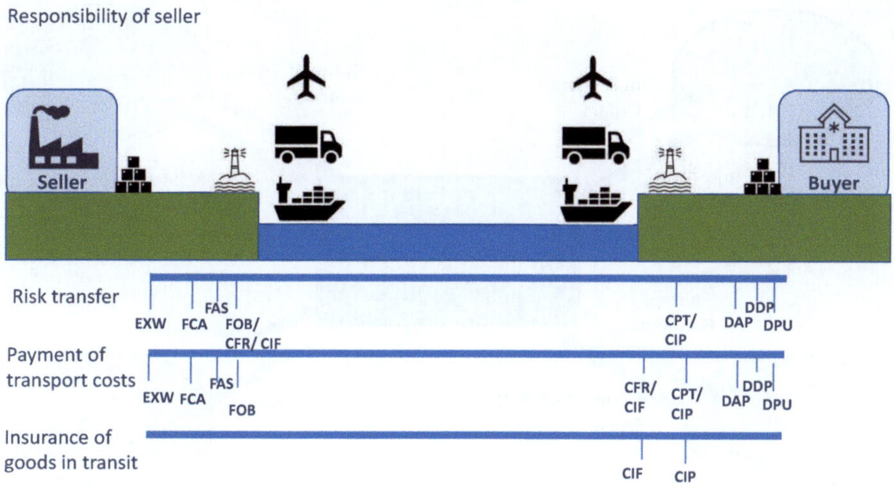

Fig. 13.7 Incoterms 2020: Seller's responsibilities. Source: According to (IncotermsExplained, 2020)

13.5 Case Study: SHEIN's Cross-Border Supply Chain

SHEIN is a Chinese cross-border fast fashion e-commerce retailer based in the Pearl River Region. Its fundamental business model is referred to as DTC (Direct to Consumer) by the company SHEIN itself and sometimes as SPA (Specialty retailer of Private label Apparel) by some fashion business advisers. This business model is characterised by the vertical integration of all supply chain processes from raw material procurement to delivery of products to customers, that is, to obtain maximal cost leadership by eliminating all possible 'middlemen' along the supply chain. The core element of the business model is the supply chain management, covering market analysis/anticipation, designing, manufacturing and sales. SHEIN's business performance is often compared with other successful fast fashion retailers such as Uniqlo in Japan and Zara in Spain.

Uniqlo starts the product design 1 year in advance. To obtain additional bargaining power, Uniqlo will reduce the product range, so as to limit the number of contract manufacturers and increase the order quantity at each supplier. Subsequently, the garment orders placed at the contract manufacturers will be adjusted according to the market reassessment based on the weekly sales reports. In general, the Uniqlo supply chain has a classic push-based design (see Fig. 13.3) (Sina, 2022).

Zara's supply chain combines the push- and pull-based strategies. On average, Zara offers approximately 11,000 items in its worldwide stores every year and renews the designs every 2–3 weeks. To speed up the internal design process, the company hires fashion agents to scout for new fashion trends at clubs, social gatherings and high-fashion stores. The central element of Zara's global supply

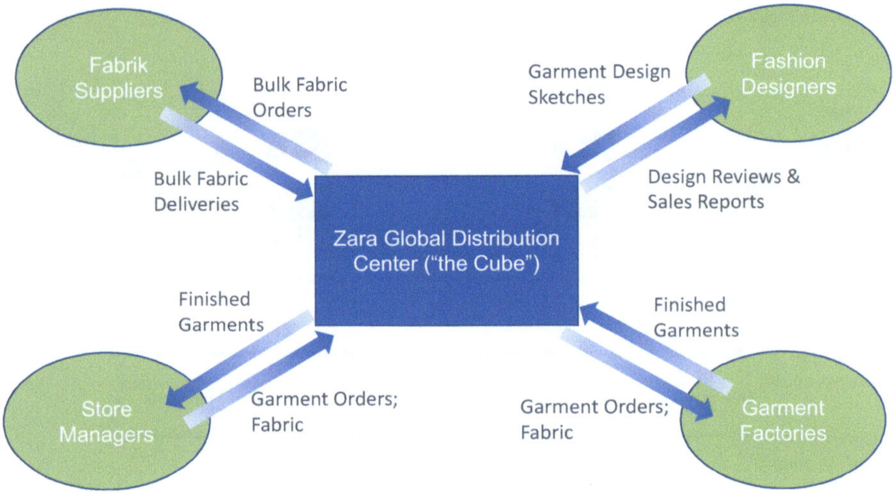

Fig. 13.8 Sketch of Zara Global Distribution Centre ('the Cube'). Source: Adapted from (SCM Globe, 2020) with modifications

chain is the Zara Global Distribution Centre ('the Cube'; see Fig. 13.8). While the basic products, such as T-shirts and sweaters, are outsourced to Asian contractors with cost advantages, other production orders for new designs in small batches are mainly sent to garment factories in Spain and Portugal nearby the Cube, so that a variety of new products can be quickly introduced to the market (average time to market is 4–6 weeks for new products and 2 weeks for modification to existing products). Customers are encouraged to visit the offline stores. Based on customer feedbacks, additional orders may be added to increase existing production quantity. To utilise the hunger marketing strategy, the sold-out product models are sometimes not reproduced. The products are priced according to market demand, not manufacturing costs (SCM Globe, 2020).

In 2022, SHEIN ranked No. 10 on Top 50 Chinese Global Brand Builders released by Kantar and Google (Kantar, 2022). The business covers more than 230 countries and regions in Europe, America, the Middle East and Southeast Asia. In order to be able to offer the impressive 2000–5000 new products on a daily basis, SHEIN cooperates with more than 1000 SME suppliers (among which approximately 300–400 are core suppliers), using a unique supply chain strategy called 'Small Order Quick Return', which has become well known in the garment industry (Sina, 2022).

Especially during the screening phase, SHEIN requires suppliers to accept small orders of 100–500 units. Although the low order volume causes higher manufacturing costs, SHEIN attracts the suppliers with favourable payment terms (from weekly to monthly, according to the supplier status), and more importantly, upon positive market feedbacks, new orders may be added to the small batch orders,

Table 13.1 SHEIN: types of supplier partnerships

Type of partnership	Cooperation partners	Requirements on supplier
FOB	Factories with sufficient production capacity	SHEIN provides designs and garment samples, stable order volume and fast payment for deliveries to orders Supplier responsible for material sourcing (at designated bulk fabric providers) and production
OEM	Factories with or without their own distribution channels	SHEIN provides designs, stable order volume and fast payment for deliveries to orders Supplier responsible for garment samples, material sourcing (at designated bulk fabric providers) and production
ODM	Factories, traders or factories with their own distribution channels that have the capacity for: • Independent product design. • Professional visualisation of products (photo shooting). • Reliable technical capacity and quality management.	SHEIN conducts product screening and guarantees fast payment for deliveries to orders Supplier responsible for product design, visualisation, processing and inventory
OBM	Suppliers with their own brands and trademarks: Traders and factories with their own distribution channels/supply chains	SHEIN guarantees fast payment for deliveries Supplier responsible for product design, screening, visualisation, processing and inventory
VMI	Suppliers for non-garment products	SHEIN guarantees fast payment for deliveries Supplier responsible for inventory

Information source: (SHEIN, 2023)

sometimes even before the previous orders have been fully processed, so that the effective order volume is much higher (Sina, 2022).

To maximise the supplier value, SHEIN offers all potential suppliers a variety of partnerships (see Table 13.1). Noticeably, SHEIN also cooperates with suppliers with their own brands in the OBM partnership model, for example, with Unifee, Jazzevar, Genanx, etc., which also own stores on the Chinese e-commerce platform Taobao (Sina, 2022).

SHEIN's comprehensive global supply chain is built on cutting-edge digitalisation technologies, covering the core systems such as user app, supply chain management system, AI-driven online shopping, internet-driven fashion trend analysis system, warehouse picking system, data mining, fabric management, garment visualisation and smart marketing. For example, SHEIN's fashion trend analysis tool operates based on special web crawlers that capture real-time fashion elements from new pixel materials. Subsequently, it takes another 2 weeks to start mass production after finalising the design. This is a significant advantage in the management of upstream supply chain over Uniqlo's prediction of fashion trends in 1 year's time or Zara time to market in 2 months. In addition, the inventory management system GMP (Give Me Products) with user-friendly WeChat interface enables SHEIN to notify its suppliers of all supply chain transactions in real time. GMP is the technical foundation for the 'Small Order Quick Return' supply chain management concept (Sina, 2022).

Unlike other fast fashion retailers such as Uniqlo and Zara, SHEIN restraints from offline stores to concentrate on the online sales platforms. Compared the multinational e-commerce platforms like Amazon, SHEIN also has downstream supply chain advantages.

At Amazon, cross-border merchants need to bear various logistic costs such as procurement, domestic transport, cross-border transport to target country, transport in target country to Amazon warehouse (Fulfilment By Amazon, FBA warehouse), delivery from FBA warehouse to consumers, commissions, promotional fees, etc. Moreover, they are challenged by series of questions, such as (Sina, 2022):

1. Which quantity of goods is to be initially shipped to the FBA warehouse (market prediction)?
2. Which transport means (sea freight, air freight, railway, etc.) is/are the most appropriate?
3. What to do if customers return the goods?

In cooperation with SHEIN, on the other hand, suppliers only need to bear two types of logistic costs: the manufacturing costs and the domestic transport from the factory to the SHEIN Central Warehouse. By centralising large-scale international goods deliveries of hundreds of suppliers, SHEIN gains power in negotiations for logistic costs, which in turn also benefits its business partners (economies of scale) (Sina, 2022).

The successful business model of SHEIN could be inspiration for entrepreneurs in other business settings.

References

China-CEE Institute. (2022, December). *China's status as the world's factory: Who is the real challenger?* By XU Qiyuan in China Watch Vol. 2, No. 43. Retrieved January 16, 2023, from https://china-cee.eu/2022/12/06/chinas-status-as-the-worlds-factory-who-is-the-real-challenger/

CIO. (2021, August 13). *What is SCOR? A model for improving supply chain management.* By Sarah K. White. Retrieved January 16, 2023, from https://www.cio.com/article/222381/what-is-scor-a-model-for-improving-supply-chain-management.html

Dathe, T., & Helmold, M. (2018). *Erfolgreich im Chinageschäft: Strategien und Handlungsempfehlungen für kleinere und mittlere Unternehmen (KMU).* Springer Gabler Verlag.

Financial Times. (2022, November 15). *Foreign companies adopt 'China for China' strategy*. By Thomas Hale and Wang Xueqiao. Retrieved January 10, 2023, from https://www.ft.com/content/e3d871cf-6ae7-4e64-8ab3-26c8f007df4a

Helmold, M., & Tracy, D. (2022, April 20). *Wettbewerbsvorteil: Kaizen im Einkauf*. By Procure.ch. Retrieved January 15, 2023, from https://www.procure.ch/magazin/artikel/wettbewerbsvorteil-kaizen-im-einkauf/

Helmold, M., Yılmaz, A. K., Dathe, T., & Flouris, T. G. (2022). *Supply chain risk management - cases and industry insights*. Springer.

ICC. (2020). *Incoterms® 2020*. By the International Chamber of Commerce (ICC). Retrieved January 15, 2023, from https://iccwbo.org/resources-for-business/incoterms-rules/incoterms-2020/

IMF. (2022, October). *World Economic Outlook Report October 2022: Countering the cost-of-living crisis*. By International Monetary Fund (IMF). Retrieved January 15, 2023, from https://www.imf.org/en/Publications/WEO/Issues/2022/10/11/world-economic-outlook-october-2022

IncotermsExplained. (2020). *Incoterms 2020 versus Incoterms 2010*. Retrieved January 11, 2023, from IncotermsExplained.com: https://www.incotermsexplained.com/the-incoterms-rules/the-eleven-rules-in-brief/delivered-duty-paid/

Kantar. (2022). *Kantar and Google's Top 50 Chinese Global Brand Builders Report 2022*. Retrieved January 16, 2023, from https://www.kantar.com/en-cn/inspiration/brands/2022-kantar-and-google-top-50-chinese-global-brand-builders

Laudon, K., & Laudon, J. (2021). *Management information systems: Managing the digital firm* (Global Edition). Pearson.

SHEIN. (2023). *SHEIN Recruitment Portal*. Retrieved January 16, 2023, from https://zhaoshang.sheincorp.cn/help/doc?id=1407584302067691522

SCM Globe. (2020, January 4). *Zara Clothing Company Supply Chain*. Retrieved January 16, 2023, from https://www.scmglobe.com/zara-clothing-company-supply-chain/

Sina. (2022, June 30). 复刻SHEIN, 中国跨境供应链大突围 by finance.Sina.com, https://finance.sina.com.cn/tech/2022-06-30/doc-imizirav1308503.shtml

Sinha, D., Bagodi, V., & Dey, D. (2020). The supply chain disruption framework post COVID-19: a system dynamics model. *Foreign Trade Review, 55*(4), 511–534. https://doi.org/10.1177/0015732520947904

Service Industry in China 14

14.1 Industry Sectors

In economics, a nation's economy is generally divided into primary, secondary and tertiary sectors (or industry sectors). The National Bureau of Statistics of China divides the national economy into the following three sectors (National Bureau of Statistics of China, 2022a, b, c):

- *Primary sector* includes agriculture, forestry, animal husbandry and fishing (excluding services for agriculture, forestry, animal husbandry and fishing).
- *Secondary sector* includes mining industry (excluding mining auxiliary activities); manufacturing industry (excluding metal products, machinery and equipment repairing industry); electricity, heat, gas and water production and supply industry; and construction industry.
- *Tertiary sector* or the service industry creates value by providing services or intangible goods. According to the classification of the National Bureau of Statistics of China, the service industry includes:
  - Wholesale and retail, transportation.
  - Transportation, warehousing and postal services.
  - Accommodation and catering (hotels and restaurants).
  - Information transmission, software and information technology services.
  - Finance (including banking, financing, insurance, etc.)
  - Real estate.
  - Leasing and business services.
  - Scientific research and technical services.
  - Water conservancy, environment and public facilities management.
  - Living services (including household help, nursery, laundry service, hairdressing, event organisation, photography, etc.), repairs and maintenance and other services (including pet services, security, cleaning, moving service, etc.) (Government of China, 2019).
  - Education.

T. Dathe et al., *Business Opportunities and Risks in China*, Management for Professionals, https://doi.org/10.1007/978-3-031-31933-4_14

- Health and social work.
- Culture, sports and entertainment.
- Public management, social security and social organisations.
- International organisations.

The classification of economic sectors by the National Bureau of Statistics of China is slightly different from that of some European countries. For example, according to the online encyclopaedia Britannica, animal husbandry is a branch of agriculture, and mining, quarrying and the extraction of minerals are branches of primary industry. Besides, Britannica also specifies a quaternary sector as an extension of tertiary sector that includes suppliers of information- or knowledge-based products and services (Britannica, 2022).

14.2 Trends in China's Service Sector

Over the past two decades, China's service sector has grown faster than the primary and the secondary sectors. Since the economic reform, the national economic structure has evolved from '2–1–3' (i.e. 'the secondary sector is the leading industry sector, followed by the primary sector, and the tertiary sector is the least developed sector') to '2–3–1' and then, in recent years, moved towards '3–2–1' (National Development and Reform Commissions of China, 2021). At present, the service sector contributes more than the half of China's GDP, and the proportion of the service sector in the national economy is expected to further increase in the future (see Fig. 14.1).

One reason for the fast growth of the service sector is the overall improved living standard and the growing middle class in China. China's share of global wealth middle-class population increased from 29% in year 2000 to 40% in year 2020 (Statista, 2023). The continuous urbanisation and the improved disposable income of the residents have permanently changed the lifestyles of the residents and increased the market demand for service industries, such as retail, catering, real estate, education, culture and sports and healthcare, and in turn the supporting services such as finance, logistics, information technology, etc. The latest development brings huge opportunities for service suppliers (National Development and Reform Commissions of China, 2021).

In 2021, China was the second largest luxury retail market worldwide (Statista, 2022). According to a recent analysis by Bain & Company and Altagamma, China will be home of 40% of worldwide consumers of luxury goods by 2030, including watches, jewellery, fashion products, cosmetics, leather products, eyewear, etc. According to the researcher Claudia D'Arpizio, China would be the most important market for Western brands of luxury goods. 'An over-dependence on China is risky, but not as risky as not being there at all' (The New York Times, 2022).

Some new trends can be observed on the Chinese luxury retail market (Vox-China, 2022; Statista, 2022):

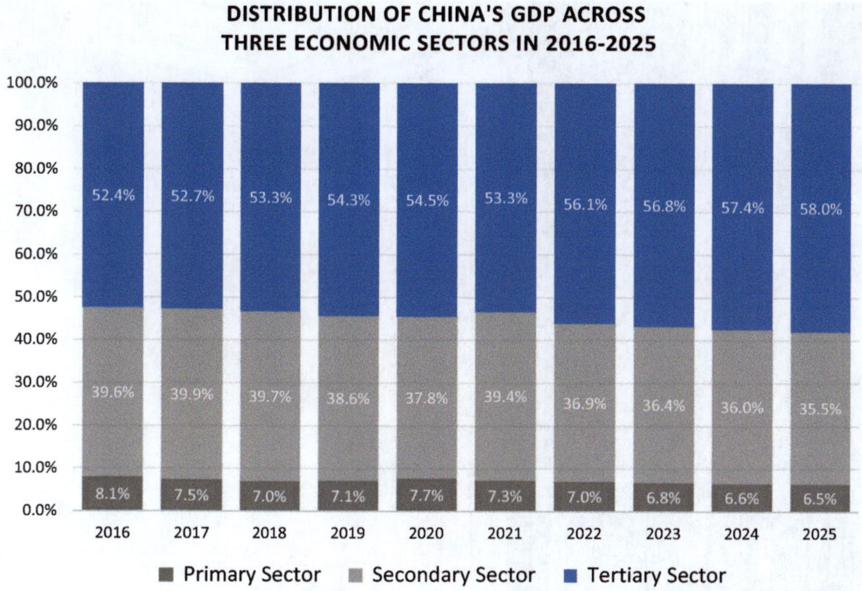

Fig. 14.1 Distribution of China's GDP across economic sectors from 2016 to 2025. Source: (National Bureau of Statistics of China, 2022a, b, c) (National Development and Reform Commission of China, 2021) (*The data of 2016–2021 are based on the statistics from the National Bureau of Statistics of China, **The data of 2022–2025 derive from the forecast by the National Development and Reform Commission of China)

- Chinese consumers have turned to e-commerce due to the long-term containment of the Covid-19 outbreak. In 2020, Chinese consumers' purchase through internet sales portals accounted for 23% of total sales revenue of luxury goods, whereas the share of e-commerce sales in 2019 was 13%. This trend is expected to continue after the pandemic period ends.
- The purchase decisions of Chinese consumers are widely influence by livestream sessions.
- Chinese consumers buy increasingly from domestic locations, for example, from the Hainan offshore duty-free zone. The domestic duty-free zones will probably remain competitive after the Covid-19 travel restrictions are lifted.
- Chinese national brands for luxury goods are on the rise. Chinese consumers believe that the local brands have a better understanding of the Chinese consumers and offer a better after-sales service (e.g. Chinese-style wedding dresses like shown in Fig. 14.2 are becoming increasingly popular in the recent years, rather than the Western-style white wedding dresses that were introduced to China since the early days of the economic reform).

Worldwide, tourism is among the business sectors most affected by the unprecedented Covid-19 pandemic. Due to the travel restrictions, the domestic tourism was hit hard, and the remaining passenger flow was mainly confined to local regions (see

Fig. 14.2 A bridalwear shop in the southern Chinese city Suzhou. Source: author

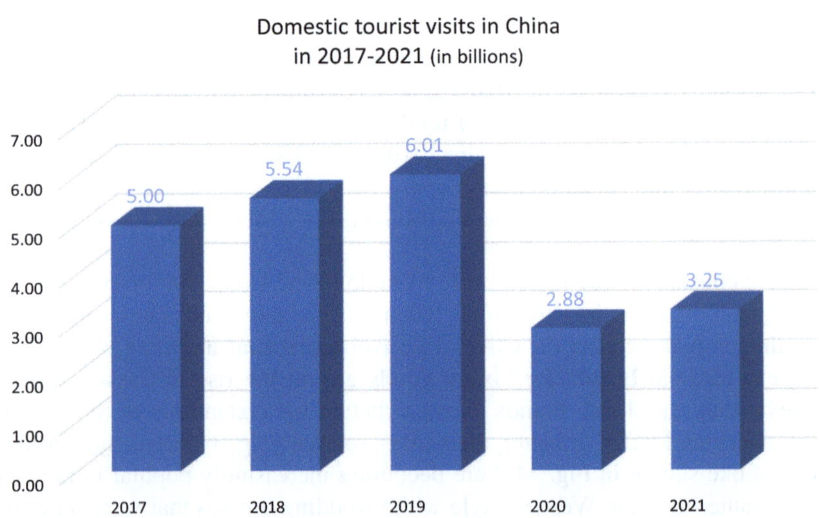

Fig. 14.3 Domestic tourist visits in China from 2017 to 2021. Source: (National Bureau of Statistics of China, 2022a, b, c)

Fig. 14.3). In 2022 and 2023, 81% of all tourists travelled within their own province, and 81% of the inter-provincial tourist destinations were in the neighbouring provinces (China Tourism Academy, 2022).

In particular, outbound tourism suffered huge losses. Before the pandemic, China had the world's highest number of international travellers. In 2019, 155 million Chinese tourists spend about US$250 billion during their trips abroad (CNN, 2023). Overall, the cumulative number of outbound tourist visits has dropped by more than 400 million in the following 3 years (China Tourism Academy, 2022).

After the Chinese government announced the reopening of the border to international travellers and the lifting of quarantine rules starting on 8 January 2023, Chinese tourist bookings for outbound travels during the Chinese New Year jumped by 540% compared with 2022. The top destinations are in the Asia-Pacific region, including Australia, Thailand, Japan, Vietnam, Singapore, Hong Kong, etc. The influx of Chinese tourists is expected to significantly boost the economic growth of the above countries and regions (CNN, 2023).

The full recovery of the outbound tourism will still take some time. Most Chinese tourists are fighting to find the balance of safety concerns, attractiveness of the travel destinations, travel convenience, travelling costs as well as the trade-offs between long-distance and short-distance travels. According to a recent survey study by China Tourism Academy (Data Centre of the Ministry of Culture and Tourism of China), more tourists are interested in long-distance travels to Europe and the United States than before the pandemic (China Tourism Academy, 2022).

At the end of 2022, the Chinese population was 1.4 billion, a decrease of 850,000 from the previous year for the first time in decades. The birth rate in 2022 was 6.77‰, and the death rate was 7.37‰, so the net population growth rate decreased by 0.60 per thousand. The declining birth rate was mainly caused by the decreasing number of women of childbearing age and the change in lifestyle (later marriage, lower willingness to have children, etc.) (National Bureau of Statistics of China, 2023). On the other hand, the average life expectancy of Chinese residents continuously increases. The average life expectancy was 78.2 years in 2021 and is expected to exceed 80 years till 2035 (Xinhua News Agency, 2022).

The aging problem of the Chinese society continues to intensify with the ongoing declining birth rate and increasing life expectancy. By the end of 2022, the working-age population aged 16 to 59 was 875.6 million, accounting for 62.0% of the total population, and the population aged 60 and above was 280.0 million, accounting for 19.8% of the total population (see Fig. 14.4). Due to the demographic development, the Chinese government has shifted the focus of the national strategy to upgrading of the domestic economic structure and the sustainable improvement of production efficiency (National Bureau of Statistics of China, 2023).

In the recent years, the Chinese government has successively introduced new policies to boost the birth rate, including moving away from the one-child policy, however with moderate effect. At the rate of the current low birth rate, the age group of 65 and above would exceed the total working-age population around 2080 (BBC, 2022).

In addition, there is an enormous demand for medical and health services. By the end of 2021, there were more than one million medical and health institutions nationwide, with 11.23 million technicians in medical and health service sectors, including 4.27 million licensed physicians and licensed assistant physicians, and

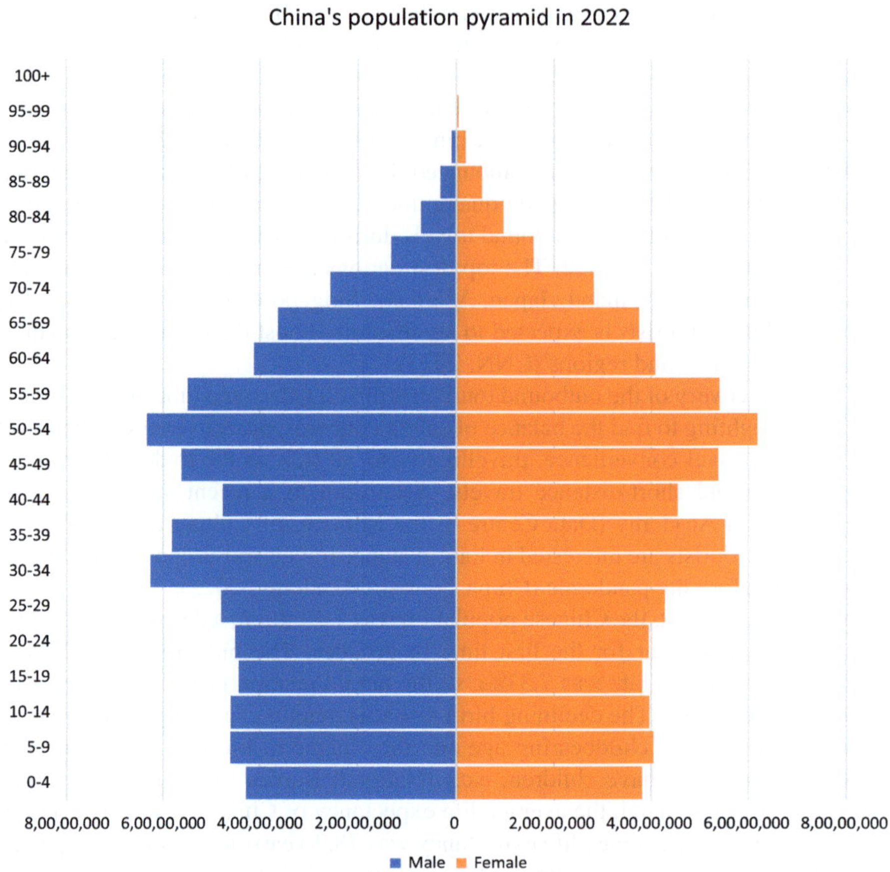

Fig. 14.4 China's population pyramid in 2022. Data source: (PopulationPyramid.net, 2022)

5.02 million registered nurses (see Fig. 14.5) and 9.57 million beds. A total number of 8.53 billion diagnosis and treatments were offered during the year 2021. Altogether, the health expenditure accounted for 6.5% of China's GDP, while 27.4% of the amount comes from government funding, 44.9% from social insurance and 27.7% from private expenses. The average medical expenditure per capita in 2021 was 5348 RMB yuan (National Bureau of Statistics of China, 2022a, b, c).

Due to the growing geopolitical tension and international trade barriers, China has shifted its strategic focus towards the domestic economy. With the declining labour supply caused by an ageing population and overall improvement of living standards, the service sector with high added value could compensate the slowdown of agriculture and manufacturing industry (VoxChina, 2022).

The service sector suffered a severe setback during the Covid-19 epidemic. However, the changed environment also brings opportunities for new business models and service formats, such as online shopping, online entertainment, movie-

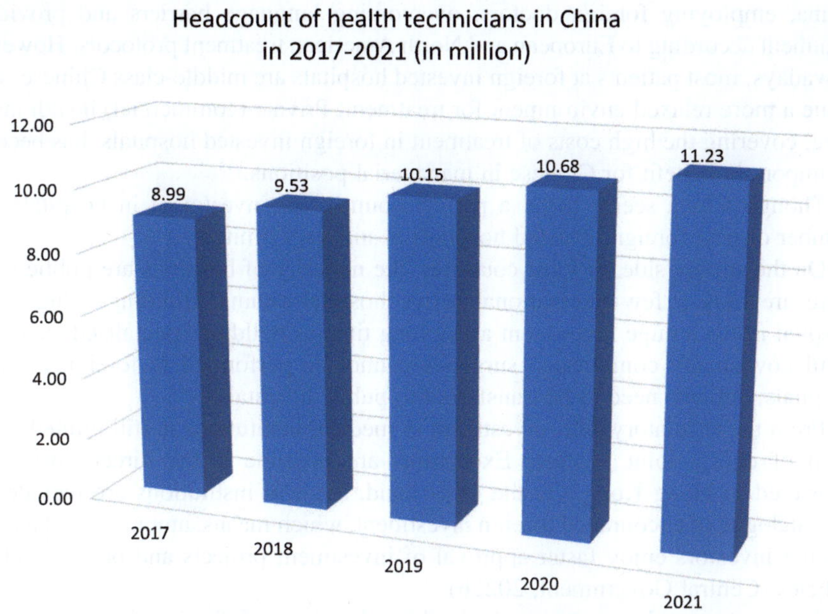

Fig. 14.5 Headcount of technicians in China's medical and health service sector from 2017 to 2021. Source: (National Bureau of Statistics of China, 2022a, b, c)

streaming, online games, online education, online medical care and online and offline fitness and healthcare services. Those ongoing trends also increase the demand on telecommunication and logistic services (National Development and Reform Commissions of China, 2021).

14.3 Case Study: Healthcare and Senior Citizen Care

In a country with 1.4 billion inhabitants and a rapidly ageing population, healthcare including homecare and retirement homes are a huge market for service providers. Despite very sophisticated services in the most developed economies, so far there is very limited engagement of international private service providers in China.

In late 2021, China had 36,570 hospitals, thereof about one third public ones; however, the public hospitals offer more than 70% of the hospital beds (Central Government, 2022a). Private hospitals focus on outpatient treatment and treatment of less severe diseases. In 2018, there were only 110 foreign invested hospitals in China (Wenku, 2019). Private Chinese hospitals serve the low-end market, public hospitals the medium- and high-end market, and foreign invested hospitals a very small top-end market.

Though nowadays many public hospitals are very well equipped, they are often overcrowded, leaving doctors little time to care for patients. When in 2000 China allowed foreign investment in hospitals, they mainly served foreigners living in

China, employing foreign doctors, overcoming language barriers and providing treatment according to European and North American treatment protocols. However, nowadays, most patients at foreign invested hospitals are middle-class Chinese, who value a more relaxed environment for treatment. Private (commercial) health insurance, covering the high costs of treatment in foreign invested hospitals, has become an important benefit for Chinese in managerial positions.

Though China seems to be a perfect country for investment in hospitals, the number of new foreign invested hospitals is still very limited.

On the supply side, in most countries, the majority of hospitals are public ones; there are only a few international active hospital chains. Building a high-class hospital needs a huge investment and a long time to build up specialised expertise. Until now, many complicated surgeries cannot be performed in foreign invested hospitals; patients need to be transferred to public hospitals.

From the regulatory side, investment in medical institutions is still limited to the form of equity joint venture. Exceptions are possible if the direct investor is registered in Hong Kong. On the other hand, medical institutions are included in the catalogue of encouraged foreign investment, which means, among other benefits, foreign investors enjoy faster approval of investment projects and preferential tax policies (Central Government, 2022b).

A recent notable exception from the reluctance of foreign investors is the Singapore-based Raffles Group. Since the opening of its first hospital in Chongqing in early 2019, it has founded hospitals in Shanghai, Beijing and Hainan (Raffles, 2022).

Compared with complete hospitals, international investors are much more active in specialised clinics, especially dentists and ophthalmologist clinics. This follows a general trend in China; these departments are dominated by private healthcare providers. For example, the Arrail Group with Goldman Sachs as a shareholder operates 50 dental clinics in 15 cities (Arrail, 2021). Another tendency: Chinese dentists who worked or studied in developed economies found their own clinic when they return to China, registering their clinic as a foreign invested medical institution.

China is one of the fastest ageing countries of the world. In 2020, the number of senior citizens 60 years old and above reached 264 million, 18.7% of the population. It is estimated that in 2033 the number of senior citizens will reach 400 million and peak in 2053 at about 487 million people, about 34% of the population (CN Healthcare, 2020). Above 90% of the senior citizens live with their families. According to Chinese tradition, it is the family's responsibility to care for their parents; only a small, but growing, number of senior citizens are living in retirement homes. Public and private support for senior citizens is a relatively new, but rapidly developing, phenomenon. In Beijing, the first public elderly care community centre opened in 2017. Now, the capital city has over 1000 such centres in residential areas. These centres provide support in daily life and basic health check-ups.

In addition, private nursing homes offer short time stays in case health of senior citizens deteriorates for a limited period. Companies offer nurse visits and let them perform basic medical care at home; there are special online platforms to book such services (CGTN, 2021) (Xinhua, 2021).

Senior citizen care is a rapidly developing market; state regulations need to catch up. For example, quality standards for homecare must be defined; it must be decided which kind of medical services can be provided at home. One shortcoming is a lack of communication between medical institutions and homecare services. As a result, patients need to stay longer in hospitals to ensure that discharge from hospitals is safe. In the first 4 months of 2022, in China, the average length of stay in hospitals was 8.8 days (CN Healthcare, 2022), for example, 1.6 days (22%) longer than in Germany.

Most Chinese, including its senior citizens, are technology- and internet-savvy. On the market, there are many affordable homecare medical devices that monitor physiological signals of the body, possibly sending an alarm if the user's health deteriorates. However, currently, most homecare service providers are not ready to provide adequate response in case homecare monitoring devices send an alarm.

The Chinese government is aware of the importance of senior citizen homecare. Public healthcare insurance shall include medical homecare in its reimbursement catalogue. In late 2022, 49 cities with 145 million inhabitants participated in trials to add long-term care insurance as a new element of public social security, similar to the system in Germany. For example, in Shanghai, residents over the age of 60 who cannot care for themselves can benefit from the long-term care insurance. The new insurance is financed by a mix of employer's contributions and funding by the city government (Shanghai Government, 2021).

Senior citizen care is included in the catalogue of encouraged foreign investment. In the current situation of rapid growth and lack of quality standards, international providers bringing their best practices into the Chinese market are very welcome; however, so far, there are hardly any international service providers present on the Chinese market.

There are quite obvious reasons for that (China Briefing, 2018):

- In developed economies, most homecare providers serve a local community; they are not ready to explore international markets, especially not the distant Chinese market.
- Homecare is a direct person-to-person service. If an international company wants to offer their service in China, it must train local nurses and constantly monitor the quality of service.
- Homecare is strongly influenced by culture, for example, senior citizens in China will expect access to traditional Chinese medicine. Best practices from Western countries cannot simply be transferred one to one to China but must be adapted to local conditions.

Despite these challenges, senior citizen care in China is a basically untapped market, providing ample opportunities for international companies. One possible approach: as there is a severe shortage of nurses in many developed countries, it is feasible to employ Chinese nurses near the company's headquarters, let them learn the language and best nursing practices and then employ them to work for the company's Chinese subsidiary, when they return to China.

References

Arrail. (2021). *Group Introduction*. Retrieved January 3, 2023, from http://www.arrailgroup.com/en/about/brand.html

BBC. (2022, June 20). 中国人口会"越来越少":原因和影响. By Peng Xiujian. Retrieved January 31, 2023, from https://www.bbc.com/zhongwen/simp/chinese-news-61828528

Britannica. (2022, October 21). *Economics & Economic Systems: Industry*. By Britannica. Retrieved January 31, 2023, from https://www.britannica.com/technology/industry

Central Government. (2022a). *Statistical Report about the Development of the Healthcare Industry 2021* (in Chinese). Retrieved January 3, 2023, from http://www.gov.cn/xinwen/2022-07/12/content_5700670.htm

Central Government. (2022b). *NDRC and MOFCOM: Catalogue of Encouraged Foreign Investments (2022) (In Chinese)*. Retrieved January 3, 2023, from http://www.gov.cn/zhengce/zhengceku/2022-10/28/content_5722417.htm

CGTN. (2021). *China's stay-at-home seniors accessing elderly care*. Retrieved January 3, 2023, from https://news.cgtn.com/news/2021-05-18/China-s-stay-at-home-seniors-accessing-elderly-care-10mUfZtsAzC/index.html

China Briefing. (2018). *The Senior Care Sector in China: Is it Time to Think Differently?* Retrieved January 4, 2023, from https://www.china-briefing.com/news/the-senior-care-sector-in-china-is-it-time-to-think-differently/

China Tourism Academy. (2022, December 11). 我院发布系列研究成果总结展望2022-2023旅游业. By China Tourism Academy (Data Center of the Ministry of Culture and Tourism). Retrieved 31.01.2022, from http://www.ctaweb.org.cn/cta/gzdt/202212/2dd38dd0d423424ca368e4be1ef0b992.shtml

CN Healthcare. (2020). *In 2050 it will reach 34%!The aging of the population in China is double as fast as in the World Average* (in Chinese). Retrieved January 3, 2023, from https://www.cn-healthcare.com/article/20201016/content-544189.html

CN Healthcare. (2022). *Announcement of the Situation of Medical Services January – April 2022!* The average cost of public hospitals has decreased. Retrieved January 3, 2023, from https://www.cn-healthcare.com/articlewm/20220824/content-1423520.html

CNN. (2023, January 19). *What the return of Chinese tourists means for the global economy*. By Laura He, Juliana Liu and Cheng Cheng. Retrieved January 3, 2023, from https://edition.cnn.com/2023/01/06/economy/china-tourist-boom-post-covid-impact-intl-hnk/index.html

Government of China. (2019). 统计局关于印发《生活性服务业统计分类(2019)》的通知. By the State Council of the People's Republic of China. Retrieved January 3, 2023, from http://www.gov.cn/gongbao/content/2019/content_5425338.htm

National Bureau of Statistics of China. (2022a). *Gross Domestic Product*. Retrieved January 31, 2023, from https://data.stats.gov.cn/easyquery.htm?cn=C01

National Bureau of Statistics of China. (2022b, February 28). *National data*. Retrieved January 20, 2023, from https://data.stats.gov.cn/easyquery.htm?cn=C01

National Bureau of Statistics of China. (2022c, November 18). 三次产业划分规定. By 国家统计局设管司. Retrieved January 30, 2023, from http://www.stats.gov.cn/tjsj/tjbz/201301/t20130114_8675.html

National Bureau of Statistics of China. (2023, January 18). 王萍萍:人口总量略有下降 城镇化水平继续提高. Retrieved January 30, 2023, from http://www.stats.gov.cn/tjsj/sjjd/202301/t20230118_1892192.html

National Development and Reform Commission of China. (2021, October 12). "十四五"时期我国产业结构变动特征及趋势展望. Retrieved January 30, 2023, from https://www.ndrc.gov.cn/wsdwhfz/202110/t20211012_1299485.html

PopulationPyramid.net. (2022). *Population Pyramids of the World from 1950 to 2100: China*. Retrieved January 30, 2023, from https://www.populationpyramid.net/china/2022/

Raffles. (2022). About us. Retrieved January 3, 2023, from https://www.rafflesmedicalchina.com/en/about-us?

Shanghai Government. (2021). *Notification of the Shanghai City Government on Promulgation of the "Trial Regulation of Long-term Care Insurance in Shanghai" (in Chinese).* Retrieved January 03, 2023, from https://www.shanghai.gov.cn/202202bgtwj/20220120/d679bd209c7248aca27227023e46edc3.html

Statista. (2022, April 19). *Luxury goods market in China - statistics & facts.* By Yihan Ma. Retrieved January 30, 2023, from https://www.statista.com/topics/1186/luxury-goods-market-in-china/#topicOverview

Statista. (2023). *Share of the global wealth middle class population in China in 2000 and 2020. By C. Textor.* Retrieved January 30, 2023, from https://www.statista.com/statistics/918468/china-share-of-global-wealth-middle-class/

The New York Times. (2022, December 7). *In China, luxury shopping faces ongoing headwinds. By Elizabeth Paton.* Retrieved January 30, 2023, from https://www.nytimes.com/2022/12/07/business/dealbook/covid-china-luxury-shopping.html

VoxChina. (2022, October 12). *Is China becoming a service economy? By Xilu Chen; Guangyu Pei; Zheng Song; Fabrizio Zilibotti.* Retrieved January 30, 2023, from https://www.voxchina.org/show-3-292.html

Xinhua. (2021). *Xi Focus: China develops community-based home care services for elderly.* Retrieved January 3, 2023, from http://www.news.cn/english/2021-08/26/c_1310150921.htm

Xinhua News Agency. (2022, July 12). 国家卫健委发布统计公报 我国居民人均预期寿命提高到78.2岁. Retrieved January 31, 2023, from http://www.xhby.net/index/202207/t20220712_7613832.shtml

Wenku. (2019). *The development of foreign invested medical institutions is winding and slow* (in Chinese). Retrieved January 3, 2023, from https://wenku.baidu.com/view/b5783f512a4ac850ad02de80d4d8d15abf2300fe.html

Sustainability Management 15

15.1 Corporate Social Responsibility (CSR)

The American economist Howard R. Bowen mentioned the term corporate social responsibility (CSR) in his book *Social Responsibilities of the Businessman* in 1953, demanding a greater contribution to the civil society by the large corporations in the United States, on the grounds of their significant economic power and the major influence of their business endeavours on lives of the ordinary people (Bowen, 1953). Since then, the concept of corporate social responsibility evolved continuously alongside the social movements in the following decades, especially the civil rights movement, the consumer movement, the environmental movement and the women's movements (Carroll, 2016). Today, public opinion about the social performance of companies in many business sectors has become a critical aspect of their social license (McKinsey, 2022).

Although there is no universally accepted definition for the term corporate social responsibility (CSR), the four-step pyramid model developed by A. Carroll in 1979 is commonly used as the fundamental framework for academic research and business strategy for ethical management. In this model, Carroll describes the social responsibility of companies in four hierarchical levels (see Fig. 15.1):

1. *Economic responsibilities*. The society demands that the companies stay profitable. Only economically successful businesses can serve society by providing useful products and services to the market, creating jobs and paying taxes to fund government social activities. Economic responsibility forms the basis for corporate social responsibility.
2. *Legal responsibilities*. The business organisations, like all other members of the society, are subject to the laws and official regulations. The society demands that companies only use legal means to achieve their economic success.
3. *Ethical responsibilities*. The society expects furthermore that the companies meet ethical standards beyond legal standards, for example, by implementing

T. Dathe et al., *Business Opportunities and Risks in China*, Management for Professionals, https://doi.org/10.1007/978-3-031-31933-4_15

Fig. 15.1 Carroll's CSR pyramid. Source: (Dathe et al., 2022)

environment-friendly technologies in the production process or providing ergonomic working conditions and fair pay to their employees.

4. *Philanthropic responsibilities*. Philanthropic responsibility is a voluntary contribution that represents the highest level of corporate social responsibility. The popular form of this type of social contribution is influenced by the regional cultures, for example, funding social projects in the local community in North American cultures or making large donations for natural disaster victims in the Chinese culture.

Carroll's CSR pyramid model has the benefit of a simple structure which facilitates the communication of ethical management concepts. However, the demarcation of the different CSR categories is not ways easy. In addition, possible conflicts of interest need to be addressed in business practice, for example, the relocation of domestic production sites in low-wage countries benefits the host countries with job creation, new sources of tax revenues, etc., while the original home countries would suffer from a rising unemployment rate and the deteriorating social division (Dathe et al., 2022).

15.2 Corporate Sustainability

Sustainability has long become an integral aspect of corporate ethical management. A prominent definition for the term sustainability comes from the Brundtland report of the World Commission on Environment and Development (WCED) 'Our Common Future' as a 'strategy of social development that meets the needs of the present

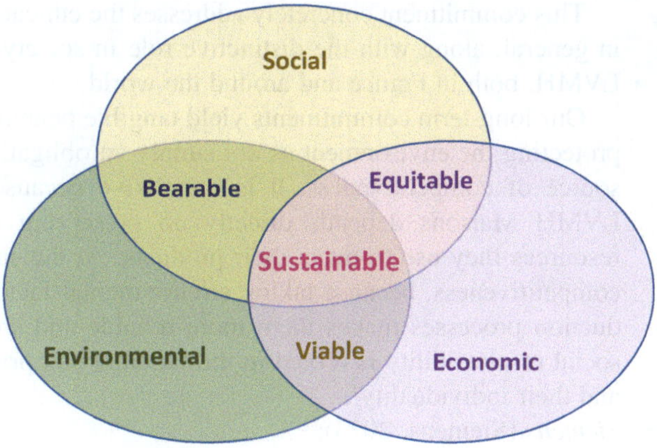

Fig. 15.2 Three-dimensional model of sustainability. Source: According to (Elkington, 1998)

without compromising the ability of future generations to meet their own needs' (United Nations, 1987).

Till this date, the environmental sustainability remains a major aspect of the sustainability concept. Prominent climate activists like Greta Thunberg use their popularity to call for acceleration of environment protection (especially carbon neutrality) and take influence on politics across the world.

Today, most large corporations coordinate their CSR strategy by addressing the three aspects of sustainability according to the three-pillar model ('triple bottom line') coined by Elkington (see Fig. 15.2). The above model depicts the optimal sustainability approach as a healthy balance between environmental, economic and social goals (Elkington, 1998).

Below are some examples of the headlines of the corporate sustainability statement that communicate the current sustainability understanding in business practice:

- *Volkswagen* (Volkswagen, 2023):
  'For Volkswagen, sustainability means pursuing economic, social, and ecological objectives simultaneously and with equal energy. It is our aim to create lasting values, offer good working conditions, and conserve resources and the environment.

  With our sustainability concept we want to ensure that opportunities and risks associated with our environmental, social and governance activities are identified as early as possible at every stage of the value creation process. In keeping with this aim, we are determined that our corporate social responsibility (CSR) activities will have a lasting, positive impact on the Company's value and reputation'.
- LVMH (LVMH, 2023):
  'SOCIAL & ENVIRONMENTAL RESPONSIBILITY—LVMH has made sustainable development a strategic priority since its founding.

This commitment concretely addresses the ethical responsibility of businesses in general, along with the distinctive role in society played by a group such as LVMH, both in France and around the world.

Our long-term commitments yield tangible benefits for society. LVMH views protecting the environment as not simply an obligation, but an imperative and a source of competitiveness. It is imperative because the long-term success of LVMH Maisons depends directly on preserving and respecting the natural resources they use to make their products. At the same time, this policy drives competitiveness, because taking environmental factors into account in our production processes makes them more reliable and sharpens our leadership. Our social responsibility is rooted in the fundamental principle of respect for people and their individuality'.

- *Siemens* (Siemens, 2023):
  'The Journey to a Sustainability Lighthouse awarded by the World Economic Forum.

  The Siemens Electronics Works in Amberg, Germany, has been awarded as Sustainability Lighthouse by the World Economic Forum. It is considered a pioneer for the future of sustainable manufacturing and an incubator for innovations that accelerate decarbonization'.

15.3 SDG and ESG

Politics provides the framework for society and the economy as a whole. In 2015, the United Nations General Assembly (UNGA) formally formulated the strategic targets for the global development from 2015 to 2030 in the 2030 Agenda for Sustainable Development as 17 Sustainable Development Goals (SDGs) (United Nations, 2015) (see Fig. 15.3). Since then, the SDGs have become the guidelines for sustainable development on the highest platform of world politics. In turn, they are often used to guide the development of CSR strategy and the measurement of progress in business practice.

The main focus of the Sustainable Development Goals (SDGs) by the United Nations is to lead the lower-income nations to higher economic, social and ecological standards in the long term. However, the SDG framework is sometimes criticised for its structural weaknesses such as:

- Too many unstructured goals (the positive correlations between the ecological, societal and economic goals are ignored).
- Not attending to trade-offs between the competing goals (e.g. improvement of climate goals consumes resources that can no more be spent on social goals such as good health and well-being).
- The specific goals are not ambitious enough, especially for the countries with strong economic power.

Fig. 15.3 The Sustainable Development Goals (SDGs) by the United Nations. Source: (UNSTATS, 2022)

In the age of digitalisation, the risk of a company's breach of ethical standards poses a major risk for investors. To deal with such public image risks, rating agencies (e.g. MSCI, FTSE4Good, IMUG, Inrate, Oekom Research, Sustainalytics, etc.) offer ESG (environmental, social and governance) rating service to evaluate the CSR performance of companies in various industry sectors and regions. The ESG approach creates a new dimension of business valuation in addition to the classic methods based on economic criteria.

The ESG ratings are manifest of corporate social responsibility (CSR) performance that directly connect the corporate social performance with its financial performance, integrating the following aspects in the concept of responsible investment (RI) (Dathe et al., 2022):

1. *Environment (E)*. The ecological performance can be measured by emissions, share of renewable energy, etc. in business operations. A company is considered particularly sustainable if, for example, the main product uses environment-friendly technologies (e.g. electronic vehicles).
2. *Social (S)*. The social performance can be reported in terms of diversity and inclusion measures, production safety and workplace design, as well as human rights issues such as prohibition of child labour.

3. *Governance (G)*. The term governance stands for the processes intended to ensure compliance with the internal ethically sustainable standards.

The ESG ratings directly impact the behaviour of a plethora of stakeholder groups (Dathe et al., 2022):

- *Investors* use ESG key performance indicators (KPIs) and key quality indicators (KQIs) to measure opportunities, risks and trends of the ESG strategy and performance of the companies of interest. Such information plays an important role in their investment decisions. The ESG performance information needs to be calibrated by industrial sector and region. A customised ESG assessment framework as a working model is sometimes provided by professional brokers and asset managers, mainly based on benchmarks with well-positioned companies in the relevant business branch as ESG role models in terms of their overall environmental and social performance.
- *Large financial institutions* like Goldman Sachs and JPMorgan Chase are committed to the development of generally accepted standards that are suitable for the assessment and control of ESG performance in both business practice and academic research, so as to facilitate the analysis of opportunities and risks to support investment decisions. As a result, ESG is integrated in the corporate culture, while members of the senior management teams increasingly drive forward their own ESG leadership skills and build up ESG knowledge base within the institutions.
- *Pension funds and pension trusts*, in commitment to its clients and customers in the role of fiduciary, use ESG risk-based approaches to assess the potential investment risks, in order to invest the fund safely.
- *Specialised consulting firms* such as the Big Four accounting firms (PwC, Deloitte, Ernst & Young and KPMG) consciously focus on ESG process and regulations and support corporates with their consulting service. Their worldwide networks are important merits for their professional service.
- *Non-profit organisations (NGOs)* also participate in the development of generally accepted ESG standards. Independent from the market participants, the NGOs develop their own assessment models by monitoring various business sectors, especially the stock-listed companies. Many NGOs mainly focus on environmental targets such as CO_2-neutral operations in the next future; reducing plastic components; climate-neutral electricity sources ('green power') like wind, water or solar energy supply; and sol heating.
- *Regulators* including worldwide governments and governmental institution and central banks (such as the US Federal Reserve or the European Central Bank or the Bank of England) responsible for regulating the financial systems supervise the development of ESG standards and ESG practice by providing guidelines or regulations.
- *Stock exchanges* are places where stockbrokers and traders buy and sell securities (shares, bonds, etc.). Influential stock exchanges such as the New York Stock Exchange (NYSE), Nasdaq and Euronext actively communicate ESG

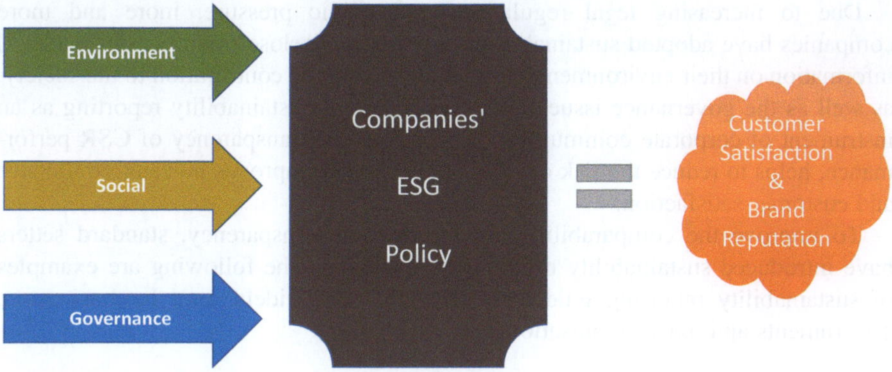

Fig. 15.4 CSR, ESG policy and sustainability reporting. Source: (Dathe et al., 2022)

requirements with their listed companies and promote the cooperation with specialised rating agencies such as Standard & Poor's, Moody's and Fitch. Especially MSCI plays an important role in ESG implementation with its MSCI indices, e.g. MSCI World or ESG derivatives.

The ESG ratings are sometimes criticised for lack of transparency and susceptible to manipulation and greenwashing, since the rating result is largely based on the self-declaration of the corporations themselves. In addition, there is no consensus among the rating agencies for the assessment methods. In fact, ratings for the same company by different rating agencies sometimes turn out very differently.

Initially, the implementation of the ESG framework in corporate disclosure was voluntary. The companies share their performance and progress in terms of fulfilling corporate social responsibilities in annual reports for the communication with investors, customers and other business partners. The implementation of ESG framework helps the companies to operationalise their corporate social responsibility strategy (see Fig. 15.4). A systematic process based on the ESG framework can guide the company to identify reporting items such as (Dathe et al., 2022):

- Environment-friendly products (e.g. electric cars, collaborative consumption such as shared transportation means, etc.)
- Production process using environment-friendly technologies (reducing carbon footprints).
- Business operations using renewable energy.
- Observing environment regulation.
- Employee-friendly working conditions and fair pay (equal pay, tariff payment, etc.)
- Anti-discrimination efforts.
- Diversity and inclusion.
- Managing fluctuation of employees.

Due to increasing legal regulations and public pressure, more and more companies have adopted sustainability reporting to disclose (mainly non-financial) information on their environmental, social and economic contribution to the society, as well as the governance issues on a regular basis. Sustainability reporting as an instrument of corporate communication increases the transparency of CSR performance, helps to reduce the risk of image damage and improves investor confidence and customer satisfaction.

To improve the comparability and information transparency, standard setters have introduced sustainability reporting frameworks. The following are examples of sustainability reporting guidelines that are most widely used by businesses, governments and other organisations:

- IFRS (International Financial Reporting Standards) Sustainability Disclosure Standards, developed by the International Sustainability Standards Board (ISSB).
- EU CSRD (Corporate Sustainability Reporting Directive).
- Global Reporting Initiative (GRI).
- TCFD (Task Force on Climate-Related Financial Disclosures).
- CDP (Carbon Disclosure Project, a global environmental disclosure system).
- B Corp.
- SASB (Sustainability Accounting Standards Board).

15.4 ESG Practice in China

Since the economic reform, China successively established comprehensive infrastructure networks for the manufacturing industry, benefiting from its well-trained low-wage labour force. To achieve the astonishing economic growth rate, China paid a huge ecological price. As the world's factory, China is currently the largest emitter of greenhouse gases, while its per capita emission level is comparable with the industrial countries (see Fig. 15.5). Given its size, China is a key factor in many global development issues. Global environmental problems cannot be solved without China's engagement.

With its deep integration in the global supply chain, China has also widely adopted the global ESG trends, including sustainability reporting. A recent survey study by the Chinese Business Network (CBN) Research Institute, which identified the top high-frequency words in the sustainability reports of 350 randomly selected Chinese companies, shows regional priorities of ESG concerns in China (see Table 15.1).

The findings of the above survey study indicate the largely common characteristics of the core principles of ESG practice in China and Western countries, for example:

- Focus on corporate communication: 'suppliers', 'consumers', 'investors', 'risk management', 'cooperation partner', 'public relations', etc. by private enterprises.

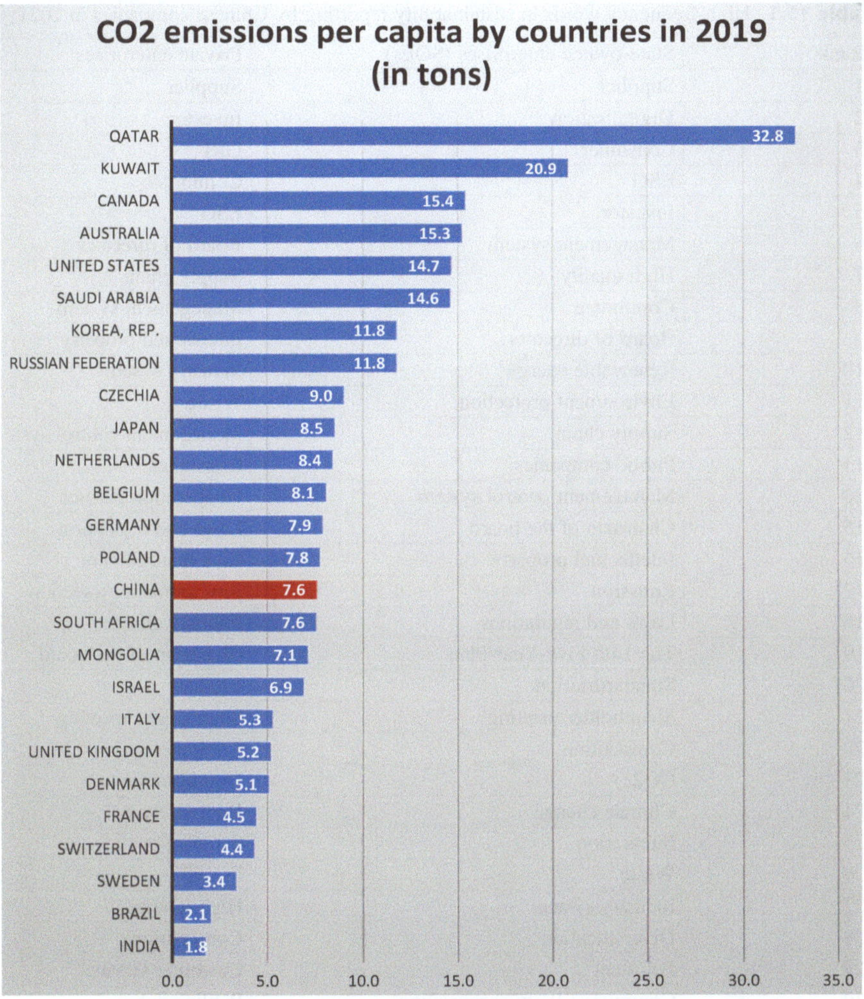

Fig. 15.5 CO_2 emission per capita of selected countries in 2019. Information source: (World Bank, 2022)

- Environment protection: 'environment protection', 'waste', 'renewable energy', 'emission', 'CO_2', 'climate change', 'pollutant' by SOEs.
- Social performance: 'public welfare' by private enterprises.
- Governance process: 'management system', 'management control system', 'laws and regulations', 'ESG', 'committee', etc.; 'standardisation' by SOEs and 'GRI' by private enterprises.

The social responsibility concerns in China also reflect a closer tie of Chinese firms to the government compared the Western countries. Not surprisingly, terms like '14th Five-Year Plan' and 'Communist Party organisation' are at the forefront of

Table 15.1 High-frequency words in sustainability reporting by Chinese companies in 2021

Rank	State-owned enterprises (SOEs)	Private enterprises
1	Supplier	Supplier
2	Digitalisation	Investor
3	Consumer	GRI
4	ESG	Committee
5	Investor	ESG
6	Management system	Board of directors
7	High quality	Supply chain
8	Committee	Management system
9	Board of directors	Intellectual property
10	Renewable energy	Industry system
11	Environment protection	Waste
12	Supply chain	Management control system
13	Public companies	Consumer
14	Management control system	Cooperation partner
15	Chairman of the board	Laws and regulations
16	Intellectual property	Risk management
17	Emission	Environment protection
18	Laws and regulations	Public welfare
19	The 14th Five-Year-Plan	Chairman of the board
20	Standardisation	Creditor
21	Shareholder meeting	Shareholder meeting
22	Competition	Computerisation
23	CO2	Digitalisation
24	Climate change	Data safety
25	Integration	Satisfaction
26	Waste	Patent
27	Industry system	High quality
28	Diversification	Competition
29	Pollutant	Customer service
30	Communist Party organisation	Public relations

Source: (Chinese Business Network (CBN), 2022)

reports by state-owned enterprises (SOEs), showing the consistency of their business strategy with the national politics. At the same time, the large number of overlapping keywords of both groups of companies indicates a convergence of ESG strategy of state-owned enterprises (SOEs) and private enterprises towards the national strategy.

The following targets were defined in the Fourteenth Five-Year Plan for the National Economic and Social Development of the Chinese government ('14th Five-Year Plan') (Government of China, 2021):

- Economic development.
- Technical innovations.
- Public welfare (improvement of overall living standard).

- Green ecology (environment protection).
- National security (improvement of food self-sufficiency and energy self-sufficiency).

In addition, a strong focus on economic achievements and technical innovations can be observed in the ESG understanding in China:

- Economic achievements: 'competition'.
- Technical innovations: 'digitalisation', 'industry system', 'intellectual property', 'high quality', etc.

There is a higher social expectation from the public companies and the personal liabilities of the business executives ('board of directors', 'chairman of the board', 'shareholder meeting', etc.).

As in many other countries, environmental protection is an important issue in ESG practice in China. For decades, China refused to curb emissions over fears that doing so would slow down domestic economic growth. In September 2020, to the surprise of many environmentalists, President Xi Jinping pledged in his speech to the United Nations that China would peak carbon dioxide emissions by 2030 and aim to achieve carbon neutrality by 2060. The motivation for this change of policy is generally seen in not only the international pressure but also the increasing frequency of extreme weather conditionals and social costs of environmental pollutions in China. The climate goals are a great challenge, since China's manufacturing industry remains highly dependent on low-cost fossil fuels (The New York Times, 2020). On the other hand, responding to climate change also provides opportunity for new technologies and business models in China.

References

Bowen, H. (1953). *Social responsibilities of the businessman* (p. xi).

Carroll, A. B. (2016). Carroll's pyramid of CSR: Taking another look. *International Journal of Corporate Social Responsibility, 1*(3), 1–3.

Chinese Business Network (CBN). (2022). 从高频热词看中国企业最重视哪些社会责任? |《2022中国企业社会责任研究报告:内生的力量》解读(三). By Li Hua. Retrieved January 26, 2023, from https://www.yicai.com/news/101652842.html

Dathe, T., Dathe, R., Dathe, I., & Helmold, M. (2022). *Corporate social responsibility (CSR), sustainability and environmental social governance (ESG)*. Springer.

Elkington, J. (1998). *Cannibals with forks: The triple bottom line of 21st century business*. University of Michigan: New Society Publishers.

Government of China. (2021, March 13). 中华人民共和国国民经济和社会发展第十四个五年规划和2035年远景目标纲要. By Xinhua News Agency. Retrieved January 26, 2023, from http://www.gov.cn/xinwen/2021-03/13/content_5592681.htm

LVMH. (2023). *Social & environmental responsibility - LVMH has made sustainable development a strategic priority since its founding*. By LVMH group. Retrieved January 26, 2023, from https://www.lvmh.com/group/lvmh-commitments/social-environmental-responsibility/

McKinsey. (2022, August 10). *Does ESG really matter—and why?* Retrieved January 25, 2023, from https://www.mckinsey.com/capabilities/sustainability/our-insights/does-esg-really-matter-and-why

Siemens. (2023). *Sustainable industries that grow forward.* By Siemens Aktiengesellschaft. Retrieved January 25, 2023, from https://www.siemens.com/global/en/products/automation/topic-areas/sustainable-industries.html?gclid=Cj0KCQiA_bieBhDSARIsADU4zLdU_DMubWDE4_C-aZgTEzMWiTBqEtfQs2eqdj2YJ0QVCk2Yzkggv6oaAhxSEALw_wcB&s=1

The New York Times. (2020, September 23). *China's Pledge to Be Carbon Neutral by 2060: What It Means.* By Steven Lee Myers. Retrieved January 27, 2023, from https://www.nytimes.com/2020/09/23/world/asia/china-climate-change.html

United Nations. (1987). *Our Common Future, From One Earth to One World.* Retrieved January 24, 2023, from https://sustainabledevelopment.un.org/content/documents/5987our-common-future.pdf

United Nations. (2015). *Transforming our world: The 2030 agenda for sustainable development.* By United Nations Department of economic and social affairs. Retrieved January 24, 2023, from https://sdgs.un.org/2030agenda

UNSTATS. (2022). *The sustainable development goals report 2022.* By the United Nations - Department of Economic and Social Affairs. Retrieved January 23, 2023, from https://unstats.un.org/sdgs/report/2022/

Volkswagen. (2023). *Sustainability.* By Volkswagen Aktiengesellschaft. Retrieved January 23, 2023, from https://www.volkswagenag.com/en/sustainability.html#

World Bank. (2022). *World Development Indicators: CO2 emissions (metric tons per capita).* Retrieved January 25, 2023, from https://data.worldbank.org/indicator/EN.ATM.CO2E.PC

Risk Management 16

16.1 Theoretical Approach of Risk Management

Risk management is essential for enterprises to survive the fierce competition in our fast-changing world (Helmold et al., 2022). Being part of the traditional business administration, new trends have emerged in risk management in recent decades, particularly in the context of increasing global competition, rapid technological progress and short product life cycles. The Covid-19 pandemic gives rise to a universal new assessment of the global supply chain resilience. Last but not least, the geopolitical conflicts force the enterprises to rethink their global business models to mitigate political risks (Helmold & Tracy, 2022).

In risk management of a business organisation, risks are usually divided into two major groups (Helmold et al., 2022) (see Fig. 16.1):

- *Internal risks* can be controlled and prevented by the organisation itself, including:
  - *Employee-related risks*, for example, the risk of losing strategically important knowledge or customer/supplier loyalty due to change of key personnel.
  - *Technology-related risks*, for example, the risk of choosing inefficient manufacturing technologies, unsuitable enterprise software, etc.
  - *Process-related risks*, for example, the risk of inadequate process for strategic decision-making, financial management, production planning and control, safety, quality control, supply chain management, public communication, etc.
  - *Physical risks*, for example, the damage to essential production facilities, etc.

Sustainability performance-related risks have become one of the major management issues in times of globalisation and digitalisation. A scandal can cause lasting damage to a company's reputation and, in the worst case, threaten its existence. On the other hand, the increasing demands of the society and legal requirements also enable a series of new business models and concepts (see Chap. 15 for more details).

T. Dathe et al., *Business Opportunities and Risks in China*, Management for Professionals, https://doi.org/10.1007/978-3-031-31933-4_16

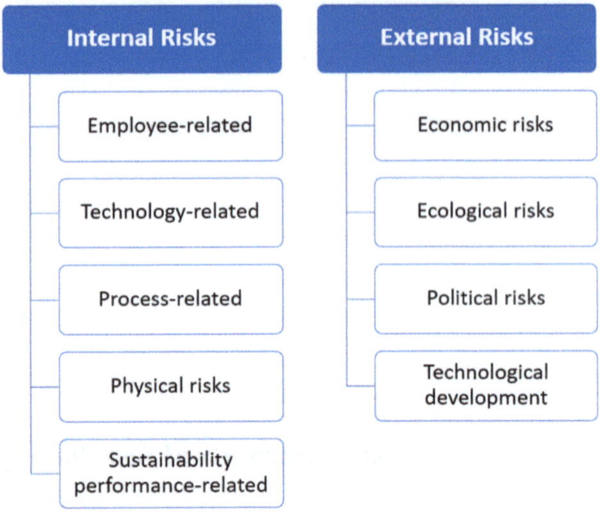

Fig. 16.1 Main types of enterprise risks

- *External risks* are caused by factors beyond the control of the enterprise, including:
  - *Economic risks*: For example, financial crisis, recessions leading to overall declining disposable incomes and rising unemployment can cause collapses in consumer demand.
  - *Ecological and natural risks*: For example, extreme weather conditions and climate changes affecting business operations, such as production stoppage caused by delivery delays or major supply chain disruptions.
  - *Political risks*: Changes in laws and regulations have become a main influence factor of business success. For example, the embargos and punitive import tariffs imposed due to the ongoing trade war between China and the United States have increased the costs and market pressure of certain types of products for international trade. The introduction of a carbon tax can change the cost and price structure of many products. Or, the regulation of the housing market through rent caps can significantly reduce the return of investment on the housing objects.
  - *Technological development*: Emerging new technology could make existing products/business models obsolete, for example, Eastman Kodak Company (commonly known as 'Kodak'), a multinational manufacturer for analogue photography (in particular, photographic film), lost its complete market due to the invention of digital photography.

The process of risk management can be divided into three stages (Helmold et al., 2022) (see Fig. 16.2):

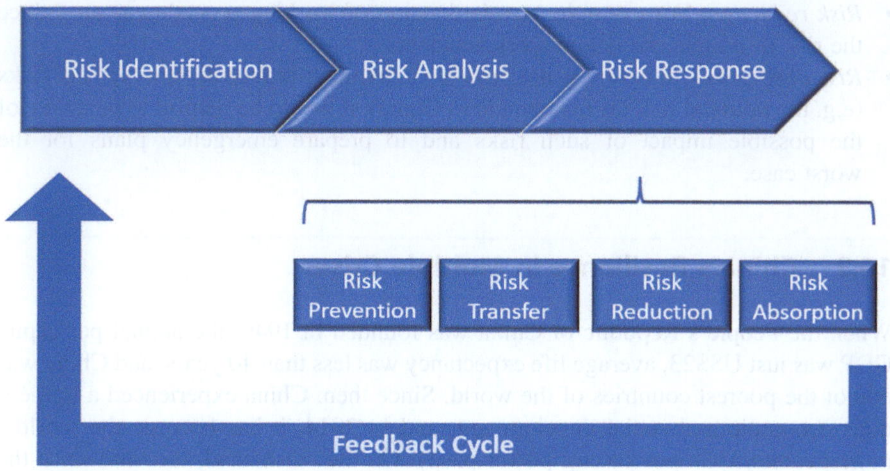

Fig. 16.2 The process of risk management

1. Risk identification.
2. Risk analysis.
3. Risk response.

Risk identification. This is the initial step of risk management. The identified risk factors can be defined with a series of characteristics, such as (Helmold et al., 2022):

- Nature of risk (description).
- Type of risk.
- Diver(s) of risk.
- Likelihood of occurrence.

Risk analysis. There are different techniques to further quantify the risk factors, for example, sensitivity analysis, SWOT analysis, stochastic analysis, etc. The risk analysis is very helpful for the identification of the major risk factors, thus the focus of risk management.

Risk response. Depending on the nature of the risks, various risk response strategies can be developed. Possible risk response can be viewed in the following groups:

- *Risk prevention*. In rather rare cases, it is possible to avoid the potential hazards (risks) by altering the business concept or the internal processes, for example, by implementing automatic production technology to avoid human errors in manual production.
- *Risk transfer*. Sometimes, it is possible to shift risks to others, for example, by purchasing insurance or requiring foreign customers to pay in home currency of the company to avoid currency risk.

- *Risk reduction.* For example, standardisation of working procedures can reduce the risk of human errors and work accidents.
- *Risk absorption.* In case it is not possible to avoid or reduce certain types of risks (e.g. the political risk for investment in China), it would be helpful to be aware of the possible impact of such risks and to prepare emergency plans for the worst case.

16.2 China's Resilience in Multiple Crises

When the People's Republic of China was founded in 1949, the annual per capita GDP was just US$23, average life expectancy was less than 40 years, and China was one of the poorest countries of the world. Since then, China experienced a tremendous economic and social development, and in 2014, it has become the world's largest economy in purchasing power parity. On the other hand, the time since the founding of the P.R. China can be sensed as a series of crises: natural disasters (notably the earthquakes in Tangshan 1976 and Sichuan 2008), political crises, national and international economic crises, diseases and finally the serious effects of global warming.

With the help of two examples—the 2008 financial crisis and the Covid pandemic—in this chapter, we analyse how Chinese government and enterprises have developed a resilience to overcome different crises.

The financial crisis of 2007–2008, triggered by the collapse of the US housing market, threatened to destroy the international financial system and caused the worst economic downturn since the Great Depression, which started in 1929 (Britannica, 2019).

In 2006–2007, China had its own, different challenges: an overheated economy with excessive fixed asset investment, soaring energy consumption, increasing environmental pollution and an increasing risk of inflation (China Daily, 2007). However, while most major economies in the world faced zero growth in 2008 and a deep recession in 2009, China maintained an annual GDP growth of almost 10% (Fig. 16.1); business in China was hardly affected by the crisis in the rest of the world. Quite the contrary, China strongly contributed to the recovery of the world economy. In 2009, China's GDP accounted for about 8% of the global total, but the country's contribution to global economic growth reached 50%. The reasons can be summarised as follows:

Compared with China's integration in the world economy in trade of goods, influence of foreign financial institutions in China was and is limited. The pace of opening-up of China's financial market accelerated from 2018, but China is aware of the implied risks and will ensure that the risks are manageable (Bank of China, 2021). In- and outflow of capital are regulated by China's State Administration of Foreign Exchange (SAFE), limiting currency speculation.

China's financial sector is dominated by the 'China Big Four' banks: Industrial and Commercial Bank of China, China Construction Bank, Agricultural Bank of China and the Bank of China. Though these four banks are stock-listed, they are basically state-owned and closely supervised through the nation's central bank, the People's Bank of China (PBOC). The dominance by just four major players limits market competition, but first and foremost, it limits risky investment and provides the state additional tools to go against possible future crises.

Similar to most developed countries, the Chinese government approved a huge stimulus package of four trillion yuan (about 540 billion euros). However, most of this money was not used to stabilise the financial sector but for new infrastructure projects. For example, China expanded its already ambitious plans to build 16,000 km of high-speed rail by 2020, up from the initial goal of 12,000 km (China Briefing, 2020). Improved infrastructure was a decisive factor for long-term economic growth, increasing the state's financial revenue, and at least partially helped to repay the government's expenses.

For a period of 3 years, the *Covid-19* pandemic threatened both the development of the Chinese economy and the health of the population. In December 2019 in the central China city of Wuhan, among the large number of pneumonia cases that in winter appear daily in the city of 13.6 million inhabitants, local doctors discovered an unusual pattern of symptoms, resembling SARS that struck several Chinese cities in 2003. Within a few weeks, scientists sequenced the virus genome and developed the first test kit to identify the new virus, later named Covid-19. Around 20 January 2020, it became clear that—different from SARS—many infections don't require hospitalisation and the virus had already spread much further than expected. Only 3 days later, on 23 January 2020, the government imposed a strict lockdown that lasted for nearly 3 months and saw all journeys in and out of the city banned. Within less than 2 weeks, two emergency hospitals to treat Covid-19 patients were erected and fully equipped, and 42,000 medical personnel from other parts of the country were sent to Wuhan. After less than 2 months, on 18 May 2020, Wuhan reported a full week without new infections; the outbreak had been contained.

Sealing off Wuhan could not stop the virus spreading to other parts of China and the rest of the world, but at least the spread could be slowed down so that—compared with Wuhan—less stringent control measures and consequent contact tracing brought infection rates in China down to almost zero. From 01 May 2020 to 31 December 2021, China reported less than 20,000 new cases and just 3 deaths (Worldometer, 2023), on the cost of strict international travel restrictions and quarantine for incoming travellers. The situation changed in 2022 with the fast spread of the Omicron variant of the Covid-19 virus. A large-scale outbreak in Shanghai in late March 2022 could be contained, but only with a strict lockdown lasting until late May. In November 2022, even more contagious—but less lethal—sub-variants of the Omicron mutant spread to Beijing and other Chinese cities. Chinese authorities came to the conclusion that the economic and social impact of long and strict lockdowns by far exceeded the benefit of keeping infections at a minimum. A gradual lifting of most restrictions led to a massive wave of infections in December 2022 that abated quickly in early January 2023.

In 2020 and 2022, China's GDP growth was 2.5 to 3.5% below the target, with a strong recovery in between in 2021. Different from other major economies, in all 3 years, China maintained positive growth of the GDP; average growth was considerably higher than in other countries. Most importantly, China's anti-Covid measures resulted in a rate of severe cases and casualties much lower than in most other countries.

Different from the stimulus package to tackle the financial crisis in 2008, infrastructure investment played only a minor role in the stimulus measures to overcome the impact of Covid-19 on the economy. During the span of 3 years, central and local governments adopted a range of targeted measures, with a focus to support SMEs. For example, on 31 May 2022, the State Council released a set of 33 measures, offering VAT tax rebates, deferring social security and housing fund contributions, increasing loan support including deferring payments of principals and interests on loans, rent reductions of state-owned property and boosting employment by offering incentives to companies that hire fresh graduates (China Briefing, 2022).

In addition to government financial support, China's relative success in curbing the pandemic was caused by a wide range of factors; to study them is helpful for risk analysis and business strategy in China in general:

- Initiative of enterprises. In early 2020, when protective masks were essential to curb the spread of the pandemic, private companies from different industries used their resources to set up mask production lines virtually 'overnight', effectively overcoming the shortage of surgical masks.
- Flexible and very fast reaction of government departments, for example, providing emergency approval for import of non-registered protective equipment and life-sustaining ECMO (extracorporeal membrane oxygenation) machines.
- Strong appreciation of medical staff shown by government, media and the public, motivating doctors and nurses to make admirable contributions at the 'front line' in the fight against the virus.
- Well-organised administration on grassroots (community) level. Neighbourhood committees, supported by volunteers, bore the main burden to organise lockdowns, virus testing and support of citizens in needs.
- High internet affinity, even in the older generation, and nationwide access to high-speed internet. In most companies and institutions, switching to work or study from home went smoothly.
- Popular internet shopping and availability of delivery services. In case of lockdowns, all daily necessities could be delivered to people's homes.
- High degree of creativity and resilience of private entrepreneurs and SMEs. For instance, small tourism bureaus specially cater to incoming international tourists. Their market was almost non-existing for 3 years. Most of these companies survived by creating other forms of income, for example, by selling local specialities from their home province on the internet.
- High degree of commitment of employees. To ensure continuing production of essential industries during lockdowns, many companies employed a so-called closed-loop management. Employees stayed at their working place, or were transported between dedicated dormitories and their working place without any contact to the outside world (See Figure 16.3).

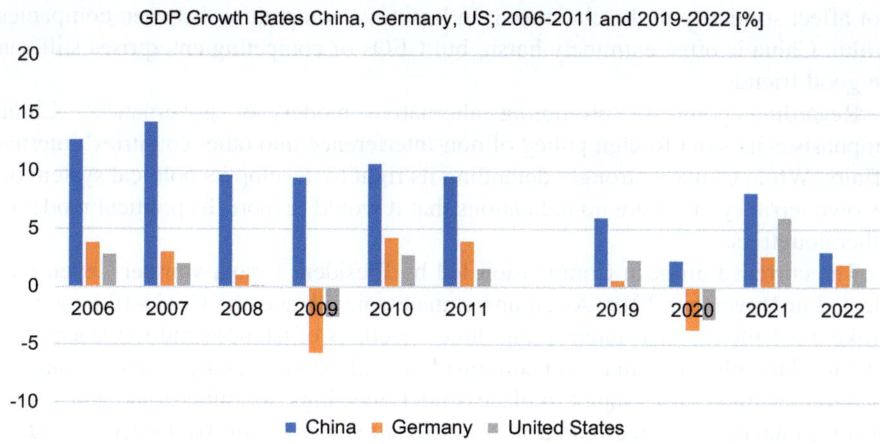

Fig. 16.3 GDP growth rates in China, Germany and the United States: 2006–2011 and 2019–2022 [%]. Data sources: (Kuaiyi Finance Net, 2023a CN), (Kuaiyi Finance Net, 2023b US), (Kuaiyi Finance Net, 2023c Ger)

16.3 EU–China Relationship

Political and economic relations between economies cannot be separated. While trade and economic cooperation foster political relations, a positive political environment is beneficial for enterprises, while political tensions may severely interrupt bilateral business.

Until a few years ago, Chinese and EU companies were serving disjunct markets, both within China and internationally: China supplied simple, low-cost products and was a source for cheap, hardworking labour, while EU companies—mainly those from Western and Central Europe—manufactured sophisticated high-end products. However, in recent years, the technological level of some Chinese companies has developed dramatically; in several sectors, Chinese and EU companies have become competitors. At the same time, in the political arena, China is no more the 'silent giant' but is increasingly assertive when defending its core interests.

In view of the EU Delegation to China, EU-China relations are characterised by (EU Delegation, 2021): 'China is, simultaneously, in different policy areas:

- a cooperation partner with whom the EU has closely aligned objectives,
- a negotiating partner with whom the EU needs to find a balance of interests,
- an economic competitor in the pursuit of technological leadership,
- a systemic rival promoting alternative models of governance'.

From the Chinese point of view, the third point 'competition' may be caused by cultural differences. In China, competition has a very positive connotation. From early age onwards, pupils are encouraged to perform better than their peers; this does not affect solidarity in the classroom. In business, competition between companies within China is often extremely harsh, but CEOs of competing enterprises still can be good friends.

Regarding point 4, 'promoting alternative models of governance', China emphasises its strict foreign policy of non-interference into other countries' internal affairs. While China is strongly defending its right to develop its political system on its own territory, there are no indications that it would 'export' its political model to other countries.

The current European Commission led by President Ursula von der Leyen was elected in November 2019. As an unfortunate coincidence, the Covid-19 pandemic broke out 1 month later, interrupting direct meetings of Chinese and EU leaders for 3 years. Though communication continued via videoconferencing, modern communication technologies cannot replace direct meetings to build trust and avoid misunderstandings. Direct contacts resumed after 3 years on 01 December 2022, when Chinese President Xi Jinping met with the President of the European Council, Charles Michel, in Beijing.

The last positive milestone in China-EU relations was the agreement on protecting geographical indications that came into force on 01 March 2021 (European Commission, 2021). The agreement protects European and Chinese agri-food names linked to a town or region (e.g. 'Champagne' against imitation and usurpation).

A big disappointment for the international business community was the freeze of the ratification of the EU-China Comprehensive Agreement on Investment (CAI). After 7 years of negotiations, on 30 December 2020, the EU and China announced their approval of the CAI. However, after the EU imposed sanctions against Chinese officials according to the EU Global Human Rights Sanctions Regime and swift retaliatory sanctions against EU members of parliament by China, on 20 May 2021, the EU Parliament passed a resolution to freeze ratification. In the latest development, Sweden, which has assumed the rotating presidency of the Council of the European Union for the first half of 2023, said it will continue to seek consultations with the European Parliament in pushing forward the ratification of the CAI (China Daily, 2023a).

In an era of increasing global tensions, the EU sees WTO regulations and arbitration as not sufficiently protecting EU interests. In recent years, the EU has adopted and is discussing a series of additional trade defence mechanisms (European Parliament, 2022). Though, in most cases, China is not directly named as a possible target, the mechanisms raise concern about a possible deterioration of China-EU relations. Main instruments in trade and political conflicts include:

- Screening and possible blocking of foreign investment. Although the final decision about approval of investment is under the responsibility of single member states, the EU is increasingly influencing the screening process (CIRCABC, 2022).

- In August 2022, the EU's International Procurement Instrument came into force, restricting access to the EU's government procurement market, if the respective market of a non-EU country is not fully open to EU companies (EUR-Lex, 2022).
- In October 2022, the EU Parliament proposed an anti-coercion instrument. The instrument—if finally approved—would allow retaliation with countermeasures comprising a wide range of restrictions related to trade, investment and funding against perceived economic coercion of a third country against an EU member state (Think Tank, 2022). This proposed measure is especially critical, as it mixes possible political differences with economic policies.
- On 12 January 2023, the Foreign Subsidies Regulation entered into force. This regulation is directed against distortion of the EU market by alleged subsidies of third countries (European Commission, 2023). The Commission can take countermeasures, e.g. exclude a bidder from a public procurement contract.

An additional main risk in China-EU relations is the policy of the United States (see Sect. 17.3). As US-China tensions intensify, the EU finds it increasingly difficult to keep good relations with both China and the United States. Because of historical commonalities, similar cultures and political systems, it is rather likely that the EU will tend to side with the United States.

China is especially concerned to be cut off from essential imports such as integrated circuits (chips). As a reaction, China adopted the policy of dual circulation (State Council, 2021), aiming at reducing imports of high-tech products by locally ones.

As a result of increasing political tensions, according to a survey by the EUCCC (EUCCC, 2022), half of the international companies report that business became more politicised.

In 2022, despite a deteriorating political environment and the third year of the Covid pandemic resulting in China's lowest annual economic growth rate since the 1970s, China-EU economic relations developed predominantly positively: China's exports to the EU grew to US$561.9 billion, an increase by 8.6%. On the other hand, EU exports to China declined by 7.9% to US$285.3 billion (Sina, 2023). Investments in China by EU companies grew by a staggering 92.2% year on year in 2022 (China Briefing, 2023).

Judging by these figures, political tensions so far had limited impact for China-EU trade and investment. For EU companies, a possible way to mitigate future political risks is an internal decoupling of the operations of its headquarters and its Chinese subsidiary, for example, by substituting international suppliers by local ones to protect its subsidiary against possible trade embargoes. However, this internal decoupling increases costs and reduces flexibility.

16.4 Special Consideration: Taiwan, Hong Kong and Macao

Political relations between Mainland China, Taiwan and Hong Kong have attracted much attention among politicians and public opinion in competing economies, especially the United States, the EU and Japan. For a historic and economic background of these territories, see Sects. 2.3 and 2.4.

To put the current status of Mainland China-Taiwan relations into a historic context: only in 1989—40 years after the foundation of the P.R. China and 10 years after the start of the opening and reform process—Taiwan allowed its citizens to travel to Mainland China. Regular direct flights between the Mainland and Taiwan resumed 20 years later in August 2009. Since 2018, Taiwan residents don't any longer need a work permit to work in Mainland China. Over time, the economies of Mainland China and Taiwan became strongly integrated; Taiwan is now a main source of investment in Mainland China. In 2022, Taiwan had by far the largest trade surplus with Mainland China. The Taiwan-headquartered electronics manufacturer Foxconn alone has an estimated 800,000 (!) employees on the Mainland. Fujian, the province geographically and culturally closest to Taiwan, specially strives to become 'first home' for residents of Taiwan (China Daily, 2023b) to promote cross-Strait's integration. Taiwan's outlying islands Kinmen and Matsu shall be connected by bridges to Fujian Province.

Despite this long-term, gradual improvement of cross-Strait's relations, risks exist and may be fuelled by global power struggle. For example, on 16 October 2022, President Xi Jinping delivered the 64-page-long *Report to the 20th National Congress of the Communist Party of China* (State Council, 2022); within the report, a full chapter focused on the improvement of Mainland-Taiwan relations and promoting peaceful reunification, but foreign politicians and media of competing economies took just a half sentence from that report out of context—'but we will never promise to renounce the use of force'—a stance that has not changed since the beginning of the reforms. While the report itself was not intended to raise tensions with China, biased reporting and interpretation created a tense international atmosphere.

Mainland China and Taiwan's industry are closely interwoven with a strong focus on integrated circuits (microchips) and electronics. In 2019, chips, electronics and IT contributed 19% to Taiwan's GDP. In 2021, Taiwan earned 26% of the global income from semiconductor production and 64% of the global revenue from foundries (History Computer, 2022). In cities like Zhengzhou, provincial capital of Henan Province with 12.7 million inhabitants, Taiwan electronics manufacturers are the largest contributors to local employment. This interdependence means that rationally, both the Mainland and Taiwan cannot be interested in increasing tension. However, if the worst case happens, a disruption in the supply of chips and electronic components would severely influence the worldwide economy.

The German-based Allianz Group, one of the world's leading insurers and asset managers, rates Taiwan a '1' (low-risk) region. In four out of five categories—economic, business environment, commercial and financial risks—Taiwan is assigned to the lowest-risk class; only political risks are rated as the second lowest risk level of six possible categories (Allianz, 2022). Credendo, a European credit insurance group active in political risk insurance, rates political short-time and midterm risks both as '1' (lowest of seven possible categories), while the risk of political violence is rated as '3' (Credendo, 2023).

Hong Kong returned to China in 1997 after 156 years of British colonial rule as a special administrative region (SAR). Hong Kong retained its own legislation and currency; the SAR is separated from Mainland China by a land border with customs and immigration control. Hong Kong residents have a different passport from Mainland China, allowing them to travel visa-free to most countries. Mainland China residents can travel to Hong Kong without a passport but need a special travel permit.

Sparked by an extradition bill allowing suspects to be prosecuted in Mainland China, a wave of—often very violent—protests erupted in 2019 that lasted until mid-2020. As a result, the 13th National People's Congress passed the National Security Law that came into force in Hong Kong on 30 June 2020 (Hong Kong Government, 2020). In a joint statement, the United Kingdom, Australia, Canada and the United States stated that the security law lies in direct conflict with the Sino-British Joint Declaration on handing Hong Kong over to China (UK Government, 2020), an interpretation the Chinese government strongly rejects. In August 2020, the United States imposed sanctions on 11 senior Hong Kong officials, including Ms. Carrie Lam, Chief Executive of the Hong Kong Special Administrative Region, who resigned in April 2022 after her 5-year term in office. In summer 2020, the protests died down; Covid-19 became Hong Kong's most pressing concern. Quarantine measures resulted in a closing of border crossings with Mainland China until January 2023.

Hong Kong's economic future is very closely linked to that of Mainland China. Given the close connection of Hong Kong's government and its business community with the Mainland, possible political risks stem from outside of Hong Kong, i.e. if Western governments impose sanctions against China, they may also cover Hong Kong.

Fifty years after hand-over from Great Britain, the existence of the Hong Kong SAR and its special legislation will cease to exist in 2047. So far, no plans have been published how Hong Kong will be administered after that date. The establishment of the Greater Bay Area of Hong Kong together with Macao and the most developed parts of Guangdong Province indicates that there will be a gradual transition. Establishment of the Hainan Free Trade Port (see Sect. 7.2) striving to reach the same degree of openness as Hong Kong shows that China has sufficiently flexible forms of administration to maintain the specific status of Hong Kong as a free-trade hub even after dissolving the SAR.

Credendo rates political short-time risks with '1' (lowest) and midterm risks and political violence risks with '2' out of seven categories. Allianz Group does not provide a special risk report for Hong Kong.

The tiny Macao with less than 700,000 inhabitants has so far managed to remain 'under the radar' in global power struggle. After Macao's return to China in 1999, China and Portugal kept a positive bilateral relationship, and there have been no notable political frictions within Macao.

Macao's weakness is its unbalanced economic structure with a strong dependence on tourism and entertainment industry, which led to a temporary economic decline during the Covid-19 pandemic. Macao's business model includes gambling services that are illegal in Mainland China and most Asian countries. An increasing harmonisation of legal regulations in the Guangdong-Hong Kong-Macao Greater Bay Area may lead to a curb of gambling. To mitigate this risk, the Macao government is encouraging casino operators to focus on non-gaming facilities, positioning Macau as a family-oriented holiday destination.

References

Allianz. (2022). *Taiwan, strong economy, tricky geopolitics*. Retrieved January 30, 2023, from https://www.allianz.com/en/economic_research/publications/country-risk/taiwan.html

Bank of China. (2021). *China's financial sector opening up*. Retrieved January 24, 2023, from https://www.bocusa.com/chinas-financial-sector-opening

Britannica. (2019). *Financial crisis of 2007-08*. Retrieved January 24, 2023, from https://www.britannica.com/event/financial-crisis-of-2007-2008

China Briefing. (2020). *Why China's COVID-19 stimulus will look different than in the past*. Retrieved January 25, 2023, from https://www.china-briefing.com/news/chinas-stimulus-measures-after-covid-19-different-from-2008-financial-crisis/

China Briefing. (2022). *China Releases 33 New Stimulus Measures to Boost Economy*. Retrieved January 25, 2023, from https://www.china-briefing.com/news/china-releases-33-new-stimulus-measures-to-boost-economy/

China Briefing. (2023). *Prospects for European Companies in China in 2023*. Retrieved January 28, 2023, from https://www.china-briefing.com/news/european-investment-in-china-prospects-for-2023

China Daily. (2007). *Economy on verge of overheating*. Retrieved January 24, 2023, from http://www.chinadaily.com.cn/china/2007-08/01/content_5447228.htm

China Daily. (2023a). *Sweden keen to push for progress on CAI*. Retrieved January 28, 2023, from https://www.chinadaily.com.cn/a/202301/11/WS63bded50a31057c47eba8d3f.html

China Daily. (2023b). *Fujian striving to become 'first home' for residents of Taiwan*. Retrieved January 29, 2023, from https://www.chinadaily.com.cn/a/202301/28/WS63d47cd2a31057c47ebab72e.html

Credendo. (2023). *Country Risk and Insight*. Retrieved January 31, 2023, from https://credendo.com/en/country-risk.

EUCCC. (2022). Business Confidence Survey 2022. Retrieved January 28, 2023, from https://www.europeanchamber.com.cn/en/publications-archive/1020/Business_Confidence_Survey_2022

European Commission. (2021). *EU-China agreement protecting geographical indications enters into force*. Retrieved February 1, 2023, from https://agriculture.ec.europa.eu/news/eu-china-agreement-protecting-geographical-indications-enters-force-2021-03-01_en

European Commission. (2023). *Foreign subsidies regulation*. Retrieved February 1, 2023, from https://competition-policy.ec.europa.eu/foreign-subsidies-regulation_en

EU Delegation. (2021). *The European Union and China*. Retrieved January 28, 2023, from https://www.eeas.europa.eu/china/european-union-and-china_en

EUR-Lex. (2022). *The EU's International Procurement Instrument – IPI*. Retrieved January 28, 2023, from https://eur-lex.europa.eu/EN/legal-content/summary/the-eu-s-international-procurement-instrument-ipi.html

European Parliament. (2022). *Trade wars: What are the EU's trade defence instruments?* Retrieved January 28, 2023, from https://www.europarl.europa.eu/news/en/headlines/economy/20180308STO99328/trade-wars-what-are-the-eu-s-trade-defence-instruments

Helmold, M., & Tracy, D. (2022, April 20). *Wettbewerbsvorteil: Kaizen im Einkauf.* By Procure.ch. Retrieved February 1, 2023, from https://www.procure.ch/magazin/artikel/wettbewerbsvorteil-kaizen-im-einkauf/

Helmold, M., Yılmaz, A. K., Dathe, T., & Flouris, T. G. (2022). *Supply chain risk management - Cases and industry insights*. Springer.

History Computer. (2022). *Taiwan's chip industry explained: Why it matters so much today.* Retrieved January 28, 2023, from https://history-computer.com/taiwans-chip-industry/

Hong Kong Government. (2020). *Promulgation of National Law 2020.* Retrieved January 30, 2023, from https://www.gld.gov.hk/egazette/pdf/20202444e/es220202444136.pdf

Kuaiyi Finance Net. (2023a CN). *China's Annual GDP Growth Rate in Previous Years* (in Chinese). Retrieved January 27, 2023, from https://www.kylc.com/stats/global/yearly_per_country/g_gdp_growth/chn.html

Kuaiyi Finance Net. (2023b US). *China's Annual GDP Growth Rate in Previous Years* (in Chinese). Retrieved January 27, 2023, from https://www.kylc.com/stats/global/yearly_per_country/g_gdp_growth/usa.html

Kuaiyi Finance Net. (2023c Ger). *China's Annual GDP Growth Rate in Previous Years* (in Chinese). Retrieved January 27, 2023, from https://www.kylc.com/stats/global/yearly_per_country/g_gdp_growth/deu.html

Sina. (2023). *Economic Observer. Review of China's In- and Export Tendencies in 2022 and Prospects for 2023* (in Chinese). Retrieved January 28, 2023, from https://cj.sina.com.cn/articles/view/1641561812/61d83ed4020015bym

State Council. (2021). *China's new 'dual circulation' development paradigm.* Retrieved January 28, 2023, from https://english.www.gov.cn/news/topnews/202103/28/content_WS60604adbc6d0719374afba4a.html

State Council. (2022). *Full text of the report to the 20th National Congress of the Communist Party of China.* Retrieved January 30, 2023, from https://english.www.gov.cn/news/topnews/202210/25/content_WS6357df20c6d0a757729e1bfc.html

Think Tank. (2022). *European Parliament. Proposed anti-coercion instrument.* Retrieved January 28, 2023, from https://www.europarl.europa.eu/thinktank/en/document/EPRS_BRI(2022)729299

UK Government. (2020). *China's proposed new security law for Hong Kong: Joint statement.* Retrieved January 30, 2023, from https://www.gov.uk/government/news/joint-statement-from-the-uk-australia-canada-and-united-states-on-hong-kong

Worldometers. (2023). *Coronavirus China.* Retrieved January 22, 2023, from https://www.worldometers.info/coronavirus/country/china/

17 Institutional Supports for Commercial Activities

17.1 Organisations that Provide Assistance

Like any other business expansion project, investment in the Chinese market needs build-up of know-how and careful planning. What is different in China from fully developed countries: because of the fast growth of China's economy and the ongoing reform process, China's business environment is constantly changing. This requires a sense of urgency, fast decisions and a flexible business plan.

17.1.1 Case Study: Consequences of Slow Decision-Making—A Factory for Infusion Solutions

Basic infusions of salt and glucose are a very common treatment method in China; the per capita application of these infusion solutions is several times as high as in Central Europe. Until 2000, Chinese hospitals mixed their own infusion solutions. To increase patients' safety, Chinese regulators decided that infusion solutions shall only be manufactured in pharmaceutical plants licenced according to Good Manufacturing Practice (GMP) standard, a giant new business for pharmaceutical companies. A leading international manufacturer of infusion solutions decided to build a factory in China to serve the local market. It took about 3 years to work out all technical details of the plant and get the budget approved by the company's headquarters. Then it took about another 3 years to build the factory and get all necessary licences from the regulators, to employ and train personnel. At that time, the market was already saturated by local companies. In a very short time, they had decided to go into that new market using their existing factories and licences to start production. It was very costly for the international company to repurpose their new plant to manufacture other medicines for which there was still demand on the Chinese market.

Information is crucial to make quick and reliable decision. On the positive side, there is a wide range of organisations that assist international companies in their

T. Dathe et al., *Business Opportunities and Risks in China*, Management for Professionals, https://doi.org/10.1007/978-3-031-31933-4_17

market entry or expansion of business in China. In addition, a large number of consulting companies specialised in China business offer their services. In this chapter, we can only give a few examples of potential non-commercial sources of information. It is recommended to obtain information from different sources. A basic level of China know-how is useful when cooperating with a consulting company so that the consultancy can be precisely instructed what service they should provide. Poor cooperation with a consultancy may be costly and delay market entry (V. Müller, 2022).

17.1.2 International Organisations

The EU SME Centre, located in Beijing, is an EU-funded initiative created to provide free first-line services to small- and medium-sized businesses from EU member states. The centre provides guidelines on how to access the Chinese market, basic market studies, events, trainings and personalised free consultation (https://www.eusmecentre.org.cn/).

The China IP SME Helpdesk supports EU SMEs to both protect and enforce their intellectual property rights (IPR) in China, including Hong Kong, Macao and Taiwan, through the provision of free information and services (https://intellectual-property-helpdesk.ec.europa.eu/regional-helpdesks/china-ipr-sme-helpdesk_en).

17.1.3 Chambers of Commerce

Companies of most developed countries have formed non-profit chambers of commerce to serve the interests of companies from their home countries; for an overview and contacts, see GlueUp (2021).

Organisation form, scope of service and range of addressees vary. Larger chambers of commerce have offices in different parts of China, possibly including Hong Kong and Taiwan. Some chambers have a China-wide organisation (e.g. the German Außenhandelskammer (AHK)), while others (e.g. the American Chamber of Commerce) have basically independent entities in each location. Most chambers focus on providing services for their member companies, while others also serve non-members.

An example of a chamber providing a broad range of services for market entry and expansion is the German AHK (https://china.ahk.de/services/market-entry-expansion), assisting companies, for example, in matchmaking with Chinese counterparts, market studies and participation in trade fairs and conferences as well as assisting business travellers to obtain business visa. During the Covid-19 pandemic, the German AHK arranged charter flights for German business people to overcome shortages in international flights.

17.1.4 Industry Associations

Because of the importance of the Chinese market, many industry associations have established a representation office in China, sharing information of the industry-specific business environment in China and supporting members to facilitate their China business.

One example of a large influential business association is the German Association of the Automotive Industry (VDA) representing more than 650 manufacturers and suppliers. In China, the VDA has founded an office in Beijing (https://vda.cn/) in 2014, arranging a wide range of Sino-German conferences and cooperation projects, for example, in standardisation.

On the contrary, COCIR, a European trade association representing the medical imaging, radiotherapy, health ICT and electromedical industries (https://www.cocir.org/), is an example of a very specialised organisation. Its only presence outside its headquarters in Brussels is a representation in China, founded in 2007. COCIR China cooperates with the NMPA, the Chinese National Health Commission (NHC) and the National Health Security Administration (NHSA) to understand regulatory reforms and improve market access for its member companies.

17.1.5 Regional Organisations

Below the national level, regional organisations have been founded in many countries to facilitate business (or cultural) exchange with China. The advantage of such organisations is their focus on regional strength of the industry, short distances to participate in working groups and events and in most cases their independence, allowing flexible setting of topics and forms of cooperation.

Baden-Württemberg is a federal country (German: Bundesland, comparable with a province) in the southwest of China. Historically, Baden-Württemberg was always a European centre of precision mechanics. For example, a famous cluster of large and SME medical device manufacturers has developed in the town of Tuttlingen. Companies from Baden-Württemberg and Chinese companies investing in the area have together formed the China Netzwerk Baden-Württemberg e.V. (CNBW) (https://china-bw.net/de). The balanced approach supporting both German and Chinese companies makes it easy to contact potential Chinese cooperation partners. The activities of the network are explicitly open to non-members.

A second example: Flanders is a region in the northern part of Belgium, with a distinctly different industry structure compared with the southern part of the country. In 2005, companies from Flanders active in business with China have founded the regional Flanders-China Chamber of Commerce (FCCC) (https://www.flanders-china.be/en), promoting economic, commercial and scientific relations between Flanders and China. Based on its network with governments, other trade organisations and companies in both China and the EU, the FCCC focuses on offering business support and information to Flemish companies looking for opportunities in China.

17.1.6 Sister Cities

Since the 1980s, many Chinese cities have established sister relationships with foreign cities. The intensity and range of activities vary. Some relationships focus on cultural activities, while others promote business activities. A very positive example is the sister city relationships Hamburg-Shanghai, founded in 1986 (https://www.hamburgshanghai.org/). Both cities have a similar industry structure with the harbours and related international trade playing a key role in their economies. The city of Hamburg has a liaison office in Shanghai, explicitly representing Hamburg business interests like the Hamburg Chamber of Commerce.

Another example of a business-supportive sister city relationships is that of Düsseldorf, capital of the Germany's most populous federal state North Rhine-Westphalia and Chongqing, the 32-million provincial-level municipality in southwestern China. The city government of Düsseldorf has established a China competency centre (http://www.duesseldorf.cn/de/partnerstadt-chongqing.html) to support local companies to become active in China. A special advantage of companies located in and around Düsseldorf is the direct freight train from Chongqing to Duisburg, just 23 km away from Düsseldorf, reducing freight time and costs between the two sister cities.

17.1.7 Chinese Organisations

Attracting foreign investment is key tasks of Chinese government departments on all levels. Each province, each city, often city district governments and most of the industry parks have established investment promotion agencies. A growing competition of China and Southeast Asian countries as well as between different locations within China resulted in a very positive service attitude of these investment promotion agencies.

On national ministerial level, the China International Investment Promotion Agency (CIPA, https://fdi.mofcom.gov.cn/EN/) under the Chinese Ministry of Commerce (MOFCOM) supports foreign investment. CIPA is especially active in Germany (https://www.ciipa.de/) with a headquarter in Frankfurt and offices in Berlin, Magdeburg, Düsseldorf and Ingolstadt. Other offices under the brand CIPA Europe (https://fdi.mofcom.gov.cn/EU/) are located in France, Hungary, the Netherlands and Switzerland. CIPA regularly holds seminars and matchmaking events, for example, on the annual medical device trade fair Medica in Düsseldorf. CIPA can establish contacts with cities or industrial parks in China to obtain specific information on local investment opportunities and business environments.

An example on investment promotion on city level is the Beijing Investment Promotion Service Center (http://invest.beijing.gov.cn/english/), with comprehensive information on questions like business registration, tax, employment of international personnel and government subsidies.

Huangpu is a city district of Guangzhou (older transliteration: Canton), the capital of Guangzhou Province. Because of its proximity to Hong Kong and Macao as well as its early and consequent implementation of economic reform policies, Huangpu is one of the most successful city districts in attracting foreign investment. As one of the first Chinese districts, it has set up its own office in Heidelberg, Germany (https://www.huangpu-europe.com/), to support European investors.

17.2 The Foreign Invested Industry's Influence on Policymaking

A large proportion of risks in business stems from government decision-making. For example, a decree to restrict or ban traditional fuel vehicle and promote new energy vehicles (NEV) completely changes the market, and manufacturers need to adapt. Because of China's fast economic and social development, state (or regional) government interventions are more frequent than in most developed economies. In addition, transitional periods tend to be shorter in China than in other countries. On the positive side, the Chinese government is aware of the importance of foreign invested industry for further development and is willing to consider the industries' concerns and recommendations.

Like in any other country, the Chinese government needs to balance the interests of different stakeholders and find compromises to satisfy the interests of different groups of the population. For example, in healthcare, the Healthcare Security Administration on national and local level represents the government, manages the funds of the public healthcare insurance and lays the framework for procurement of medicines and medical devices. The hospitals—public and private—and its medical personnel are a strong influence group that must implement healthcare policies. Manufacturers—local and foreign invested—of medicines and medical devices are essential suppliers of the healthcare system; their need to finance research and development of new treatment methods needs to be taken into account. And most important are the patients, who have also conflicting interests: access to the best possible treatment and at the same time affordable social security contributions.

In China, new or amended laws, draft regulations and standards are published on the internet for public consultation. Not only Chinese citizens and organisations but also foreign nationals and associations can submit comments and recommendations. This is not just a formality, but it is quite likely that well-founded and fact-based recommendations will be adopted. Examples of successful advocacy are given in the case study in Sect. 17.3.

In the case of already existing, unfavourable regulations, the industry can take the initiative to present its concerns and suggestions in written form or ask for a meeting with relevant authorities.

There are many channels to interact with decision-makers in Chinese government bodies. Some authorities with frequent contact with the industry organise regular events. For example, the NMPA holds the annual 3-day China International Medical Device Regulatory Forum (CIMDR) (CCFDIE, 2023), an event specially designed to align Chinese and international regulators as well as industry experts on how to ensure safety and efficacy of medical devices.

Many government departments on both national and local level hold a regular, mostly monthly, minister/director general reception day to discuss issues that cannot be resolved on working level. Most authorities are willing to hold meeting with representatives of the industry. However, access is easier for large, well-known companies and industry associations than for SMEs.

In the case of very technical issues, for example, standards, it is feasible to hold seminars to bring Chinese and international experts together to make joint proposals to harmonise regulations and adopt international best practices.

FIE can participate in Chinese industry organisations and standardisation committees. For FIE with sufficient human resources, this is a promising way to formulate their interests. Because of the sheer number of member companies, local industry organisations have enormous resources and often excellent access to political decision-makers.

Finally, all major countries as well as the EU hold a wide range of government dialogues with its Chinese counterparts. For example, Germany and China maintain around 80 different government dialogues, most of them related to trade, investment and science (Deutschland, 2021). If direct company-government dialogues in China don't provide the desired results, international companies may approach the government of their home country to include critical issues in the government dialogues. The range of these bilateral dialogues includes both rather macroscopic topics and tangible, practical issues. For example, the German Federal Ministry for Economic Affairs and Climate Action (BMWK) has entrusted the Deutsche Gesellschaft für Internationale Zusammenarbeit (GIZ) to lead the Global Project Quality Infrastructure (GIZ, 2022) with China as one of the major participating countries. Target of the project is to reduce barriers to trade and increase product safety. Delegates of German companies active in China are regularly invited to participate in the Sino-German dialogues.

17.3 Case Study: The European Union Chamber of Commerce in China

When China opened up in the 1980s, its economy was basically unregulated; the legal framework ensuring that stakeholders 'play by the rules' was only rudimentary. Since then, China is striving to establish its own legal system. For FIE and local companies alike, it is essential to staying informed on legal changes and, if necessary, avoid that new regulations have a negative impact on the industry.

This requires communication channels with Chinese government departments on all levels. Most Western and Central European countries had formed chambers of commerce, but they remained relatively uninfluential, especially compared with the American Chamber of Commerce. In another development, in the 1990s, the EU developed into a single market with free movement for people, goods, services and money within its territory. This implied that decision-making in foreign trade policies was transferred from member states to the EU administration in Brussels.

As a consequence, on 19 October 2000, 51 initial member companies founded the European Union Chamber of Commerce in China (EUCCC) with a special focus on building a bridge between Chinese government departments and the European industry.

For Chinese government departments, it is an important advantage to have a single point of contact with the European industry when feasibility of new regulations and compliance with them must be ensured. In addition, companies from 27 countries have an extensive knowledge of best practices within the EU, a unified economy with an unbalanced level of economic and social development, comparable to the situation in China.

By early 2023, the EUCCC has developed into an organisation with 1800 member companies with 9 offices in Mainland China (EUCCC, 2022b). The EUCCC has adopted a matrix-shaped management: offices are responsible for local questions, while working groups care for industry-specific issues in whole Mainland China. Each working group is responsible for a specific industry, for example, automotive, energy or railways. A working group consists of an employee of the EUCCC and delegates from FIE active in the specific industry.

The EUCCC is a consortium partner for projects funded by the European Union such as the China IPR SME Helpdesk and the EU SME Centre. It offers a platform for European industry associations to establish a physical presence in China, for example, the medical equipment association COCIR and the Association of the European Heating Industry (EHI) (EUCCC, 2022a).

Influencing political decision-making in China is completely possible, if it is constructive and fact-based. Two examples of advocacy success in different industries (EUCCC, 2022c) are as follows:

For several decades, in most developed countries, **animal testing** had been a precondition to allow non-special cosmetics on the market to protect consumer safety. In China, this requirement has been imposed in 1989. However, with alternative test methods evolving, animal testing became redundant. In 2013, the EU promulgated a general ban on animal testing of cosmetics. The Cosmetics Working Group of the EUCCC organised a wide range of activities, providing evidence for Chinese experts that compared with animal testing, alternative methods provide the same or better level of safety. On 04 March 2021, the NMPA released the *Provisions for Management of Cosmetic Registration and Notification Dossiers*, which basically waives the requirement for animal testing of non-special cosmetics. For the industry, China's new policy means reduced costs and avoidance of possible conflicts with legal requirements in the EU; for China, waiving the request of animal tests enhances its image in foreign countries, where public opinion is opposed to animal testing.

In another example, restriction on **international cargo relay** has been greatly eased as a result of advocacy activities by the industry. In the shipping industry, cargo relay means re-loading of containers from one ship to another owned by the same company. For example, in the case of export from China: cargo is shipped from one domestic harbour to another before being moved onto a different vessel to an international destination. Until recently, Chinese shipping services had to be used for shipping between different domestic harbours. This not only did exclude foreign shipping companies from part of the business (that within China) but also considerably reduced efficiency and often resulted in higher CO2 emission. Cargo relay within one company is highly optimised, but IT systems of different companies are not integrated, resulting in long transfer times at the port of re-loading. Often, the only feasible option for international shipping companies was to ship the containers to other international ports, such as Busan in South Korea or Singapore, and re-load them there. After years of intense contacts of the responsible working group with different Chinese government departments, on 18 November 2021, the State Council announced the launch of a cargo relay trial at Yangshan Port in Shanghai. In a pilot programme, cargo relay is now allowed for containers originating from or destined for Dalian, Tianjin and Qingdao, three of the most important harbours in China. As a result, shipping companies calculated that transit times have been reduced by a week to an average of 20 days.

These two examples show that it is possible for international companies to participate in the Chinese reform process and achieve improved market access.

References

China Center for Food and Drug International Exchange (CCFDIE). (2023). 13th China International Medical Device Regulatory Forum. Retrieved January 15, 2023, from https://www.medcircle.cn/meeting/index/4443?lang=en

Deutschland. (2021). Deutschland und China im Dialog. Retrieved January 15, 2023, from https://www.deutschland.de/de/topic/politik/deutschland-china-5-fakten-zu-den-beziehungen

EUCCC. (2022a). Joint Initiatives. Retrieved January 18, 2023, from https://www.europeanchamber.com.cn/en/joint-initiatives

EUCCC. (2022b). About the Chamber. Retrieved January 18, 2023, from https://www.europeanchamber.com.cn/en/european-chamber-background

EUCCC. (2022c). Advocacy Success. Retrieved May 13, 2023, from https://www.europeanchamber.com.cn/en/advocacy-success

GIZ. (2022). Reducing barriers to trade and increasing product safety. Retrieved January 15, 2023, from https://www.giz.de/en/worldwide/72555.html

GlueUp. (2021). List of Chambers of Commerce in China. Retrieved January 09, 2023, from https://www.glueup.com/zh/blog/china-chambers-list

V. Müller. (2022). We must talk – How to increase China expertise in European headquarters to improve communication with Chinese subsidiaries. EURObiz March/April 2022, pp. 6–8. Retrieved January 13, 2023, from https://www.eurobiz.com.cn/we-must-talk/

18 Outlook

The atmosphere in China in the first half of 2023 following the end of the Covid-19 pandemic is akin to racehorses finally being unleashed. Business delegations from the eastern provinces of Jiangsu and Zhejiang couldn't wait for regular flights to resume, but readily took the initiative to charter flights to Europe. Engineers from abroad are flown in to put machines into operation, and delayed conferences and meetings are now taking place throughout the country. Foreign chambers of commerce report that investment promotion agencies from every part of the country are contacting them on an almost daily basis to arrange events to attract international companies. Companies pursuing business collaborations in China now will undoubtedly find a red carpet being rolled out for them.

The Chinese government has made promoting economic growth a top priority. Despite being the world's second largest economy, China's per capita GDP is still below that of Romania. The government is determined to close the gap and catch up with the most developed nations. At the same time, the Chinese people aspire to reach the living standards of their role models in the European and American upper middle class, and they are working extremely hard to achieve this goal.

However, the necessary reform of China's economic model is facing headwinds. The real estate market, previously one of the main drivers of growth, has reached saturation. Public infrastructure in the densely populated parts of China is excellent; further government investment will not automatically induce more growth. The upper middle class has reached a consumption pattern similar to that of the most developed economies. Furthermore, China's agriculture and hydropower generation are threatened by global warming and changing precipitation patterns. In response, China is committed to becoming carbon neutral by 2060, which is a faster de-carbonisation timeline than any other economy. This has resulted in numerous environmental protection and emission control regulations, posing both an enormous challenge for local manufacturers and great opportunities for multinational companies specialising in green technologies.

Political conflicts and trade wars may exacerbate China's economic situation. However, economic sanctions are a double-edged sword. China has a vast number of

T. Dathe et al., *Business Opportunities and Risks in China*, Management for Professionals, https://doi.org/10.1007/978-3-031-31933-4_18

engineers, surpassing the EU and the USA combined, and, in the long run, will be able to replace essential imports, especially integrated circuits (chips), with locally manufactured products.

China's strategy for future growth consists of several key components, including:

- Advancement of its high-tech industry to foster innovation for a diverse range of products.
- 'Common prosperity', stimulating consumption by boosting the earnings of its huge low-income population. This goal requires improving efficiency in both the production and service sectors through automation, leaner processes and enhanced education.
- Expanding its international presence by tapping into emerging markets and developing countries with rapidly increasing populations and higher economic growth rates than the most developed countries.

Much like in the previous 40 years of reform, China continues to undergo rapid changes, and both local and foreign companies need to adapt. There are encouraging signs that at least the large multinational companies have already started to modify their China strategy, no longer viewing China solely as a vast market and source for low-cost labour, but also as a wellspring of inspiration for innovations. As the CEO of German automotive manufacturer BMW, Mr. Oliver Zipse, stated in early 2023, 'A lot of things happening in the tech world are starting in China, and then are being extended to the world'. China is actively encouraging the establishment of R&D centres within its borders, and many multinational companies are taking advantage of this opportunity.

As China becomes an increasingly crucial component of companies' global strategies, the associated risks also escalate. Today, it is more critical than ever for international companies to implement a well-crafted risk management strategy that includes extensive due diligence prior to investment decisions, a review of all relevant legal and regulatory frameworks as well as careful monitoring of political developments before and after investment. Manufacturers, whether producing in China or in their home country, need to strengthen the resilience of their global supply chain.

Given the sheer size of the market and the countries' innovative capabilities, staying away from China is not an option for multinational companies and also not for most SMEs. As Claudia D'Arpizio, researcher of Bain & Company, puts it: 'An over-dependence on China is risky, but not as risky as not being there at all'.

MIX
Papier aus verantwortungsvollen Quellen
Paper from responsible sources
FSC® C105338

If you have any concerns about our products,
you can contact us on
ProductSafety@springernature.com

In case Publisher is established outside the EU,
the EU authorized representative is:
Springer Nature Customer Service Center GmbH
Europaplatz 3, 69115 Heidelberg, Germany

Printed by Libri Plureos GmbH
in Hamburg, Germany